BELFRY OFFENSE

BELFRY OFFENSE

≡

DARRYL BELFRY
ILLUSTRATIONS BY CATHERINE LOSI
EDITED BY SCOTT POWERS

Copyright © 2023 by Darryl Belfry

All rights reserved. No part of this publication may be reproduced, stored in a retrieval system, or transmitted, in any form or by any means, except as may be expressly permitted by the 1976 Copyright Act or by Darryl Belfry in writing.

ISBN: 979-8-8530-2752-7

Whilst every effort has been made to ensure that the information contained within this book is correct at the time of going to press, the author and publisher can take no responsibility for the errors or omissions contained within.

I would like to dedicate this book to my Wife Ruth, my Daughter Ella and my Son Easton ... for without their support none of my career would be possible.

———

To all the great players whom I've had the great privilege to work with ... I thank you for leaving so many clues to your greatness.

———

To the many great influences I've had in my career, who have introduced me to many of the ideas, concepts and tactics you will read about. A book like this isn't written without influence and a career of collecting and interpreting.

Please visit *www.belfryhockey.com* under the **Belfry Offense** book page, as all the videos that I reference in the book are there. While I did my best to describe the clips in detail ... I'm sure you'll find it easier to follow the text by watching the video.

CONTENTS

Preface Logo Origin Story	1
It's not what you know, it's how you know it	5
Pervasive Mindsets	13
Interconnected Game Model	24
Offensive Zone Possession	36
Possession Line Change	167
Offensive Zone Exit Kill	182
Neutral Zone Transition Re-Entry	204
Rush Entry Denial	218
Retrievals	228
Coverage Exit to Rush Entry	238
Play of the Center	278
What Makes Them Great	283

PREFACE LOGO ORIGIN STORY

When I committed to writing *Belfry Offense*, I spoke to my long-time branding and visual identity designer Colin de Jersey about having a logo for the book that really encapsulates how I acquired the understanding of offense, and I thought immediately of the October 7, 2018 game between Patrick Kane of the Chicago Blackhawks and Auston Matthews of the Toronto Maple Leafs. Now before I get into the significance of that particular game, let's step back a little over a month before:

In August of 2018, we had the 2nd Annual Belfry NHL Camp in Tampa, Florida. This is a preseason camp we do for some of the best players in the world, where they all get together to collaborate, compete and spend time together before the grind of the season starts again. This was also the first year for the 88 Summit which took place at that camp, over the course of which Kane and Matthews played on the same team and were linemates; it was what we hoped was a sneak preview of the chemistry they could build if they played together in the Olympics.[1] The two of them worked together during the camp alongside the other NHL superstars we had there. There was a lot of buzz about the 88 Summit and the camp in the weeks that followed, and Alex Prewitt of Sports Illustrated wrote a fantastic article on September 19, 2018 painting the picture of just how special that event truly was. Now back to the game.

The Leafs are in Chicago at the United Center on October 7, 2018. It was the third game of the season for both teams, just a few days into the start of the season. I had the game circled on my calendar as a must-watch as I was interested to see the extent of the training-to-game transfers I would see from both their individual training programs and

---

[1] *https://www.si.com/nhl/2018/09/20/88-summit-darryl-belfry-hockey-film-breakdown*

the carry-over skill effects from what they learned from each other at the camp.

We pick it up with the Blackhawks leading 2-0. Matthews wins the puck on a brilliant stick takeaway in the Leafs' defensive zone and rounds the net before using a high flip to send Kasperi Kapanen on a breakaway to make it 2-1 Blackhawks. Then on his next shift, the Leafs win the puck back after an offensive zone faceoff loss and Matthews reloads high in the OZ before taking a brilliant downhill route through the slot and goes with the catch of an interior pass from Kapanen to tie the game at 2 with two goals in the last six minutes of the first period.

With 2:09 left in the third, the Blackhawks are down 5-4. Chicago pulled its goalie and Kane is on the left circle as his center Artem Anisimov wins the puck back to him. Kane works down the wall in a down route to the goal line and tries to surprise the Leafs goalie with a high dead-angle shot that just misses. Kane follows the missed shot to that side of the ice and climbs the wall as he often does before settling on the right dot while Chicago works the puck to the left side. After taking a shot, the Leafs get a clear and Chicago has to organize a re-entry. Kane ends up with the puck on the re-entry rim recovery in his familiar right corner; he works it to the top to the D to set up his position between the two checks, the strong-side D and the strong-side defensive F. Kane attacks the dot before using a back-cut skating skill to hold the puck on his forehand while sliding off the dot toward the corner in a slight diagonal, changing the angle. The Leafs goalie doesn't adjust his feet and looks around the Blackhawks net screen to the goal line side of the body. Kane keeps the puck in a dual-threat (shooting and passing position) and threatens to pass with his eyes and his body language before shooting on the opposite side of the screen to tie the game 5-5 with 1:25 left in the game.

Matthews is on for the next shift immediately following Patrick's goal. After working the puck from the defensive zone to the offensive zone, the Leafs have control of the puck in the left corner. Matthews is the third Leaf into the offensive zone and heads straight to the net front. The Leafs go low to high for a quick point shot. The point shot gets deflected and as soon as Auston sees Patrick Marleau going to get to it, he reloads to the slot backward in perfect position for the carom and he goes backhand to forehand over the goalie's glove. Once he sees it go in the net, he skates directly to the sideboard's crowd and brings his left hand to his ear as the crowd quiets with the Leafs retaking the lead 6-5 with 1:02 remaining in the game.

On the next faceoff with 1:02 remaining, Kane is on the ice. Similar to the previous Matthews' shift, the Blackhawks have to start in the defensive zone. Once they gain possession, the puck goes to Kane in the middle of the ice with the goalie sprinting to the bench for the extra attacker. Kane weaves deliberately through center looking for an entry opening as he skates diagonally through the neutral zone; he sells he's going outside and attacks the heels of the pivoting Leafs forward defending the blue line, taking the middle of the ice. Once he has the middle, he finds a Blackhawks forward attacking down on his off wing for a one-timer. Kane continues his route and gets to the loose-puck rebound on the right side of the Leafs goalie on the back wall and sends it again to the top. This, in peak Kane fashion, allows him to work the backside of the ice up the wall while the puck moves to the left side. Kane positions himself on the top of the circle on the right side and calls for the puck. He gets a pass he can shoot with a one-timer and scores to tie the game with 30 seconds remaining Kane immediately after scoring skates towards the sideboards and raises his left hand to his ear, perfectly replicating the Matthews' celebration from 30 seconds earlier. This time, rather than quieting the crowd, the crowd erupts as the roof comes off the United Center.

Auston leaves the game with two goals: one to answer Kane's game-tying goal with a minute to go in the game and two assists, including an assist on the Morgan Rielly OT winner just 19 seconds into OT), while Kane finishes with two late game-tying goals in the last 90 seconds of regulation.

What was fascinating in this game was how dialed in both players were on multiple puck touches in the same possession sequence, which was a prominent theme of ours in the camp. Working to get the puck, improve the conditions of the puck, and relocate into better ice to get another puck touch with improved opportunity was a focus that I was keen on watching for ... and these two didn't disappoint all game long and in the goals they were responsible for.

I was watching the game live, going completely nuts watching the drama unfold between two of my longest and best clients. Immediately following the game, I put them both on a group text sharing my enthusiasm for the game, and they shared a great moment together.

It was a heavyweight tilt between two of the best American-born players ever to play the game. From where we were in the camp just over a month earlier, it was a storybook battle with a befitting ending as they both wouldn't give an inch. The game was an extension of the camp in many ways, both players performing at the highest level and utilizing skills and tactics that are critical to their own individual offensive game structure.

When I decided I wanted to write a book on what I know about offensive hockey, I kept thinking about this game. When we were designing a logo for the book, the image of both players with their hands to their ears emerged to both silence and ignite the crowd. For me, this was the image that captures best how far the development of my understanding, ability to articulate, and teach offence has come over the course of my career. Now for the upcoming launch and the summer camps based on what will be in the book: *Belfry Offense*. [2]

---

[2] *https://www.youtube.com/watch?v=FSMTdBc8lRE&t=2s*

IT'S NOT WHAT YOU KNOW, IT'S HOW YOU KNOW IT

On April 12, 2023, Metallica was on Howard Stern. There was a segment where Stern asked: "I don't understand how songwriters come up with a riff ... how do you know what to sing over it?" James Hatfield, Metallica's lead singer, responded by saying, "For me as a vocalist, I try to insert where the guitar isn't." He added, "You simplify the riff so the vocal has its pace to jump around." There's an exchange between Hatfield and lead guitarist Kirk Hammett discussing how their iconic song "Enter Sandman" came to be. Then Hatfield talks about Lars Ulrich, the drummer, on his critical role in the songwriting process. He said, "Lars doesn't know how to play guitar and he will just arrange stuff, and he will say, can't you do that thing in another key, something that I wouldn't do ... then it becomes a challenge." Then Lars and James talked about each other, James not knowing how to play guitar, and Lars not knowing how to play drums, asking themselves questions. Then Lars talked about how they leave their ego at the door and allow each other to ask questions of each other "... and there's that freedom, because there is trust, and where there is trust there's the love." This segment talking about unlocking the genius of songwriting, perfectly encapsulates my role in player development working with the best players in the world. [3]

I've been asked, "What could you possibly teach Patrick Kane or Sidney Crosby or Nathan MacKinnon? These guys were all great before they met you. What is it you do that could possibly add value to them?" I specialize in "the space between" and I ask the questions that they would not think of to open up an entire new realm of skill possibility. I've learned how to have a valuable perspective from "outside the arena."

---

[3] *https://www.youtube.com/watch?v=sv-yU78-oRU*

One of the most important people in my personal hockey development journey has unquestionably been Bill Gillmeister, a trial lawyer from Buffalo, NY. His son JP was a client of mine when I was doing hockey schools in Niagara. Bill has since kept in regular contact over the years by sending me parallel concept-type articles I wouldn't have thought to have read or been able to see the relationship to player development. Bill is extremely well read in a number of disciplines and has an ability to find books, articles and studies of people and organizations who are pioneering breakthroughs in excellence in other professions, and the lessons make sense when you look through a player development lens. As an example, Bill was the one who got me started on the parallels between teachers teaching vocabulary and player development which I detailed in *Belfry Hockey*.

He recently sent me an email with "It's not what you know, it's how you know it" in the subject line and went on to detail an idea about how it's the lessons we learn, but never quite know, that matter most. To synthesize the genesis of the idea, it's the ability to learn something, but not have it become a cognitive drag , so you can perform without being in your head, which is not a skill that can be taught, but a capacity that can be developed. The development talent is being able to bubble something into focus for the player to learn the lesson and then recessing the lesson into the subconscious and trusting that it will automate in the poetry of their game execution.

That subject line encapsulates my player development approach. I get triggered when I hear rhetoric surrounding players thinking too much and imploring coaches to "simplify" so the player isn't overburdened with thought. Which when it's expressed casually comes across as, "don't think at all." This, of course, is absurd. The oxymoron of suggesting we need players who "don't think" … but we need to find a way to improve their processing speed. Which is it? I believe high performance is not the absence of thought (forethought, pattern recognition and prediction, keeping an eye out for strategic advantage, setting traps for the opposition), it is the ability to think without it affecting movement speed or execution quality. If a player is "thinking too much," it means when they are processing information, they aren't able to move at the same time or with the same fluidity of execution. The entire game of hockey is played in forethought, players seeing patterns, predicting situations and taking control and dictating play to their favor. That's a lot of thinking, that's a lot of processing, it is anything BUT an absence of thought. The objective is not to eliminate or reduce thinking and processing, it is to be able to think and process while playing at pace. From a development perspective, we don't want our players to think less, we want them to play with forethought and move with pace simultaneously. This is why progression (skill introduction, tactical application variance, game-situation recall and manipulation or bending the game) is so important in development. It's not isolated skills, it's not just randomness of game play, it's the combination of the progression and multiple exposures to the skills and tactics that offer the richest development opportunity for our players. For this development, it's not what you know, it's how you know it.

My career is built largely on understanding how the game is being played, how my client plays when he's playing at his absolute best, and what other layers he could learn that would greater impact his results. You can bet, I'm promoting a lot of thinking … while moving at pace simultaneously. Kobe Bryant captured this brilliantly when he said, "Reading the game will make you a good player, understanding what you're reading will make you a great player, but … BUT, if you can write the game that others read, you become a champion. That's a different level of understanding, where you are not reacting to situations, you are the one creating the situations that others react to. That is the whole key." [4]

There is a process to being able to play at that level. You don't just wake up one day and you play with no thought and it all just works out. You need to understand the game at a deeper level than everyone else. The advantage comes from more thought, not less. The advantage

---

[4] *https://www.instagram.com/reel/CqGONXZp_YT/?igshid=MmJiY2I4NDBkZg==*

comes from taking the time to truly understand how something works at a ridiculous level, to where you can explain it simply. Players who enjoy an achievement gap when they are younger, the ones who are reflective on what's leading them to success and tinkering with different approaches, these kids are adding layers and are creating the conditions of true development. It comes from thought … forethought, pattern recognition, habits, leveraging advantages and then reflection. From reflection, they have a chance to see different nuances in the patterns and that gives them other ideas, then they work on these ideas and skills. It's a lot of thought that goes into it. Great players remember everything, their recall ability is beyond ridiculous. We all remember LeBron James baffling the sports world recalling the details of the entire last couple minutes of a game without having the benefit of watching it back and studying it. [5] In a postgame interview, he chronologically rattled off the details of every play. He's not the only one who can do this. I work with many players who have this capacity.

I've said this many times, I am so fortunate to have had the career I've had and worked with the quality of players I've had the privilege to work with. The richest part of the experience is the number of different types of players I've worked with and the different situations that each of them were in that prompted them to want to work with me – the different pathways to success and the different challenges they've had to overcome to reach their goals. I've had players who were young prospects just trying to make the NHL. I've had young players who are NHL players who are trying to establish themselves as NHL players. I've had clients who were solid NHL players who were ready to take a step to become stars or superstars in the NHL. I've worked with generational talents who crave new ideas and want someone to collaborate with to reinvent. I've had players who were NHL stars at some point and now their role is changing and they are trying to apply their talent to a diminished offensive role. I've had players come back from serious injury and try to

---

[5] *https://www.youtube.com/watch?v=eNVJFRI6f6s*

regain their previous level of performance. I've rode shotgun alongside players who have set records, who have won the Stanley Cups, who have won individual NHL awards. I've worked with players who have been considered the best player in the world at a given time. The level of player when I look back is beyond absurd.

If you separated all my clients into individual seasons and you only took the number of seasons they finished in the top 100 in NHL scoring, I have been a part of over 100 of those seasons, including 21 of those years the individual season performances they were in the top 10 in scoring. If you took just those seasons and added up the goals scored, that's 2,807 goals and 6,953 points. I have clients on teams that won eight Stanley Cup winners. That's a lot of offence to be a part of. You could say I've seen some sh ... goals.

- 1 Conn Smyth winner for Stanley Cup MVP
- 2 Hart Trophy winners for regular-season MVP
- 4 Calder Trophy winners for rookie of the year
- 1 Art Ross scoring champion
- 2 Maurice Richard NHL goals leader
- 2 Ted Lindsay award for players' choice for MVP

If it's not what you know, it's how you know it, then it's important to share what I've learned and how I have learned it.

I've been working closely with many of the top NHL players of this era. Many of them have been my clients for their entire NHL careers, so I've witnessed every one of the highs of performance excellence and all the missteps and lessons. At the same time I am experiencing the highs, the missteps and lessons, while we are both on their journey, I am still on my own experience. Their experience is being the actual "man in the arena" and all that comes with that. Most of the aspects surrounding performance at that level in the magnitude of the environment they do, I'll never begin to understand. My experience is to interpret their performance on video and what they articulate to me of their experience and qualify all my statements regarding something they are doing is working, something they are doing is not working, or something they could do may work better if done differently.

The single greatest high for me in my role with the player is when transfer leads to actual production. When I can teach a new skill to a player who previously never executed that skill, then they leverage that skill in an NHL game and it leads to a goal. That skill, leads to winning. Or, a player has a high-frequency situation they create, but the success rate of the situation is very low and my research revealed this area of opportunity they wouldn't have been able to find on their own, I identify why the success rate is low and suggest a different way to execute that event. Then the player leverages that suggestion into creating an actual NHL goal. I have many of these situations happen every year with every client, and it never gets old. I have the same level of excitement tear through my body every time I see it. The follow up text of acknowledgement, let's me relive the exhilaration, and the probability that it'll happen again skyrockets. It's impossible to put into words to really capture what it means to me, but there is a validation of contributing in a small way to their greatness that leaves a permanent imprint on my soul. The highest level of what I just described is when the player does it in the very next game. There just isn't a better professional feeling for me.

I'll detail one of these examples that may encapsulate it. Patrick Kane on the rush comes down the right side, and after exhausting his passing options, decelerates using a right skate slide deceleration skating technique, slowly preserving the shooting space, then looks off the goalie, disguises his shot intentions by looking at his rush support and then he will shoot inside the deception. In the previous stretch of games, he had quite a few of these situations and he was either shooting high-blocker (to the far side of the net) or trying to go 5-hole. I could see in the way I track his games that this was a high-frequency event with a low-success rate. I quickly pulled all video instances of these events and included them in my segment report for him. My suggestion was rather than go high-blocker or 5-hole, to try going just above the pad on the blocker side. My suggestion was to keep everything the same, just change the shot location. Then … the next game, he does exactly that, and as fate would have it, he scores. Then the follow up text of acknowledgement, and I'm on cloud 9 until the next one.

My knowledge has expanded with every new client. Each one has different reasons for wanting me to study their game and suggest game execution subtleties that will make them more productive in their habits. I have to ensure their habits produce at a higher percentage. I also have clients who are looking for new ideas and applications of skill. They want to approach situations with a different perspective, so they share an incredible amount of detail on their perspective on a recurring situation with me. They detail the situation, the variables, the "if this, then that" expected responses, the manipulation strategies of defenders as they move the pieces around the rink to their favor, and then they share questions they have about how they might do it differently, things they have tried that haven't worked. They expect collaboration from me, that will include a different perspective and ideas that have logic and are in concert with their environment and their assets. Now I need to deliver. Over the years having been in these situations so many times, I have developed a process that works for me that gives me a chance to bring that fresh perspective. My process is rooted in game video research and stacking questions. When I follow my process, I find myself seeing my angle to the situation reveal itself. I present my idea to the player, the player works through it in their own mind, we collaborate on it, next thing you know it takes on a life of its own. Now it's at a place where neither one of us would have expected or been able to get to by ourselves, and because of the collaboration, the ideas are coming from the athlete. I shift back to facilitator of questions or highlight skill execution aspects and we have the conditions for innovative transfer. There are three players in recent years I've had the most success with this approach. There is Nathan MacKinnon, who has rewritten his entire approach in the offensive zone. It's been a riveting process of leveraging all his best assets, the assets of the players around him, and he's found new ways to dominate the game through multiple possession sequences, like nothing I've ever seen. There is Auston Matthews, who reinvented a slant on shot release. The multi-year process of refining and reinventing components of the release allowed him to produce a unique approach that changed the game. Imagine being part of just these two processes. Then, in a completely different way, there is Jack Hughes, collaborating on the art of scoring and the nuances in chance generation. Having the privilege of watching his mind work in a completely different way I've ever been a part of. To be a part of the process of integrating his mind into his offensive assets to then watch in amazement as he blew the lid off completely during the 2022-23 season. Imagine being a part of that process for every world-class people you work with, over a 100 top-100 performances in the NHL.

Matt Damon articulated in an interview how great collaboration works. When talking about collaborating with Ben Affleck in writing "Good Will Hunting," Damon said, "One of the most profound things than anyone has ever said to me, when he [Ben Affleck] was 20 years old ... he said judge me for how good my good ideas are, not how bad my bad ideas are. That to me is one of the most important things when you embark on a collaborative process with someone. It's like you have to get the window open to throw every idea in there and not be afraid to have shitty ideas, because we all have shitty ideas. And sometimes you need a shitty idea and then you iterate on that and then they iterate on that and it builds into a good idea. You have to feel free to express it." [6]

How I've come to understand the game in the way that I do has been a very unique process. It's not lost on me how fortunate I am to have had the chance to collaborate with as many top players in the NHL as I have, many of whom I've been with them lockstep through their entire NHL careers. It really is not what you know, but how you know it.

---

[6] *https://www.instagram.com/reel/CrWH4cEpcXD/?igshid=YmMyMTA2M2Y=*

PERVASIVE MINDSETS

"Keep It Simple Stupid," or the KISS principle is the clubhouse leader for most restricting mindsets plaguing hockey at every level. The frequency of this bullshit is spewed is mind-numbing. The actual pathway to having the ability to communicate something simply is to push yourself to become a diligent student and build a depth of understanding of the intricate and complicated topics you are responsible for. Those who have a high level of understanding don't ever have to worry about spitting complicated and convoluted information and answers to their audience, their simplicity and ease of communication is revealed in the depth of their understanding. If you are worried about not being able to communicate crisp and clean, that's your best indication you don't understand the subject well enough, so it's best you don't say anything at all. The KISS principle for me is, "If you are worried about Keeping it Simple, don't be Stupid, start asking questions." In this book, you'll see sections where I am very clean and concise and can explain my thoughts very well due to the work I spent on seeking to truly understand that area. Then there will be other sections that aren't as clean, because I haven't spent quite as much time and don't have quite the same fluency, so the delivery will not be as tight. There will also be areas where I am still asking a lot of questions and along the way you'll see what level I'm at.

This is why I love offensive hockey, because for decades it has been dismissed and explained as natural talent, or reserved for only Mensa-level thinkers whom most of us will never approach the capacity to understand. Then reduced to the lowest possible expression of offence, "just get it and throw it at the net and crash the crease and hope it bounces off you into the net." For decades this is the two popular generalized extremes we have been battling against. This isn't to say great players don't do unbelievable things and create artistic magic from seemingly no advantage, and they may just be the only person in the world who could do it like that. Of course they do, but that's not the reason not to dig in and try to understand, rather the opposite.

One of the most limiting aspects of offence is believing the propaganda of pervasive perspectives. We put unnecessary and often unfounded ceilings on ourselves through the viewpoint and limited interest of others, which wouldn't be so bad if we didn't often push those perspectives onto others and create glass ceilings in their pursuit of understanding. It's only fitting that if we are going to talk about offensive hockey, we have to push past the especially egregious connotations that come from these statements. There are many of these that have somehow been adopted into truth. Here are a few that I find particularly restricting:

1. If you care about offence, you don't care about defence.

There is a train of thought that has circulated for years, that I've personally had to deal with and that is this automated assumption, that if you care about offence, you immediately don't care about defense. This, of course, is ridiculous. Truth be told, if you really care about offense, you will have to study defense to improve your understanding of where the offensive opportunities are in defending. One of the best offensive teaching methods is the illumination that comes from looking directly at the opposite of defense. For example, if good defending is deflecting the play out of the middle, then good offence must be in finding a way to attack through the middle or play on the inside. The best offense I've uncovered has often come from studying defenders. Understanding how team and individual defenders angle, use their stick, work together to discourage the puck from the middle of the ice is direct insight into how we can find opportunities with the puck. The offensive solution to a defensive problem is most often found in the exact opposite of defense. Moreover, some of the best offence created comes from great defending, that forced turnover when the offensive team is building an attack, the offensive window that comes from forcing that turnover and attacking in transition is often some of the best scoring chances you can create. All coming from transition from good defense to offence. I used to take it personally as a demeaning shot from someone who would say, "Well, you only care about offence." Now I only see the advantages that perspective has for me. I learned quickly that if I wanted to understand offense at a deeper level, I need to also study great defending. Whatever limitations you may have in your understanding of offense will create ceilings in your understanding of defense ... and vice versa.

The defensive zone is the work zone and the offensive zone is the fun zone.

The impression that the offensive zone is not a work zone couldn't be further from the truth. If you want to stay in the offensive zone and extend zone time, you better believe this is hard work, and it's getting harder and harder work with every season that goes by. Every year, defending in the offensive zone takes on a greater role in offensive zone offence. Controlling the puck, generating offense and sustaining offense is incredibly difficult. It challenges every aspect of creativity, skill, teamwork, competitiveness and determination expressed through the willingness to physically engage "going through the puck" in an effort to score. The offensive zone is fun, so long as you bring your work boots. The defensive zone is also fun, so long as you bring your work boots. Work is the same, it's consistent and detailed effort with a purpose.

2. It's not what you create, it's what you give up.

If you don't create, you'll soon be giving up. Many of the best chances in a game originate from mis-managed pucks that turn into transition against. We can't, out of one side of our mouth, say, we have to manage the puck intelligently, and then out of the other side say, attention to defending is most important. One of the best fundamental truths of defense is ... when I have the puck, it's really hard for you to score.

Understanding the difference between attack pucks and possession pucks is a critical distinction to offence that is important to defending. An attack puck is when the conditions surrounding the puck on acquisition are favorable for offence (time, space, numbers, angles or lanes to attack). A possession puck is when the conditions surrounding the puck on acquisition favor the defending team and the mindset has to be on possessing the puck and changing the point of attack in a collective effort to improve the conditions.

3. Offense is separate from defense, they are two separate entities.

The game of hockey is so fast and fluid with 100s of changes of possession in a game. It's just not possible for every player to truly be on offence when we have the puck, and everyone to truly be on defense when we don't have the puck. In any given possession sequence, there could be any combination of players truly on offence, players still transitioning to offence from defense and players who are in a defensive position. Then when the puck turns, the configuration of the combination of players truly defending, transitioning to defense and players who are defending may not be the direct opposite of what it just was. Then as the puck moves, in an instant, each of those roles change again depending on where the puck goes. It is not often that all five players are truly playing offence or playing defense. Understanding this reality of the sport really changes how we approach coaching it. When you factor in game situation, score and time on the clock, now you really have some interesting configurations of who is really on offence and who is really on defense.

4. Accusing players of playing on the perimeter, but then repeatedly damning play attempts to the middle of the ice.

By excessively expressing risk aversion without situational context and solution suggestions, you are encouraging players to default to possession plays, even on attacking pucks. Of course, there is perimeter play linked to physical hesitation, that is something that can't be dismissed. However, we can't condemn the middle of the ice altogether and then accuse the athletes of being perimeter players. One simple way to aid in getting players more in the middle of the ice is to have one in and one out as a part of your offensive shape. Not a principle or a rule, part of the shape ... there is a difference.

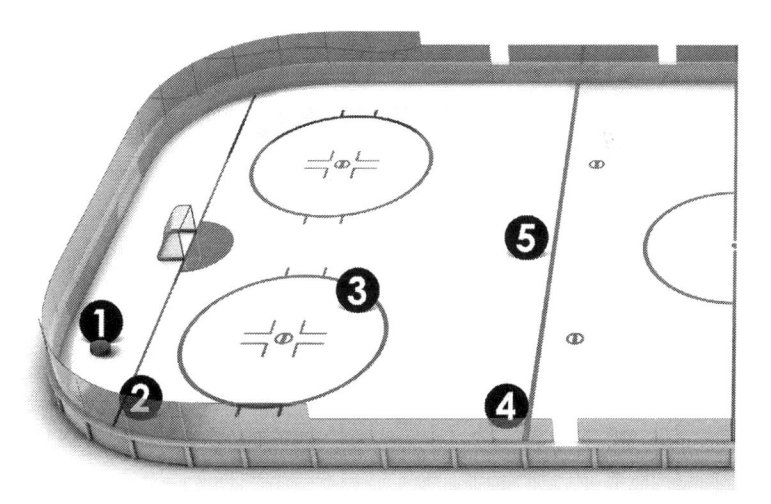

Figure 1: 1 in and 1 Out

In this first diagram, this is more like the way we used to draw the offensive zone for our players. We would have the puck carrier with the puck, a third man high and the two defenders. We would draw his support player on the boards. This directly is promoting perimeter play as we are suggesting that the puck be moved on the perimeter. In the diagram, we have three of the five players on the outside, and that's not counting the weak-side D, whom you could argue is also perimeter in this diagram.

BELFRY OFFENSE

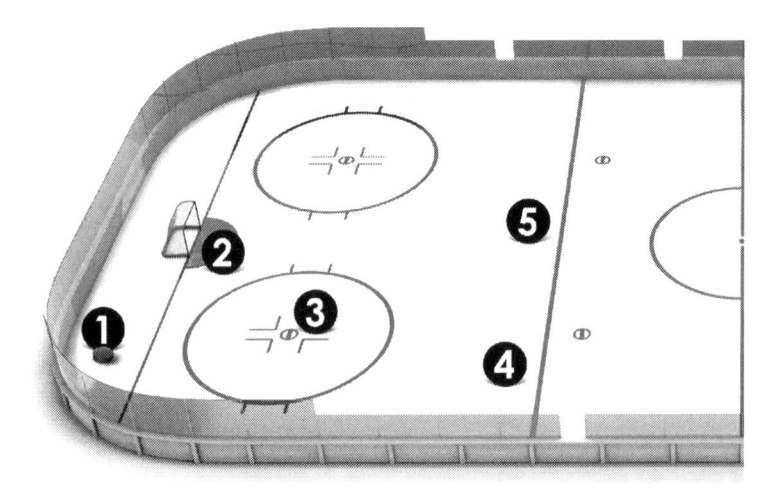

Figure 2: 1 in and 1 Out

In this second diagram, we have moved the primary support player inside, indirectly promoting interior play.

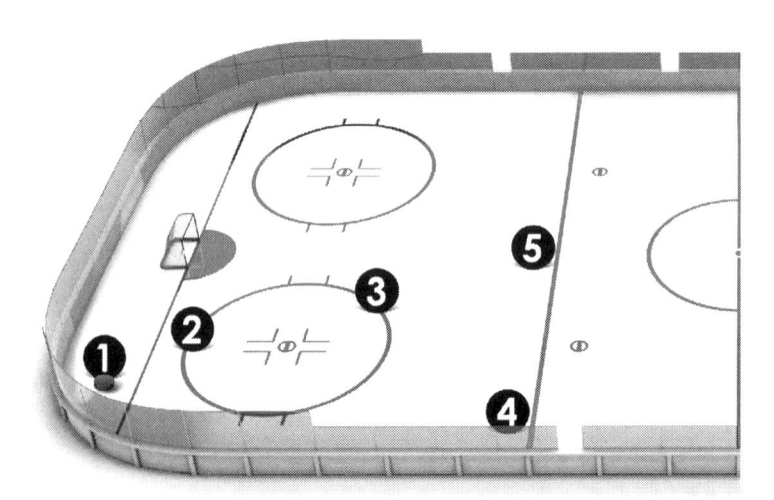

Figure 3: 1 in and 1 Out

18

PERVASIVE MINDSETS

In the third diagram, we have the support players at the net and on the strong-side dot, again promoting more interior play. The net presence carries a dual role, as he could be used for a backwall side change.

The one-in-and-one-out shape is part of the offensive shape. One of the biggest culprits to endless perimeter play is that the first player in direct support of the puck carrier moves to the wall. The immediate pass option is on the outside and can lead to stopped pucks and chains of perimeter or board play. To disrupt this, we change our shape to have one in and one out, now the puck support is inside the first layer of pressure. This will help that first play get off the wall more frequently, if nothing other than intent.

5. Confusing the achievement gap with projectable offence.

The deceiving challenge is deciphering between a player benefitting from the achievement gap and projectable offensive habits. I wrote about this in my book *Belfry Hockey*,[7] as I described what I feel is hockey's version of the achievement gap, players whose physical tools are ahead of the league they play in, allowing them to leverage those advantages and hide some long-term development deficiencies. Moreover, by holding tightly to their achievement gap advantages and running roughshod over their competition, they inadvertently block their own development of learning true hockey sense (the ability to control play with others), and worse, blocking their linemates' ability to do so as well.

6. Labeling players too early based on the flimsy relativity of role and without investing in them.

In a practice as old as time, we can't wait to put artificial ceilings on players' potential. With a fraction of the information needed to make such a

---

[7] *https://www.amazon.com/Belfry-Hockey-Darryl/dp/162937928X/ref=sr_1_1?hva did=472173589640&hvdev=c&hvlocphy=9054499&hvnetw=g&hvqmt=b&hvran d=14010753910694787035&hvtargid=kwd-454162681646&hydadcr=2732_10398- 893&keywords=darryl+belfry&qid=1684675148&sr=8-1*

determination, and even less qualifications, we all, including me, seem to be quick to insert ourselves in these assertions on what a player is and isn't capable of. The damage of these definitive statements is they tend to take a life of their own and can wreak havoc with player development. Where we see the most harmful restrictions is in the development of offence. When role labels get haphazardly assigned, we run the risk of the player believing their role is their identity. Your role is relative (to the players available to the coach) and has nothing to do with your identity. To illustrate my point, take a player in your league who is the third line center on the top team in the league. Now put him on the worst team in the league, is he their top player or close to it? This is the relativity of role. The player's identity is their personality, habits, skill set, mindset, and how they are within the group, and … their personal, interpersonal, physical, mental, emotional, social, skill development and coachability. There are so many moving parts, it's pretty difficult to just unilaterally label anyone, especially at the young ages we tend to do it.

Players being resistant to labels, both favorable and restricting labels, and just staying the course trying to get better in every area as much as they can, that's an indicator of mental toughness. We have to be much more careful with what we say to players about "who we think they are." The odds of any of us really knowing what that actually is incredibly low, to the point where we should probably not even get involved in that kind of talk. Rather, find ways to develop players in all areas, and if there are offensive hockey sense questions, then rather than dismiss the player as incapable, invest in him/her and let's see. One of the lowest hanging fruit in hockey, and easily the best examples of this is in assessing and developing hockey sense, is in women's hockey. If you were ever looking for a space that was riddled with restricting labels, pop psychology assertions, hardened opinions on capacity, devoid leadership in all the key positions, and ridiculous "out-to-lunch" takes … women's hockey is a goldmine. The entire sport is plagued with half-truths and misinformation further perpetuated by a complete lack of depth of talent in management, coaching, player development and talented athletes worldwide. The complete lack of actual competition on the world stage creates no impetus for those at the top to develop and evolve. Therefore, it falls further and further behind.

Offensive hockey in the women's game is in its infancy. The "ocean" analogy still isn't big enough to accurately describe the potential for the women's game. One of the first tasks to unlock it is to STOP labeling women's hockey players too early based on flimsy relativity of role and without investing in them. We have to find ways to invest in the talent surrounding the game and provide real development opportunities for them, so they can actually take ideas and run with them. The people who have the most capacity to positively change the course of the entire sport haven't developed yet, and, therefore, haven't arrived in the positions of great influence yet ... but I hold out hope that it is coming. And when it does, it's going to be amazing to watch these women take off and explore the true art this game has to offer them. Once they have a fair chance to explore these ideas, imagine what else they will uncover. It's exciting to think about and is the best example to illustrate this point. It's so sad that these wonderful athletes have no way to gain access to some of the most interesting aspects that the game has to offer them.

7. Connecting points of understanding in offence.

There will be more about this coming up later in this book, but briefly, most people in the game have a very fragmented understanding of how offence works. There are bits and pieces of information scattered in the understanding and that's how it's then communicated. Then because it's communicated in a convoluted way, we tell everyone to abide by the KISS principle which keeps not just the communication simple, but the quality of the ideas are also deducted down to a ground floor level. This would be awesome if we used this deduction to create a baseline to build from, however, that's not how it's often done. We deduct it down and then wallow there. There is in fact no development of ideas, because ideas have to be connected to be developed. The information stays fragmented, and worse, passed along to the next generation.

One of the best things we can do to generate offence is have group discussions on offence that offers everyone in the group to connect the fragments and fill in the gaps, to play with concepts and to encourage their players to do so as well. The intent of this book is to do just that, to try to connect common fragments of offensive understanding, show the lineage of how things have developed thus far and offer the opportunity for a deducted baseline to grow. To push past principle-based logic models and into an interconnected equation that players can leverage to express true creativity, as a collective.

8. Rules that we impose on our players that make good sense for defending, but no sense to generating offence.

In *Belfry Hockey*, I referenced the absurdity that we sometimes operate under. On the one hand, we instruct all our D to deflect everything, keep everybody outside and to not give up the middle, then on the other hand, we tell our offensive group to attack on the outside, use the boards and don't use the middle. Or how about we instruct defensemen that the forward is most vulnerable when they turn their back, and when they do, jump them quickly to close space. Then we tell the puck carrier to turn with the puck when in small space. We forecheck to take away the walls, and when we break out, use the walls. When we break out, we want slash support, but the slash support player is going into small space and on an island. In the defensive zone, the scheme is built with layers to ensure fail safes and that there is someone to cover if the primary defender gets beat off the wall. But offensively, we put the closest support player to the puck-carrier on the wall. We know point shots have a shot-recovery rate that is around 30 percent and point shots score under 5 percent of the time, and we design the offensive zone based on point shots with traffic, but we are frustrated when our team isn't able to generate offensive zone time. We know the goalie has the hardest time with shots where the puck travels distance across the offensive zone or on diagonals, but all we hear is north, north, north. When we are in player acquisition, we value players who express creativity and offensive instincts. But when they arrive on the team, anything that could be an application of creativity is considered a bad risk.

There are so many of these "offensive rules" that actually inherently favor the defensive team, and while the emphasis is to generate more team offensive production, we still perpetuate these rules that are counterintuitive to generating offence. They make no sense offensively. When dealing with offensive hockey, there is a need to take the time to review all these areas that are disconnected and streamline them for our players.

INTERCONNECTED GAME MODEL

Interconnected Game Model refers to teaching the team tactics through an interconnected and interdependent lens. Teaching through this lens is different because it emphasizes the relationship between team tactics rather than each in isolation. The objective of teaching in an interconnected game model is to further drive the greater strategy of game control. The practical application of the model from the player's perspective is that the quality of the team's play in one aspect of the game directly impacts every other area.

Each aspect of the game is connected and dependent by the play patterns of the event that happens before and after. Once in game control, the objective is to not allow the opponent to advance to the next one, but to continually retake possession and control of the puck, the play and the team tactics to maintain the advantage.

There are seven aspects of the Interconnected Game Model:

1. OZ Possession Offense
    a. Controlling the puck, creating chances and recovering the puck. The combination of offensive zone time and generating scoring chances. Extending the opponent in their DZ to evaporate their shift.
    b. In Game 5 of the 2023 Stanley Cup Final, the Vegas Golden Knights score their third and fourth goals of the game to put the game out of reach. They have a four-minute stretch of hockey that encapsulates the best of what I can describe OZ Possession Offense. The clip is featured in our "Belfry Offense Support Clips" section of our website.[8]

---

[8] www.belfryhockey.com

INTERCONNECTED GAME MODEL

2. Possession Line Changes
   a. Maintaining control of the puck while executing line changes. The value of possession line changes can't be overstated. Offensive zone, neutral zone re-entry changes, DZ exit turn backs into regroup changes and penalty kill changes. By consistently executing possession line changes, we can go a long way to both out-changing our opponent in an effort to win the energy battle, as well as affecting their ability to change or more importantly catch them trying to change when we have the puck, which can lead to great scoring chances.

3. OZ Exit Kill
   a. Killing exits (regaining the puck while the opponent tries to break out) is a critical link to extending OZ Possession Offence and facilitating the opportunity for possession line changes. An exit kill is a loss of possession or a loose puck situation in which the opponent has a chance to break out and exit the zone, however your offensive zone defending - reloading, tracking, back pressure, pinching, weak-side folding, either in isolation or in combination, wins the puck back sustaining offensive zone time and pressure.

4. NZ Transition Re-Entry
   a. When the opponent is able to clear the zone, but not able to formulate an attack, we can transition quickly and re-enter. Whether it's a chip-out recovery, a track takeaway or defensemen defending skating forward to force the change of possession, we can turn that into offence. Re-entry is an under-utilized and therefore underdeveloped aspect of rush offence. There are tactical advantages more readily available in re-entry rush entry than in rush entry. The tactical advantages are in speed differential and in defenders contesting the line. In re-entry, few teams' defensemen are aggressive in working to re-gap to contest the

entry, so there are more uncontested entries and the possession entry offers a chance to sustain pressure.

b. The 2023 Florida Panthers scored a re-entry goal in overtime in Game 3 of the Stanley Cup Final vs. the Golden Knights.[9] It started with offensive-zone defending as Sam Bennett, No. 9, for the Panthers has an F2 track disruption in the middle of the ice forcing a loose puck in the neutral zone. Bennett's route discipline is phenomenal, he finishes his check as F1, as he tracks back, the puck is undetermined, so he goes right to the net. Then as soon as Vegas gets control, he starts his F2 track to disrupt, and then once he sees the loose puck in the neutral zone, he heads right over to the anchor position. That loose puck is recovered by No. 19 Matthew Tkachuk, who is the Panthers F3. He bumps it back to the strong-side defender (Gustav Forsling, No. 42) who immediately whips it cross-ice to Bennett, who is the anchor on the re-entry. On the re-entry, Tkachuk is the middle speed which insulates the shooting space for Carter Verhaeghe who scored the goal through the Tkachuk middle driver speed. Also on the play is the weak-side defender who is No. 5 Aaron Ekblad, who does a great job offering a secondary shot off the pass option for Verhaeghe if he didn't like the shot. The reason the re-entry was so effective was because the Vegas D Zach Whitecloud, No. 2, overruns his position upon the puck exit leaving the forward Mark Stone to challenge the anchor, Bennett. In the challenge, Stone's pursuit angle is underneath Bennett, giving him full access to the middle of the ice. On re-entries, defensive spacing and responsibilities can get stretched more so than on a rush entry. Therefore, the opportunity can be greater to attack through the middle of the ice. It was a beautifully executed example of a NZ transition re-entry on the biggest stage, in the most important game of the season to that point for Florida.

---

[9] *https://twitter.com/belfryhockey/status/1667046250556817409?s=20*

INTERCONNECTED GAME MODEL

5. Rush-Entry Denial

    a. If the opponent can successfully exit their zone and possess the puck in the NZ, then we move to rush-entry denial. The hard and fast back pressure of the forwards allow the defensemen to hold their gap to contest the entry. The engagement rules are key here in rush-entry denial so the defensemen and the forwards work in unison to deny the entry creating the lucrative turnover for rush transition, or at the very least forcing an icing or an offside.

    b. I put together a quick montage of clips on Jaccob Slavin of the Carolina Hurricanes on rush-entry denial in our clip support for the book. [10]

6. Retrievals

    a. While not the desired outcome, it's the next best thing to an outright denial is forcing a dump-in. Now we move to retrieval priorities. The first priority is "quick to 3." It doesn't matter what retrieval scheme you prefer, you want three players involved to convert the retrieval to initiate an possession exit. My preference is quick to 3 with the weak-side D on the strong-side post.

7. Coverage Exit to Rush Entry

    a. If we were unable to win the puck back in the OZ, deny entry or force a retrieval we were able to recover, we have either conceded a possession entry or the opponent has recovered the forecheck. Now we dig in to win the puck back through DZ coverage and gain a coverage exit. Now we execute our DZ coverage scheme to win the puck back with an exit plan. This is different from teaching DZ coverage and breakout separate, we link the two.

---

[10] *https://twitter.com/belfryhockey/status/1667056036656689155?s=20*

The philosophical difference in the interconnected game model is that we view the game tactically from the offensive zone back to the defensive zone, rather than the goaltender or defensive zone out. When our season starts, in an interconnected game model, we would start the tactical development of our team from the offensive zone.

When we teach the interconnected game model, we start with centrally teaching all that goes into the offensive zone and bookend the development by connecting the play before (rush entry) and after (exit kill).

This is a great video clip depicting the interconnected game model, in this game in which the Colorado Avalanche are visiting the Los Angeles Kings, Los Angeles has a brilliant investment shift that details the elements. The clip starts off with a retrieval to breakout where the Kings are able to connect their exit to the entry. They get a self-chip to start the offensive zone. Once in the offensive zone, the puck is originally stopped. They work hard to "inside the puck" and get it moving. They get an interior shot in the high F3 spot with their weak-side D activating down the wall to win the puck back. Once they win it back, they get the puck off the wall and generate a second shot. They win the shot recovery and maintain possession. They temporarily lose the puck on the back wall, only to win it right back with a strong-under-stick takeaway. They are able to go low to high for a third shot and the flash screen recovers the puck as they are trying to set up their stack screen. Then they work the boards of the offensive zone before generating a fourth shot walkout wrap attempt. They track the puck with their high F3 to force the dump in and maintain control of the puck. [11]

Offensive Zone Ice Geography

Before we get going too far in the offensive zone, it is best to clearly define the ice geography terms. Ice geography is a critical communication tool with players and important to coaching the offensive zone. The

---

[11] Great example by the LA Kings of connecting the play in the offensive zone - *https://twitter.com/belfryhockey/status/1660288444692561922?s=20*

INTERCONNECTED GAME MODEL

sooner you can align your coaching staff and your players on the terminology you will use, which may be different than the ones I use, the easier it is for everyone to understand clearly what you, your coaches or other teammates are referring to. In hockey, there are a lot of terms everyone uses and is familiar with, then there are terms that have evolved for each individual. Over time, we have all adapted or invented terms to describe different things. Every year my terms change a little bit as I find better words. For the book, it is important you know what I'm referring to, so it makes sense to review those terms before we get started:

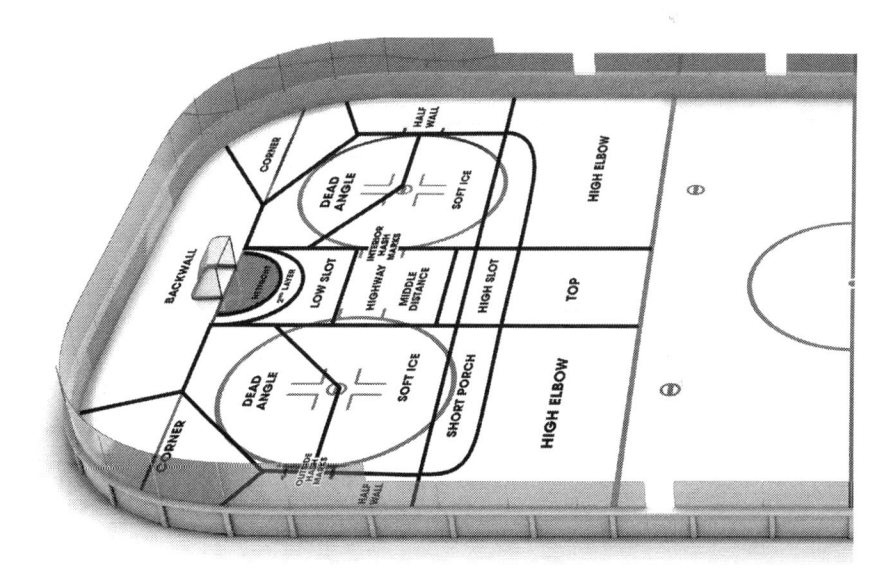

Figure 4: Ice Geography

- **Backwall**

    The space on the wall behind the net, usually defined by the inside of the trapezoid

- **Corner**

    Obviously the corner of the rink

29

- **Half-wall**

  The space between the corner and the top of the circle

- **Outside hash marks**

  Often referred to as good ice markings for decision-making.

- **High elbow**

  The top corner of the offensive zone at the blue line.

- **The top**

  The top is the middle of the blue line between the top of the circle and between the two elbows.

- **The highway**

  The interior section of the ice, commonly referred to as the house, or home plate, I refer to it as the highway because it captures the moment I want to see in this area.

- **Net-front**

  Right at the blue paint of the crease

- **Second layer**

  A three-foot band at the edge of the crease, usually refer to this area as a rebound area for the net-front or for players landing at the net

- **Middle distance**

  The high and low slot, there is a strong correlation to scoring and middle-distance shooting. Most recently for scoring defensemen, they tend to find themselves shooting from middle distance at high frequency

- **Interior hash marks**

  Good ice marking to guide players to get into the middle distance area

- **Low hash mark**

    The ones closest to the net

- **High hash mark**

    The ones closest to the top of the circle

- **Low slot**

    Space between the second layer and the low interior hash marks

- **High slot**

    Space between the high interior hash mark and the top of the circle

- **Short porch**

    The Canadians among us will refer to this as "the ringette line," which is a sport played in Canada and one of the lines they have on the ice is directly across the top of the circles. This line is red in most rinks in Canada. I call it short porch because I want the defensemen surfing down to this area often. This is also a movement line for the goalie. When the attack goes below this line, the goalie starts to initiate movement.

- **High ice**

    The high ice is the space between the short porch (top of the circle) to the blue line. The high ice is often referred to when talking about the high 3v2.

- **Soft ice**

    I used to call this the "offensive seam" but now have conceded a popular term others have used for this area called the soft ice. Soft ice is a great term because it refers to defensive presence in this area. It's a difficult area to consistently defend so you can slide into the soft ice and get some good shot chances.

- **The 45**

    Refers to the rebound angle line that goal scorers in response to a shot from the opposite side will position themselves on the 45-degree angle of the rebound.

- **Seam pass**

    Dot-to-dot passing lane going through the box.

- **Dot line**

    All the dots are in a straight line down the ice, the dot line is a great geographical area

- **Dead angle**

    The area below the offensive zone dot and the goal line. A geographical area that's received a lot of spotlight because of how difficult it can be for the goalie. The dot is a second movement line for the goalie as well, where they have to start moving once the attack goes into the dead angle.

The next aspect of the offensive zone is offensive zone spots and offensive zone movement terms.

- **Offensive zone spots**

    Offensive zone spots is a very common way to refer to baseline areas that we want to have constant player presence. So net-front presence and F3 are easy ones to identify with because of the frequency those spots are referenced. These vary, depending on the coach and how he likes his offense run. For our purposes, it's a good starting point.

INTERCONNECTED GAME MODEL

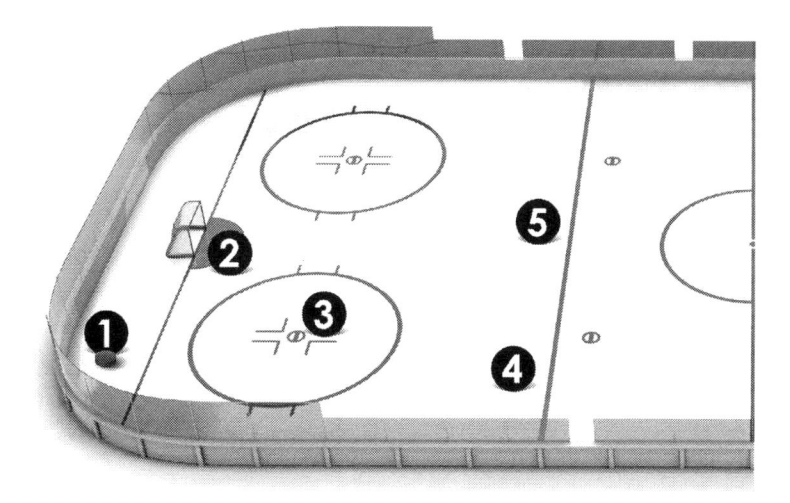

Figure 5: Offensive Zone Spots

- **Player at the net**

    Constant net-front presence

- **Player on the puck**

    Player on the puck and in control of the puck. When drawn we always seem to draw this player in the corner.

- **Player in F3 spot**

    Depending on the coach, he will position this player in different areas - in the soft ice, in dot release, between the two D at the top. This player, depending on situation and coach, can be in many places, but the expectation is once it's defined that the player is reliable and constant.

- **Stack Screen**

    The stack screen is the net-front presence and F3 are stacked or in a line from the net to the point.

- **Dot Release**

BELFRY OFFENSE

A geographical position as well as a spot

- **Strong-side point**

    A position as well as a spot

- **Weak-side D**

    A player position and well as a spot

- **Offensive movement terms**

    Offensive movement terms are terms that identify a player position or spot followed by an action word describing what is expected.

- **F1**

    The F1 action is depending on whether we have the puck or not. If we have the puck, F1 is the puck-carrier. If we don't have the puck, F1 is pressure.

- **F2 track**

    This is the player at the net in the offensive zone who must defend from under the puck, looking for immediate back pressure, tracking and steals once possession is undetermined or has changed hands.

- **Weak-side fold**

    The weak-side defense position whereby the weak side D is surfing the short porch in a dual-threat position and on exit recognizes that the winger is on an island and attaches to that check skating forward to pressure and kill the play. Leaving the strong-side D to back up and support the transition plays that follow.

- **F3 track**

    The F3 is in the high forward position and tracks the puck to disrupt the breakout, also responsible for containing the puck on the strong side. F3 can't have the puck go through him.

- **Strong-side pinch**

    The strong-side defensemen attacks down on the opposition's strong-side winger to contest the puck, disrupt the breakout and keep the play alive in the offensive zone.

- **Weak-side pinch**

    The defensemen away from the puck is on the weak side of the ice, when the puck changes sides attacks down on the oppositions winger to contest the puck, disrupt the breakout and keep the play alive in the offensive zone.

- **F3 support**

    When either of the two defensemen pinch, F3 supports the pinch by assuming the vacating D's responsibility at the point.

OFFENSIVE ZONE POSSESSION

When we think of the offensive zone, it's normal to immediately think about being on the puck and being on offence, but you can't think about offence in the offensive zone without thinking about offensive zone defense and transition response. It all starts for me with acknowledging the duality of the offensive zone – offensive zone offence and offensive zone defense and the speed at which we can transition between the two. The most important part in understanding the offensive zone is knowing that while we are in possession of the puck, we are also organizing our defense when the puck becomes loose or we lose it, so we can get the puck back as quickly as possible to sustain offensive zone pressure. When in the offensive zone and you force a turnover, you have three seconds or less to create a high-danger chance before the opponent recovers their defensive position, which is why being organized before the turnover happens is critical as that will aid in speeding up your response. There are seven aspects we can organize in our favor at any given time, the five skaters we have on the ice on our team, the utility of the boards and how we use space to our advantage. We have to be able to sustain offensive zone time, which has four blended elements:

1. Offensive zone possession
2. Exit kill
3. Shot recovery
4. Re-entry

What key factors restrict teams from attacking interior?

If your team is not proficient in offensive zone defense, that weakness will bleed into every aspect of the offensive zone play. You'll obviously struggle with exit kill, but where it becomes interesting is how it manifests itself in other ways. In offensive zone possession, you'll be reluctant to properly attack the middle of the ice ... like at all. If you are confident in your offensive defending, you'll be more inclined to want to attack interior, because it feels less "risky." There are any number of reasons why teams struggle attacking interior. One of the biggest reasons can be attributed to a fear of turnovers. The fear will outweigh the benefit, so the lack of courage is rooted truly in insecurity in their offensive zone defending. If you can become exceptional in offensive zone defending, it will positively impact your ability to attack interior. The process of alleviating the fear of transition and shifting the fear of transition to the "anticipation of transition" is the empowerment we need to pull more of our players into a willingness to attack interior. When teams struggle in attacking interior offensively, you'll see disconnects between their offensive zone puck play and their offensive zone defending. When they are attacking in the offensive zone, they don't do so with any defensive awareness, therefore when they inevitably lose the puck or the puck becomes loose, they aren't able to intelligently defend.

The heaviness now required at the puck

There is a distinct heaviness that is required to make plays at the puck. This term comes to prominence during every reference to the NHL playoffs. The playoffs are a different sport. There is an unreasonable and unnatural competitiveness at the puck that goes a long way to determining winning. In studying this and trying to make sense of approaches in how to teach it to more players, and to trickle the best of this down to players from a habit perspective, there is a realization of how much "heaviness" there really is. It's not just about being physically capable of defending or taking the puck. While being effective in playing in high traffic (dirty) areas is a part of it, that is just the beginning.

Heaviness at the puck, if you want to really understand how it works and what leads to it, can be traced back to positional discipline. The duality of positional discipline has two faces - when we have the puck and when we are trying to get it back. When you are trying to get it back, it's difficult to be heavy if you can't get there. So it starts with team shape, are you moving collectively whereby no matter where the puck goes one of you is in position to have "pressure presence" The pressure presence in large part is trying to establish the defensive puck recovery shape BEFORE the offensive team can get puck support. This is a major part of the battle. On the other side, when you have the puck, does your positional discipline offer you a chance to alleviate pressure through puck movement? If you think the consistent solution to strong pressure presence is skating the puck in self-escape, you will find you'll skate the puck into a turnover more often than you'd like. The offensive answer to heaviness starts with making plays. Making plays is rooted in positional discipline, the puck carrier needs clear outs and people moving in advance of the play. Nothing about heaviness is reactive, it's all proactive on both sides and it's the crux of the battle. The next puck-carrier needs an opportunity to make the next play, we have to have an attitude of improving the conditions of possession. Heaviness starts with the group.

There is a clip of Colorado in a game vs. Winnipeg that is a great example of this.[12] Colorado has become one of the best teams in the NHL with its offensive zone heaviness through positional discipline. In this clip, the play starts with an offensive zone faceoff. Upon winning the draw, Colorado goes right into a high 3v2 with Mikko Rantanen walking up the wall and Bowen Byram activating on the weak side. MacKinnon

---

[12] Pressure Presence Example *https://twitter.com/belfryhockey/status/1660300674331025411?s=20*

OFFENSIVE ZONE POSSESSION

and Artturi Lehkonen set up a stack at the net. Makar, shoots the puck and MacKinnon recovers the shot and moves it back to the top to Rantanen, who shoots, again MacKinnon recovers. Now in both situations with the high shot, they have MacKinnon on one side and Byram activating down the other side in anticipation and structure for recovery. When MacKinnon recovers, Lehkonen makes himself available for the low-side change behind the net in anticipation. MacKinnon makes the play to the top again to Rantanen who shoots again with Lehkonen at the net and Byram again activating down on the weak side. This is the third time Byram activates on the weak side on a shot, and this time he recovers the puck. When the puck gets stopped on the back wall, they have MacKinnon, Byram and Lehkonen working to win the puck back. This time they win the puck to MacKinnon, who works the left corner 1v1 vs the D. Rantanen and Lehkonen set up the stack at the net. MacKinnon walks up the wall and Byram moves to the middle and shoots the one-timer from the top. Both Rantanen and Lehkonen and MacKinnon crash the boards to win the puck back. Upon winning the puck again, they find Makar coming downhill on the weak side. The shot is blocked and Makar recovers it and rims it down behind the net to Rantanen. During this time, Colorado initiates a possession change as Nikolishin replaces Lehkonen. Now they start working the high 3v2 to find the interior to the high forward in the stack. Byram and Makar have changed sides and the three forwards rotate in and out of the corners through the slot and to the net. Eventually Byram runs a give and go with Nikolishin on the half wall and rolls over to the weak side. Nikolishin finds Byram going downhill on the weak side. Byram then finds Rantanen for a net-front redirect. The entire offensive zone sequence is one minute and 33 seconds of complete offensive zone dominance.

 The dominance comes from their positional discipline and continual rotation in and out of the key spots, the net-front the stack high forward and the high 3v2 with active flanks. They recover five shots and they score on the sixth shot of the sequence. They are able to win pucks back because positionally they have the offensive zone covered no matter where the puck goes they can get immediate pressure on the puck as they are always in close vicinity. Eventually, they wear Winnipeg down with positional discipline, recovered shots and offensive zone movement.

What goes into "Pressure Presence?"

Pressure presence limits the puck-carrier's options and encourages the puck-carrier to slow down, to move into small space or punt it. Once the pressure presence gets on top of the puck-carrier, now there is a clear process that anyone and everyone should learn. Learn to become great at it. Angling to reduce space, skating angle combined with an active stick to take away passing options until you get in range. Once in range, now it's personal discipline to habits, a commitment to play through traffic and a relentless mentality. This isn't someone running around chasing the puck. This is someone who understands and leverages their team shape, anticipates puck movement and role changes and moves in advance of the play. They also know the triggers of vulnerability and attacks. Vulnerability includes the moments just as the puck carrier gets the puck. It's difficult to catch the puck and protect it simultaneously. These are usually done in two steps no matter how great the player is. Therefore, if you can arrive as the puck arrives, you have a huge advantage and an easier time being heavy. If a player turns their back, they are vulnerable because they can't see the rink as easily as if they didn't have to turn their back. If there is a bobble, the act of having to corral the puck takes time and is a vulnerability that can and should be taken full advantage of.

Once you arrive into the takeaway space, they skate into the takeaway space, they don't reach. They skate through the puck, driving through the middle of the puck, can play through contact. The players who win pucks do so because of three connected elements. Their stick is disruptive, they knock your stick, they tic the puck, they are in your stick-handling space, the stick is a problem. They make contact when the puck is still there, the contact is also with a stick at the puck or coming down on the puck and they are going through the middle of the puck. In the takeaway, they get under sticks and they get over sticks hard. The heaviness comes from the leverage they have in the hips. When you watch, they drive their hips into the contact and down on the puck. They have great posture, they don't reach, they are in strong position and the leverage for the heaviness comes first from the posture.

The most fascinating dichotomy of heaviness at the puck is when you are competing to get it. You need to be "heavy" on your stick and skates and aggressive in the contact with an ability to pry the puck off the opponent's stick and the whole thing is willingness, attitude, determination, body position, winning the puck line and applying leverage. Now the second you have the puck on your stick and you are looking to make a play, well, now you need a "feel" for space, soft hands to navigate through tight spaces, soft shoulders and mobile hips to roll with contact, poise and calmness with an ability to "slow the game down" to see and process the advantages of the play, effectively putting the opponent on your time. Then you have the feel for how hard to pass the puck. Most players pass the puck way too hard, way too often. The best passers lead the receiver into space and make it easy for the receiver to handle the pass cleanly. One area to look at if your team is struggling to score is how hard they pass the puck to each other. Teams that struggle to score in the offensive zone have a hard time creating shots off the pass … largely because the passes are way too hard. It's artful on the puck. This split-second dichotomy of "heavy" to "poise" is what makes it so difficult to be elite.

There is a great clip of Kyle Connor of the Winnipeg Jets this year vs. the Golden Knights. The play is a back-wall board battle with Eyssimont in the corner and Connor is net-front. The puck gets knocked behind the net and just as the Vegas D touches the puck, Connor is already there. He gets his shoulder contact and follows through with his hips through the hands and then his stick follows through under the Vegas D to win the puck. The interesting technique part of this clip is that the Vegas D works quickly to get off the wall and re-establish inside position, and as soon as Connor sees him get inside, he pulls the puck on the wall and turns back, catching the D trying to recover his position and it offers him the space he needs to make the play behind the net, improving the conditions. The timing of this play is unreal. Just a brilliant job of turning contact takeaways into extended possessions. The takeaway isn't enough, it needs to lead you into the next play. [13]

If they don't get the takeaway immediately, their competitive second and third efforts are possible because of their positioning. They can move, they can bounce off contact and stay in balance to move again. The posture and balance creates the conditions for the heaviness and then the competitiveness and relentlessness. This isn't discussed enough with these players. There is a reason, it's will, but there is a lot more technique than they get credit for. The best of the Tampa Bay Lightning for me was this exact skill set. The discipline structure of their offensive zone offers them the ability to get people consistently into pressure presence situations and then they go to work to win pucks back. I think this becomes contagious on teams. It's like anything that is a direct reflection to being a great teammate, like taking a hit to make a play, blocking a shot and pressure takeaways. These galvanize a group and players whom you wouldn't think would be so inclined, all of sudden, become brilliant at it.

The backhand advantage

Your backhand is an advantage ... it may just not be YOUR advantage. Your backhand may actually be a competitive advantage for your opponent. Offensively, when we refer to the benefits of the backhand, it's generally in regards to the unpredictability value of the backhand shot in scoring. Developing a great backhand is something we all harp on all of our players. However, from a frequency perspective, it's more important

---

[13] Kyle Connor *https://twitter.com/belfryhockey/status/1660306951505604608?s=20*

to develop fluency in backhand passing. Restrictions in the backhand, both catching passes and giving passes is where you are either taking or giving an advantage. Your backhand will be an advantage for someone though.

Let's start with backhand pass reception. If you aren't comfortable in backhand catches, it usually is reflected in the puck bouncing off the stick, or "stabbing" the puck to deaden it. This is restricting. The restriction manifests itself in time and anxiety. The time is the time available to make the next play from the time the puck hits your stick before the play is contested. If you have to "stab" or the puck bounces off the stick, you'll have to locate the carom and corral the puck. This takes time and your head is down, so while the time is ticking, you will lose vision of the play and the conditions of the play will change significantly while you are getting a hold of the puck. The anxiety often comes, less about taking a hard hit, although that is an undeniable factor for many players, it's more about knowing pressure is coming and making a rushed play that leads to a turnover, or time expires and you get stripped. In an effort to improve fluency on backhand catch situations like rim collections, defensive zone pass receptions for all players and general backhand catch situations, I work on backhand "sticky catches." A sticky catch is when the player cushions the puck on reception and is able to keep the puck on their stick throughout the catch. Where this skill takes on even more importance, the number of contested pucks on the backhand a player receives that needs to be put right into protection on first touch. Just an absolutely critical skill in protection - backhand catch in protection. Backhand catches where the puck needs to be immediately moved on touch, like a sticky catch with a backhand toe-drag pull to protection or a pull on the catch to change the line (This is often a skill I work on for angle entries). The development process for "sticky catches" is often very arduous and frustrating for everyone involved. Developing the timing of the soft catch, handling pucks that aren't perfect (close to the skates or where you have to reach), different weights of the pass (how hard a pass is), pucks spinning and tumbling around the boards.

Most coaches, players and skill development coaches give up before the process is complete and the player is left with a backhand reception that takes time and causes anxiety ... not just for you, for everyone. Fluency on backhand catches leads to plays and massive offensive opportunity.

Backhand passing is equally as difficult for players as catching is. Backhand passes over distance that are accurate and have pace generally require the ability to do so inside a weight shift and/or inside a crossover, which is skill blending. Fluency in the backhand can be traced back to the timing of the lower body in coordination with the wrist roll. Backhand saucer and flip passes in traffic, backhand hook passes to keep the puck flat around a stick, through a triangle and behind skates of a check, also coming from a place of protection and inside skating.

Backhand shooting from 20-25 feet is a rare skill. Players who do this well, shoot it like a wrist shot inside skating movement, such as weight shift and crossovers. Players whose backhand shooting habit is to "chip" the puck on the backhand have a very narrow scope of opportunity to use the backhand and will often not use it in situations where it is advantageous to do so. Getting the backhand to get upstairs on a goalie's shoulders and in the 6-hole under arms and off the pants is where goals can be created. Now if you can shoot the backhand from distance, around the hash-mark level and it has any pace on it, well, that's where Sidney Crosby has enjoyed an unmatched advantage. That's embedded in his skill set and offensive habits.

Backhand passing and backhand-pass reception would be everyday practice skills for me. I think it's that important. Players need daily work on it, rim collections, breakout pass reception, entries, small-space passing, backhand shots ... any and all of it. It's just that important. Backhand passing and shooting skills are a reflection of true elite hands. Fielding a tumbling rim with ease, allowing you to get your head up and make a play – that's elite hands. Your backhand is an advantage for someone ... either you and your team or your opponent.

The grit of scoring

There is a grit to scoring goals, the grit is rooted in playing with expectation. The players who score, expect to score, they have clear shot-generation habits that lead to most of their shot chances, however they are always on the lookout for an opportunity to pounce. Playing with expectation is really the epitome of leveraging habits to improve percentages. Playing with expectation is also expecting to have to play in traffic to score, handle the puck in contact, shoot through a stick and being prepared means to initiate those contacts rather than run from them. Derek Jeter has a great video clip when talking about why a game speeds up and slows down. "You hear about athletes talk about the game speeds up and the game slows down," he said. "It slows down when you are prepared, and it speeds up when you are unprepared. Every time I'm in a situation I've already gone through it in my head." [14] This is part of the grit of scoring in hockey. The preparation that makes the game slow down or speed up is how the consistency of their habits allows them to play with expectation. They know they are going to get those pucks, so they are ready and aren't surprised by a chance. They expect it and are prepared for it. I'm not someone who watches or studies other sports to figure out how we can play hockey better, I think many of the ideas that people try to pull from other sports tactically and technically can be a reach. What I do like about other sports is in their player interviews there is a lot more candid and unguarded statements made that offer great insight into how the players think and apply skill.

Goal scorers also hit the net. Since I was very young, I loved going early to watch the warmup, regardless of the level. NHL players hit the net a staggering number of times, even in warmups. The grit of scoring involves hitting the net. Forcing the goalie to stop the puck. As a team, you can do everything right and create the scoring chance, but if the puck smashes off the glass … it's all for naught. The grit part of hitting

---

[14] *https://twitter.com/TheHoopHerald/status/1590440639732539393*

the net is demanding yourself to hit the net all the time. It's so important that it is a major part of the expectation of scoring. It's hard to expect to score when you aren't sure if the shot you'll take will actually be on net. Communicating with your teammates, playing with expectation, pre-shot shape (stick available, body set up, spacing and angle preserved), pass receiving and hitting the net are all parts of the skill stack (more on this coming up) inside the grit of scoring.

When I first studied elite hockey goal scorers, I was surprised by how many different ways they score despite having an image in my mind about "how they score." I think of Alex Ovechkin, David Pastrnak and Steven Stamkos on the left side one-timer or now an Auston Matthews with the change of angle shot and Connor McDavid walking defensemen on the rush and making a quick move on the goalie in tight at Mach 3 speed. However, when you pull all their goals for the season, you see out of 60 goals, they score maybe 12-15 in these signature ways, then the other 45-48 come all different ways – rush chances, backhands, net-area rebounds, tips, walkouts, seam pass shots, empty net … you name it, they score that way. They score a high number of goals in high-traffic areas inside stick and body contact. While they have a signature goal structure, this is a structure they leverage for less than 20 percent of their goals, the rest of the goals come from playing with expectation. They expect to find solutions to plays and get presented with a chance. They have a coldness to them. A frightening coldness, whereby they have a short memory and don't carry negative emotion of missed chances into their next chance. They approach goal scoring like the movie *50 First Dates*. They are able to let the emotion of chances go, positively or negatively, and prepare themselves equally for the next chance. That ability to control their emotions to continually look forward to the next chance, combined with the expectation they'll find solutions to plays that lead to scoring chances, those are big parts of the grit of scoring.[15]

---

[15] Stamkos 60 Goals *https://www.youtube.com/watch?v=YimRmMapl9s&t=2s*

The most deadly shooters score on 15-18 percent of their shots, probably half that when you include missed shots and blocked shots. Yet, they keep coming relentlessly, fully expecting for one or more of the shots to go in. They have elite creativity and determination of both shot selection and manipulating game conditions, and they manufacture shot chances. This isn't to say they don't get frustrated, because they do, but they let it go quickly and move onto the next shot and chance ... that they expect is coming very soon.

One of the biggest mental hurdles to scoring for players is our perception of others' opinions. Relative proclamations of your role stuffing you in a box. Accepting your role on the team and executing it to the best of your ability, while also resisting relativity labels, well, that's one of the great mental hurdle opportunities available to everyone in the sport. You overcome the lack of self-confidence through discipline, hard work, determination and concentration of focus to a process. The process of shooting pucks every day in your basement or your garage, that's as much mental as it is skill development. Self-ownership, impose tests on yourself through goal setting. Get a boost of self-esteem by being the best teammate in the role you are given, and then trust your process and believe in yourself as you expand the depth and belief in your capacity. Be the "coming of age" lead character in your own movie. Build momentum slowly and methodically through the skill stack of the grit of scoring and break through every glass ceiling.

The skill stack

The skill stack has been a career-long discovery process. It started during the hours of initial video study, dubbing NHL skill video clips from one VCR to the other to build "skill tapes," to start pulling the skills apart. Started with the physical properties of the skill, the characteristics of posture (shin angle and back angle), then into locating the true center of gravity. Where is the balance? What edge is the player on? Where is

BELFRY OFFENSE

the weight on the blade? How does the upper body contribute? What about the way the player leans and shifts their weight from one foot to the other? A deep dive into the top-hand elbow leads me into what the role differences between the top hand and the bottom hand. Now I'm curious about puck placement and its impact on movement. What about the player's head? Surely, it's not just about keeping your head up. What are they looking at? What about a better question ... what are they looking for? All this on a still-screen image, the player isn't even moving yet. All these questions ... still feels like I haven't scratched the surface. What's most important? What parts directly influence other pieces? Can you create a domino effect in movement? If so, how so? What are the key movement elements?

It's so overwhelming, where do I start? In my discovery process, I focused a lot on the domino effects of movement, and that's what I taught for many years. As my level of understanding of how the body is supposed to move in hockey, which is in many ways, an unnatural physical movement, I started to gain a better understanding of skill. I studied "power skating coaches" and how they taught, the attention they gave the forward stride as their critical shape. I watched hours and hours of lessons and listened to the cues and watched the progressions. Then matched that against my ongoing research and developing philosophy. The more I watched the clearer it became to me ... there is a big difference between skating and moving. The skating coaches all struggled with what to do with the puck. The intersection of skating and movement is the puck. What we do with the puck when we skate, the separation of the upper body and the lower body, the athletic reactions to changing pressure and support conditions to make a play ... this is movement. I became convinced I needed to understand movement. Movement is skill stacking. The skating is a base. The goal is not to become a great skater. Rather the goal is to leverage a foundation in skating to become a great mover. Movement in hockey is expressed and best illustrated on the puck. Early in my career, I stumbled upon the value of teaching skating with the puck and was producing results

OFFENSIVE ZONE POSSESSION

above and beyond my power skating counterparts because my players could move.

When I was coaching teams during the foundation stage of my career with Playmakers Hockey, I invested a ton of time in crossover skating with the puck. Everything we did involved somewhere, somehow crossing over with the puck. In those days, if you were on the ice with me, you were either crossing over with the puck, crossing over into the skill you were going to do (tight turn for example) and then crossing your feet coming out of that target skill. However, the sequence would include a steady dose of crossovers. Crossovers with a puck is a foundational hockey movement. Expressing a complex skill stack that offered seemingly endless opportunities to build more and more and more with the athlete. The more I stacked, the better the player could move.

I was at a minor hockey tournament toward the end of my Playmakers Hockey run and was stopped in the lobby by a longtime rival coach. As we started to talk, he said, "Hey, I saw one of your players playing in a tournament last weekend with (another) team. I knew it was a Playmaker by the way he skated ... crossovers everywhere." I was taken aback of course, but the investment in movement became an identifiable characteristic. This became the platform for my discovery into the "linear crossover," which was inside my NHL acceleration study. Another breakthrough of understanding in the space between skating and movement.

The "underhandle" challenge

The ability to leverage "underhandle" in scoring is incredibly difficult. When we talk about underhandle, it can be interpreted by the athlete that we are "simplifying" movement for efficiency in scoring. Underhandling is actually incredibly difficult and most often requires more skill from the athlete to do well. We frame it as the underhandle is a compensation for those who don't handle the puck well, when it's actually the opposite. Underhandle is the ability to get the puck quickly into the shooting position and be able to release the puck at any time when the puck is in that position. Common examples include:

- Catch-and-shoot situations, most often when the puck goes across the body on the forehand side for a shot.
- Shooting deception, when the player has the puck in the shooting position and is now looking to hide intentions or shot-release timing.

Getting the puck quickly into the shot position without handling it to put it there. Using the pass to pull the puck there or moving your body around the puck. The underhandle challenge is being able to get the puck into the shooting position without having the puck touch the backhand. Sounds easy, try it, it's really hard. Underhandle is actually an advanced puck skill. Players who don't handle the puck well, often overhandle when they should be underhandling, much to the frustration of their coaches and linemates. These are players in catch-and-shoot situations where their pass receiving habits stop the puck in the middle of their body and now they have jammed themselves. They have no shooting body shape, and they have to move the puck again to shoot. The problem is the catch. Players who overhandle in deception, handle the puck in an area in front of their body or on the forehand, but not in a shooting position, so they have to move the puck to shoot it, killing their deception. In forehand shooting situations, when the puck touches the backhand, you can't shoot, so you are now telegraphing your release.

Underhandle for me is an advanced puck skill and represents a unique advantage for those who want to take it a step further. Take Nathan MacKinnon, for example, at Mach 3 speed on the rush, just prior to shooting, he will handle the puck incredibly fast INSIDE the shooting position. The combination of the puck being in the shooting position, the speed and angles he is attacking at and the stickhandling executed so fast, overhandling is a weapon. It's a step beyond the challenge of underhandle. There are levels to this, and underhandling is an advanced puck skill. The first step is to be able to get the puck out of the middle of the body. Players who frustrate us with overhandle may not be capable, they are jammed with the puck in the middle. Developmentally, there just isn't any value of having the puck there. A lot of puck skills are restricted by the players' comfort in handling pucks in the middle of the body. If we want to make meaningful gains in underhandle, it all starts with getting the players comfortable with the puck out of the middle and only use the middle of the body as a pass through. Easier said than done.

The NHL teams that are the most effective in scoring in the offensive zone share four distinct inter-reliant pillars that provide the platform to the duality of the offensive zone, which is most critical to truly understand and execute.

OFFENSIVE ZONE

OZP SHAPE = **TRIANGULATION** + **ACTIVE DEFENSE** X **ROTATION SPEED**

Figure 6: Offensive Zone Pillars

1. OZP Shape
    a. The shape and spacing of the five offensive players hold a duality of position. Each player is able to pressure, get above their defensive speed responsibility and holds in rotation and side change, while being aware that each position offers strong offensive opportunity to threaten. Teams that struggle with offensive zone defense lose their shape and ability to quickly transition with numbers or strong positions.
    b. When I watch a team move in the offensive zone and I see the shapes moving and changing as the conditions change, there is a fascinating dichotomy at play that I don't think is given its rightful due for how important it is. Active patience vs urgency. Urgency is a term we hear all the time, but when teams express

urgency, it often looks more like rushing the play (making a play before the play develops) or pressing (just throwing pucks at the net, which feels more like hope than a strategy) rather than being urgent (elevating the collective effort to play at a speed and pace that opens the ice up for better opportunities). This is why the term I use is active patience. Active patience (a determination to maintain possession team of the puck while keeping an eye out for opportunities to attack) is where the urgency comes from being patient, but patience isn't passive. It's leveraging control until you find a seam to attack. Active, I want to be expressed as, moving from one good spot to the next good spot as the conditions change, or ... to intentionally change the conditions.

2. Triangulation

   a. When the game is 5v5 the nature of five players immediately offers two triangles:

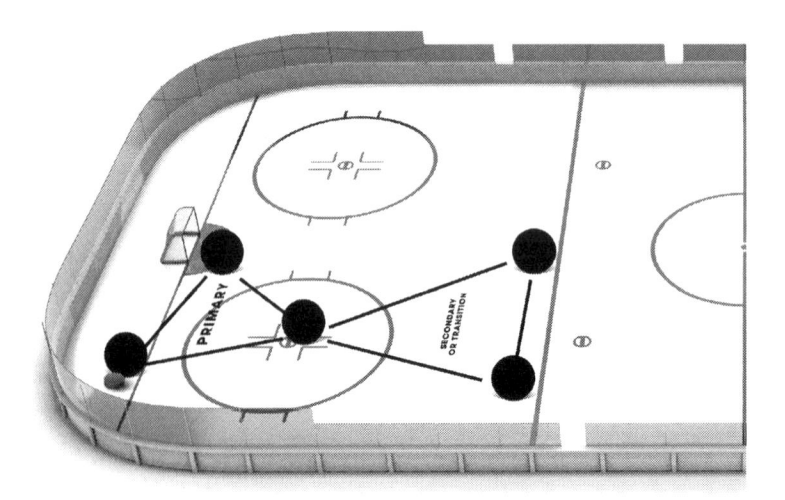

Figure 7: Triangles

   i. Primary Triangle - most immediately at the puck
   ii. Secondary Triangle - three players furthest from the puck

OFFENSIVE ZONE POSSESSION

- Transition triangle
- Player furthest from the puck has the potential to be the most dangerous both offensively and in defensive transition

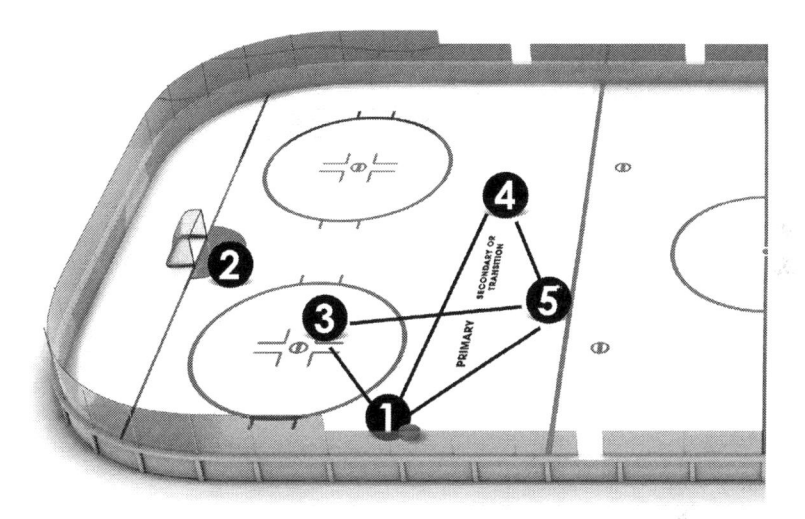

Figure 8:

What's interesting is as the puck moves around the zone, the roles and the triangles change.

In this example, if the puck carrier climbs the boards, the puck carrier (1) and the two D (4 and 5) are the secondary or transition triangle the strong side D (4) and the high forward are the primary triangle.

b. The key to understanding triangulation is that each point of the two triangles has a specific job that has two sides to the responsibility, like a coin. There is an offensive responsibility and a defensive responsibility. Roles are continually changing as the puck moves, the game situation changes and the puck changes hands or become loose. Knowing your role in the play as the puck moves and the game situation changes is essentially hockey sense – anticipating role changes by seeing the context of the play evolve, the puck moving and transition response – moving prior to the situation starting – that's a tenant elite hockey sense.

c. The roles are as follows:

PLAYER	OFFENSIVE ROLES	PLAYER	DEFENSIVE ROLES
Puck Carrier (PC)	Player on the puck	F1	Immediate pressure on the puck
Support (S)	Player directly supporting the puck	F2	Player directly supporting the pressure
F3	Dual position	F3	Dual position
Strong Side D (SSD)	Defense position on the puck side	Strong Side D	Defensive position on the puck side
Weak Side D (WSD)	Defense position on the weak side	Weak Side D	Defensive position on the weak side

Note: Throughout the book, there are many diagrams and none of them will refer to the players by traditional positions of Left Wing (LW), Center (C), Right Wing (RW), Left Defense (LD) and Right Defense (RD). The frequency of interchange of roles leads me to refer to the players as their role number. So when you are viewing the diagrams, please keep this in mind.

d. All roles are constantly interchanging as the movement of the puck and the ever-changing game situations dictate.

e. Examples include:

   i. In the first five minutes of the first period when the game is tied.

   ii. The strong-side D pinches down at the puck and becomes the puck carrier.

   iii. The puck carrier sends the puck to the weak side but the opponent cuts it off, the roles change,

   iv. Last couple minutes of a period where we are winning by one goal. Puck support plays exclusively on the defensive

OFFENSIVE ZONE POSSESSION

side. In this scenario, we have one player playing on offence and four players in defensive mindsets and there decisions are based on defensive responsibilities.

3. Active defensemen

   a. The defensemen are active and engaged because of their absolute trust in F3. F3 is not a luxury on these teams, it is a constant presence and therefore the D can rely on F3 being there all the time. It eliminates engagement hesitation. Teams who defend well in the OZ shift the responsibility of pinching engagement off the defenders and onto F3 whether directly or in its effect. There is no "only pinch after checking to see if F3 is in position." F3 is in position ... that's a constant, don't hesitate, just go! The only considerations of the activity of defensemen is reflected in score and time on the clock. In my offence, I'm less inclined to take my foot off the gas, although I could see some situations where it may make some sense. One specific situation would be to purposely engage in more re-entry or rush defense situations because tactically there are greater offensive advantages to be exploited in that particular game, juncture in the game, etc.

4. Rotation speed

   a. Teams who defend well in the OZ sprint off the puck. They just do. They anticipate role change and move without hesitation. When they are on offence, they also value movement in the OZ that is above the speed of the defenders. This is a critical interdependence element to OZ defending. The faster the team plays on offence, the more space they use in the OZ - side changes and low to high to low - the movement speed, if above the speed of the defenders creates the opportunity to defend effectively in the OZ. Rotation speed is both reloading ... but also before that, it's when we have the puck. The best time to set up your defensive play is when you are on offence. The best time to set up your offensive play is when you are on defense. Rotation speed is sprinting to the next best position. As the conditions of the play change, each player is decelerating or accelerating. We have five players on the ice, so three players may be accelerating, while two players are decelerating. Or one player is accelerating while four are decelerating, or any combination thereof. The collective changes of speed impact the timing of rotation speed. It's not five guys whipping around the offensive zone at top speed. It's better when their five players are accelerating at different times and for different reasons. When the players know how the shape (two-connected triangles) move, then each player can either be sprinting to the next best spot as they anticipate their role change, or they could be decelerating to hold a good spot a little longer to preserve space to either be open longer or to open more space to accelerate into next. It's rotation, but it's more than that, it's sprinting and decelerating in anticipation of the best conditions for the play. This is the interconnected play model.

These four interconnected, inter-reliant and interdependent pillars drive offensive zone play. Now, let's dig into Offensive Zone Offence.

To generate consistent even-strength offense - throughout the lineup - the goal of every team. Everyone is searching for the magic formula that unlocks scoring. However, there are any number of challenges that every team has to navigate. While what follows are generalizations meant to illustrate, we can all identify with these common challenges. Scoring as a team is difficult to do through team structure because the top players are asset driven, relying on a superior depth of skill over the opposition, and leverage these inside their own personal game structure that works for them and they'll look for or manipulate repetitive creases of opportunity inside that structure. If you take them out of their assets, minimize their depth of skill and restrict their personal game maps, you run the risk of affecting their timing, rhythm and confidence. So, often times, the top offensive performers are left to their own devices so long as they remain productive. Over the years of play, they've discovered patterns and situations that lead them to success and they drive the game into those patterns and situations. Top players will also break down the defense 1v1 which will open up other opportunities.

The middle part of the lineup is where coaching the offensive zone can have the most impact. The players have enough offensive tools to finish plays, but could use a structure to facilitate the reads of their teammates to connect on plays and leverage the structure for repeatability. Then the bottom of the lineup , on most teams, isn't expected to score, and that low expectation is passed onto the players and therefore they rarely threaten unless it's outside of shots from the perimeter with a burly net presence.

The point of this over-generalized illustration is regardless of the team makeup, there is a wide variance of perception of speed, depth of skill, awareness, background knowledge and processing speed that makes it challenging to fully synchronize whereby every player is firing on all cylinders. So we have every player on the team with:

- Different backgrounds of knowledge
- Read the game at different speeds
- Have different skill assets
- Move at different speeds
- Perception of pressure is different
- Ability to see plays develop is on different levels
- And then, you have all the environmental differences, like different linemates, different D pairings, different opponents, different zone starts, different game circumstances ... not to mention all of them have different personalities and love, commitment and passion for the game.

Now through all this, in order for offence to work best, it's executed through the collective. However, if you are too hardened to your philosophy, system, structures, objectives, principles and rules of play, you will invariably alienate someone or a group of players on your team, which all but eliminates your ability to create offensive production depth.

When we talk about processing speed or reading the game, we sometimes either diminish how difficult it really is or the opposite extreme, treat it like it's a superhuman power. The best way I can describe how difficult it is, I offer you the "book club" analogy, which goes something like this: You have a book club that meets to discuss the book series they are reading, like the Hobbit, Harry Potter or any book series that is a massive undertaking. The only problem is everyone at the meeting didn't read the book the same way. It wasn't like the group decided to start at the beginning and everyone reads a chapter or two and stops at the same place before meeting again to discuss the events of the first couple chapters. That would ensure everyone is at the same spot in the book and they all read the same thing and therefore are discussing the same things at a similar level of understanding. No, if teaching hockey is a metaphor for this book club, then everyone comes to the meeting at completely different places in the book. One person read the first chapter of the first book, another person is two chapters ahead, while another is two full books ahead and yet another has read the whole series through once already and is reading it for a second time, and finally, there is one person who has read and studied the series a few times and knows it inside and out as though they are the co-author. Now we get all these people together to meet a few times a week to discuss the book or learn to play hockey together. You are the book club meeting facilitator or the hockey coach ... where do you start? Oh, and by the way, it changes every year, with every group. That's the overwhelming challenge of coaching/teaching/playing hockey. Now here you are reading this book, you have everyone at completely different places and now you need to find a way to simply explain it so everyone reading the book can follow along, but you also have to appeal to the many who know much more about it than you. Now to complicate matters even further, everyone who is at the book club didn't read the book from the

OFFENSIVE ZONE POSSESSION

beginning and read it or learn hockey skills and tactics in a natural and logical order. No, everyone at the book club has read all kinds of just random passages here and there and the odd chapter and is trying to put the pieces together in their mind. Every person at the table has fragmented understanding. This doesn't even take into account the actual reading and comprehension skills or athletic learning capacity of each person in the book club or hockey club. This is why teaching offence to a team is so incredibly hard to do.

So where do we start to influence offensive zone play?

This is where you would normally hear some version of a logic tree like Philosophy/ Structure/Objective/Principles/Reads/Tactics/Skills/ Fundamental Skills to explain the approach and deduct the level of collective understanding to the lowest common denominator. This approach has been what we've been attempting to execute and refine for decades. When we go down this path, there is an overwhelming amount of information to convey to the players. Many coaches get lost in the volume of information to understand and that's before they have to figure out how to communicate it to their players. Which forces many ambitious coaches back to the K.I.S.S. principle (Keep It Simple Stupid Principle). I'm ready to try something different.

What am I looking for here?

My mind goes to more of an equation. I have always done well with equations. I find that in searching for the equation it forces you to look for or create terms that capture the essence in very few words and perhaps the best part of an equation is that it forces you to think in relationships. Hockey is a relationship game because of the fluidity of the game and the frequency of changes of possession. So building the logic out in equations forces you to think of how things relate to or impact each other. I like it because the layers underneath tend to be more implied and open-ended rather than a pyramid structure or other type of logic tree where you feel the need to list all of the granule individual pieces, and by the time you are done, the list is as long as your arm, and with the amount of time you put into creating all the lists, it's impossible not to become both overwhelmed to the point where you confuse yourself and hardened to the logic process you finally arrived at.

My mission is for the equation to become the objective and capture how I want the players to work together to create advantages. When playing with players with high hockey IQ and creativity it can be difficult to know how to create plays with them. The equation becomes a way to govern their movement decisions so they can always meaningfully contribute to the play. How the players know when to move where.

Belfry Hockey Offensive Zone Equation:

BELFRY OFFENSIVE ZONE

ZONE CONTROL = ELEVATED SPEED OF SHAPE X HABITS + PERCENTAGES

Figure 9: Equation

The equation is based on knowing your role in the shape, reading the possession and direction of the puck which tells everyone how they can move purposefully to support the play. Habits are your skill execution techniques to become more successful more frequently, and percentages is the sliding scale that guides your next decision.

Zone control is the objective, as much as I'd like to reinvent the entire wheel, clear objective aligns people to the common understanding. Zone control for us is defined by the ability to maximize zone time through controlling how the puck can move both offensively and defensively.

OFFENSIVE ZONE POSSESSION

Elevated speed of shape is the first element to assume control of the space and it has several different intertwining aspects: establishing shape early, knowing your role in the shape and how your role changes as the puck and the conditions surrounding the puck ever change, maintaining the integrity of the shape through anticipating and sprinting through rotations which elevates the skating speed off the puck and offers more opportunity to impact collective pace with the speed of the puck or speed of pressure to get the puck back through its movement and frequency.

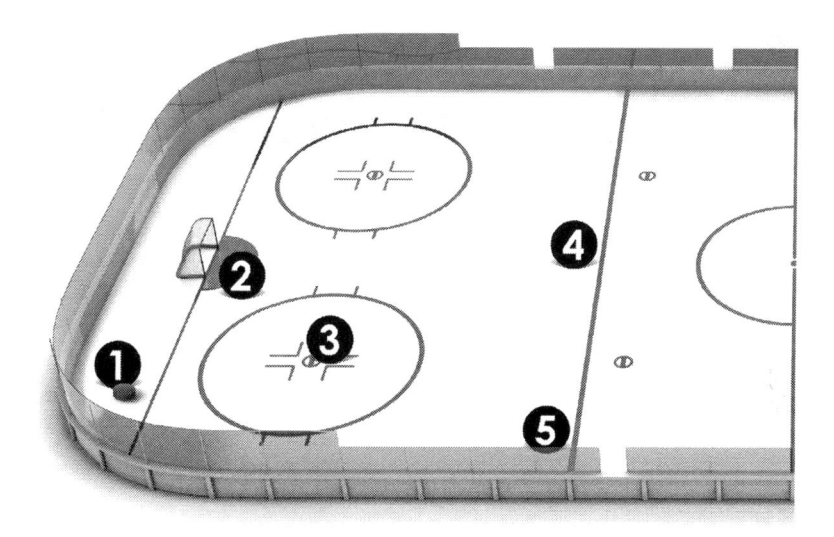

Figure 10: Elevated Speed Shape

The puck could be anywhere on the rink, we establish our shape with 1, 2 and 3 as the primary triangle and 3, 4 and 5 as the secondary triangle.

There are generally two ways the puck can move - with player movement or counter player movement. When the puck moves with player movement, it achieves the first competitive advantage - pace of play, which is critical in both offensive zone offence and offensive zone defense.

BELFRY OFFENSE

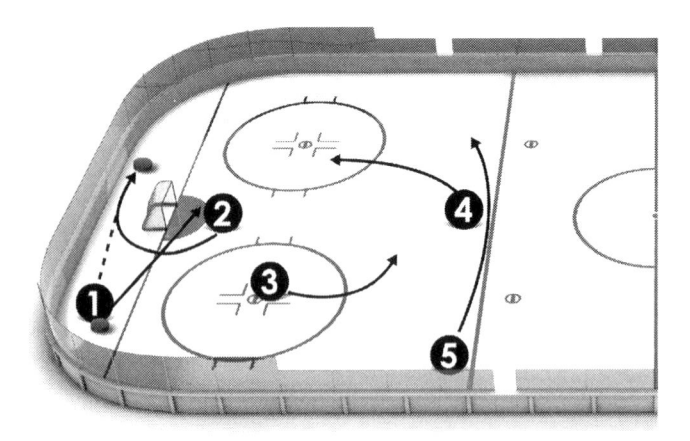

Figure 11:

If 1 passes to the net front going with the puck, that is going with player movement. As the puck moves, so do the roles, now the primary triangle is 1, 2 and 4, with 4, 3 and 5 as the secondary or transition triangle.

When the puck moves counter movement, we are looking to attack more on the inside. The shape refers to how the group of five moves together, each of the spots are completely interchangeable and rotation is not only encouraged, it's outright demanded. We don't want anyone split from the herd.

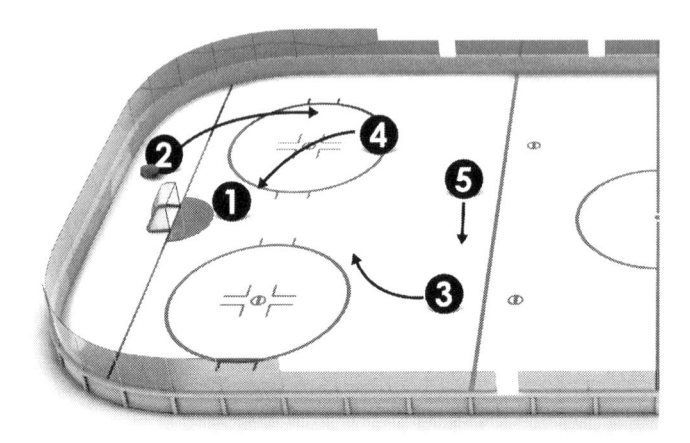

Figure 12:

62

OFFENSIVE ZONE POSSESSION

As we continue to follow the play, as 4 activates, he is moving counter to the direction of the puck, as 2 is climbing up the ice, 4 is attacking down. Now as 2 continues to climb, the primary triangle is 2, 5 and 1, with 4, 3 and 5 as the secondary triangle.

Counter movement refers to the puck and players moving on sharp angles. Generally, attacking interior works off playing off the heels of the defenders and forcing them into repetitive stops and starts. This is how active patience is practically expressed.

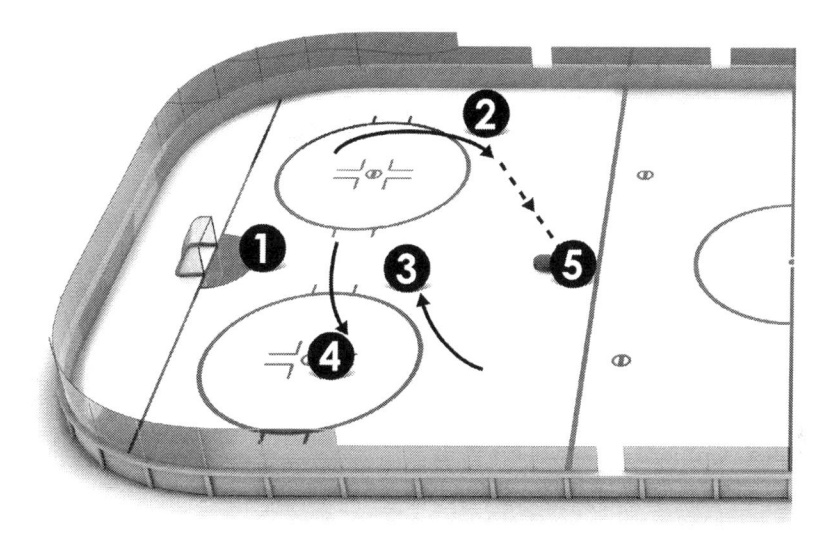

Figure 13:

Following the play to the shot chance, the play goes up to 5, who has a double stack screen at the net, or he has 4, who rotates to the weak side to maintain ice balance for shot threat and shot recovery and prepares to resume his original position at the top.

When the group starts moving WITH the direction of the puck, they are elevating speed and then trying to time opportunities to then move counter the direction of the puck to open up opportunities to attack. This is how active patience becomes embedded in the fabric of your team's mindset.

BELFRY OFFENSE

The most advantage we have offensively is when we have part of our group moving with the direction of the puck looking to elevate speed, while we have someone else moving counter the direction of the puck to open up opportunities to attack. When both directions of support are active, it maximizes the play potential. It's critical in our level of understanding that the best support is varied support that is purposeful. So when someone says, "You need to support the puck better," recognizing your role in the shape and moving either with or counter the direction of the puck for competitive advantage is what they mean.

This is where it gets interesting and may explain in part why attacking the interior can lead to defensive exposure. When you defend on exit kill, you want to move on "attach angles." Attach angles instructs the defending players to attach to their check, moving in the same direction of angle to control space defensively - tracking, folding, swinging in - these are all terms that imply attaching or same direction angles.

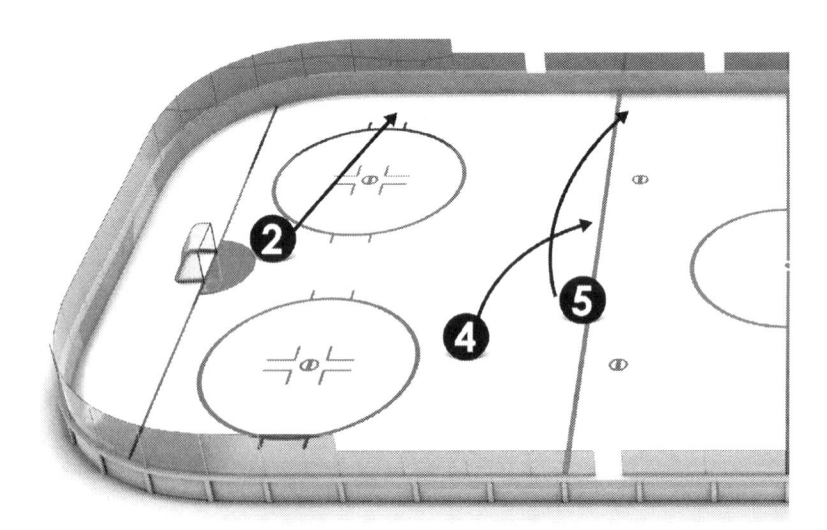

Figure 14: Attach Angles

In this illustration 2 is the F2 track at the net, 4 is an example of a weakside fold, and 5 is a swing in or surf.

OFFENSIVE ZONE POSSESSION

When you are truly attacking, you are working on counter angles with teammates and working off heels of the opponent - when the puck turns over, the offensive group has two or more players moving counter to the puck, when the defensive response has to be an attach angle - so they have to respond quickly to the turnover to quickly redirect their skating direction to get on an attach angle. This is why a shape that has life and purposeful movement is so critically important to the offensive zone. The two players above the puck have the best opportunity to immediately work on attach angles while the players at the puck who are counter the puck quickly recover their skating direction. It's a group! Sophisticated offensive zone is a group with all five moving together because the puck is going to either turn over or become loose and we have to be organized in puck recovery BEFORE our opponent organizes around possession. The best time to organize yourself defensively is when you have the puck. If you think you can react to defend, you will be late and unnecessarily concede organization, speed and numbers to the opposition making it harder and harder to timely get the puck back.

In 1990, I attended the then Canadian Hockey Coaches Certification Program, or NCCP, Level 4 conference in Ottawa, ON. During that conference, one of the speakers was a fellow named Bjorn Kinding, who had researched transition hockey. It was one of the most impactful presentations I've ever seen as it literally changed my thinking on the spot. I was never able to watch hockey the same way since. In that presentation, he cited his research of how frequently the puck turns over in a game, and along with that, he said it's unlikely to expect all five players to be on offence and then all five players defend when the puck turns over. He said, most often, you have some players who are still in offensive positions while others are asked to defend immediately, and some players are in defensive positions while you are on offence. When you really look at it closely from that lens, you also notice that there is quite a bit of opportunity for dual positioning - a player who is in both an advantageous offensive position AND defensive position simultaneously. This is often F3. F3 is in a dual position - the two defenders at the blue line are naturally

BELFRY OFFENSE

in good defensive positions and the two forwards at the puck may be in offensive positions. Now when the puck turns, who is in the best position to defend immediately to get the puck back quickly? F3 and strong side D? F3 and weak-side D? F2 at the net and F3? We have to have two in immediate position. Now the puck turns quickly again, who is in the best offensive positions F1 and F2? F3 and weak-side D? You see what I mean. This is the duality of the interconnected game model. In the offensive zone, we are on offence and defense at the same time, and depending on your place in the shape, the location of the puck and the conditions surrounding the puck (time and options of the puck carrier), that will determine your role in the shape, and as the puck and the conditions move, your role changes accordingly.

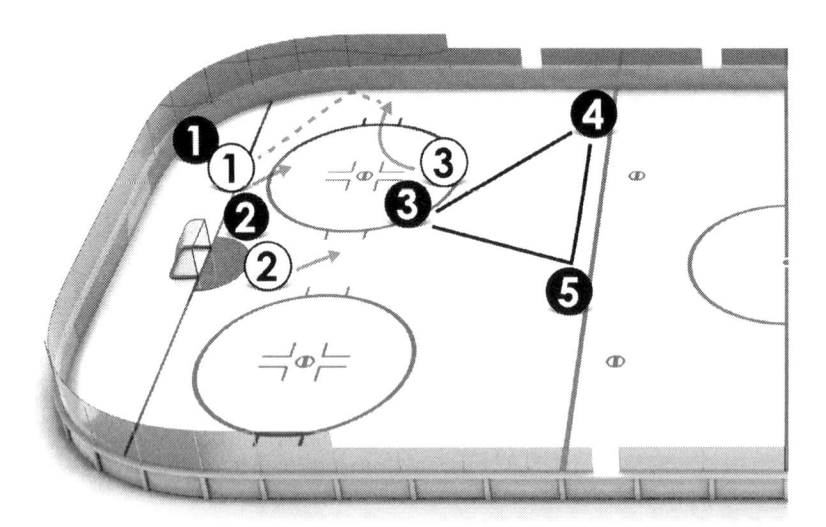

Figure 15: Dual Position

When we lose the puck in the corner to white 1, and he bumps it to white 3 on the breakout, we have our F3 and our strong-side D (4) who are in the best positions to make a defensive play on the puck. Their white 1 and white 2 are above our 1 and 2, so our 1 and 2 have to recover a defensive position as they are on the offensive side of the puck on the turnover.

66

Now that you know more about the perspective I'm coming from, you can see how now the habits (success tools) and percentages (decision-making structure) engages group creativity.

Team scoring creativity

"Team scoring creativity" is how the group reads off each other to improve scoring chances. This starts with what the collective understanding of how scoring chances are created, what we prioritize in chance generation, how a scoring position can be improved, and the need to pull the opponent's goalie into a chess match. If you've done a good job in elevating the group understanding of scoring, then you can play chess, if you haven't you'll be playing checkers.

The goal is six-foot wide by four-foot tall, and goaltenders get bigger and more skilled every year. Goaltender development has become a competitive industry around the world and the results are phenomenal. Many of the goalie brethren have executed fantastic studies of goaltending movement efficiency, developing hockey IQ for goaltenders and the physical geometry of the position as it relates to shooting, angles and positioning. Goal scoring is a million miles behind in training and development, and only recently have there been meaningful breakthroughs in terms of shooting technique and improving shot selection, release speed, changing angles, expanding the net and the geometry of shooting.

Goaltenders understand how to get square to the puck in the first place, how to move to stay square to the puck, and use positioning, movement, and proper feel of situational depth to leverage the limits in the trajectory of the puck to make the net as small as possible. When a goalie is on, it is a big challenge for even the best shooters to score. The math of goal scoring vs goaltending is tilted way in favor of the goalies. Goaltending save percentage is over 90 percent and the best shooters in the game are shooting at 15-2 percent and that doesn't take into account all the shots they take, that's just the percentage based on the shots on goal. The actual shooting percentage, taking into account shots blocked and missed shots as well as the shots on goal, the actual shot attempt percent to score ... well we don't even want to talk about it. Then, when you become aware of the clear-sight shooting percentage, and our best response is to send bodies to the net to "take the goalie's eyes away," you realize our best solution is to take the goalie who is big enough and on angle taking away even more of the net than his body would otherwise indicate, and we put more people in front of the net to shrink the net even more. By the time we have the goalie, our net-front presence, their defensemen and then probably another shot blocker at the shot, that doesn't leave a lot of net to be actually shooting at. When all things are equal and the shooter has the puck on his stick for any length of time and he's shooting from 25-plus feet out with all this traffic and the goalie has had time to get his depth and get square to the puck, your shooting strategy is reduced essentially to hope.

I've spent my entire career working closely with elite goal scorers and they have taught me everything I know about goal scoring. The first rule of goal scoring is we need to find a way to tilt the math, even just a little bit. When I say tilt the math, I mean do things that improve our chances, chisel away at the edges and pick up a percentage here and percentage there, knowing every little bit counts. When I started to try to understand goal scoring at a deeper level, I studied goaltenders. Not from a goaltending perspective, but from the flip side of their process.

A goaltender is trying to do a few fundamental things consistently on as many shots as they can.

- Read the play and understand the initial threats of the play and make a good decision on depth based on the threats.
- Get square to the puck. At the end of the day, square to the puck is a starting point to create a leverage-able advantage.
- Manage depth and optimize the position for both taking away the net and being available to get to the next play. If they are shallow with their depth, they may be able to move across the net well, but

OFFENSIVE ZONE POSSESSION

give up net to shoot at because they are too deep. If they are too aggressive with their depth, they have the primary shot covered, so long as the puck carrier doesn't dramatically change the play situation, or make a play that changes the point of attack and make it difficult to recover for the next play.

- Once square to the puck, use anticipation and movement to stay square and track the puck. Track the puck with their eyes and head down on the puck and stay disciplined with their head level to get their entire frame on the shot.
- Keep their feet as long as possible and get set upon release.
- Read the release of the puck coming off the stick, pay attention to the nuances of release and turn that knowledge into tracking the puck through the save.
- Leverage the depth, the understanding of trajectory, set your feet square to the puck, read the release, track the puck right to the body and control the rebound.
- Track the puck to be ready for the next play.

If this is basically the process of goaltending, then scoring goals must live on the opposite side of the street. If we want to score, it would stand to reason we need to:

- Change the point of attack on entry whenever possible and/or disguise the true intentions of the play.
- Invite the goalie to get square and then change the line. Unsettle his feet.
- Stagger the threats to create uncertainty in the depth, players ahead of the puck and players behind the puck. Influence depth through quality of threats.
- Move the puck east-west and on diagonals or down with change of speed to keep them chasing their position. Over rotate him or flatten him out.

- Disguise the release, change the shot angle and shoot off the pass.
- Preserve shooting space (the closer you get to the net, the shooting trajectory makes the net smaller for the goalie to cover) on initial shots.
- Vary the traffic, land on the net at the edge of his crease and compress his depth, flash screens, force goalie to find sight windows around traffic and shoot to the opposite window.
- Shoot outside the goalie's frame, force him to reach or get extended.
- Offensive box out, fall off the heels of the goalie with a redirect stick.

If this is the basics of shooting to score, then what are the details to elite scoring:

1. Expand the net

    There are many ways to make the net bigger for the goalie. Scorers employ these strategies as much as possible.

    a. Inviting the goalie to the puck line, using deception to freeze him in a set stance, and then changing the puck line (using a combination of lateral skating movement, like a hook turn, a weight shift, a crossover, an inside cut and a drag or a push of the puck) is a great process to get ahead of the goalie and pull him off the puck line.

    Back in the day, I remember the goalie coaches would periodically bring out "the ropes" to illustrate the puck line and to teach goalies to square to the puck and not to the player, which is a common challenge with young goalies. The ropes illustration essentially is four ropes tied to the top corner elbows on both sides and the bottom of the posts on both sides. The ropes extend out about 20-25 feet and you pull and gather the four ropes all together in one hand. Now, you put the goalie in the net and also in the middle of the ropes, then you pull the four ropes you've gathered into one hand down to the ice where a puck is. The goalie moves out to where he is touching the ropes and you have a

OFFENSIVE ZONE POSSESSION

great picture of "what the puck sees" when the goalie is square. Then, you move the ropes simulating that the goalie is off angle or pull the goalie back and show the impact of when they have the wrong depth. Then move the ropes to where the shooter is, show what happens when the goalie is square to the shooter and what the "stick sees." The puck (or stick) sees it very different than the shooter. If the goalie is truly on angle and square to the puck with the proper depth, then the shooter's vantage point from their eyes shows them a lot of net available short side. However, the goalie is dialed in and that is an illusion. What the shooter sees and what the puck sees are different. Now, where I took it a step further when I was doing this exercise, was I would tell the shooter, "Imagine if you could drag the puck to where the vantage point of your eyes were and make what you see with your eyes true and simultaneously changing the puck line for the goalie. How much would that impact shot quality?" Therefore it would stand to reason, that understanding the difference in vantage points and differentiating what is real and what is an illusion and turning the puck line and the sight line into a manipulative is a great start to getting a feel for how to expand the net.

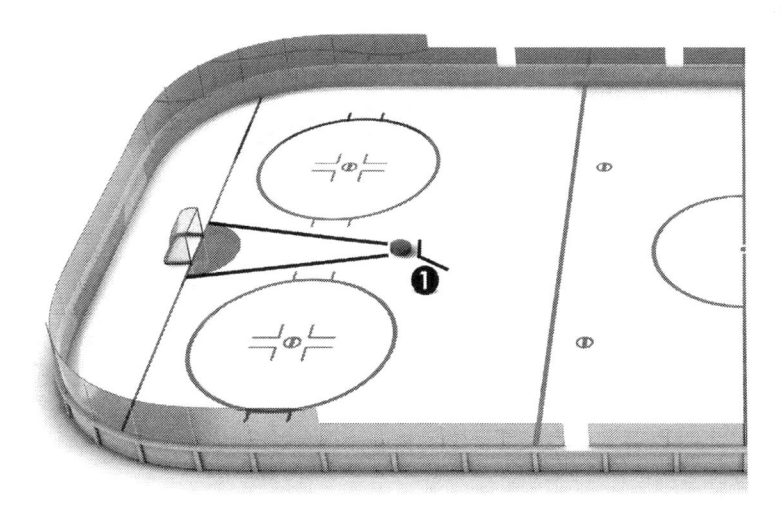

Figure 16: What the Stick Sees

BELFRY OFFENSE

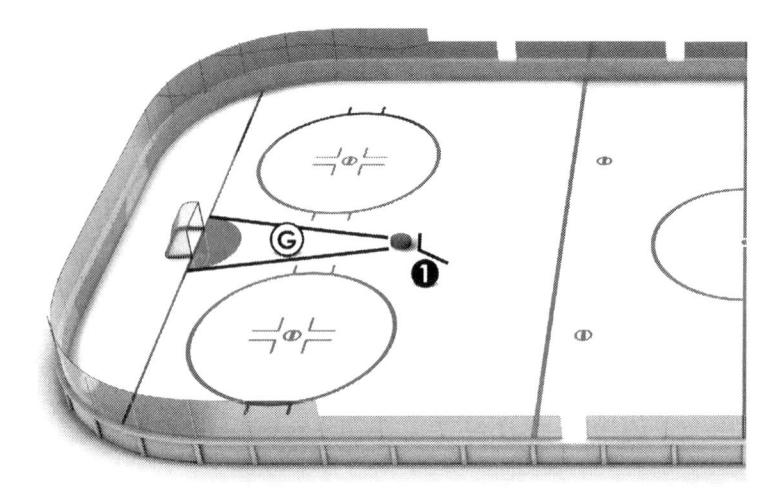

Figure 17: Basic diagram of what the puck sees

The goalie, when square to the puck and with depth take away a lot of the shooting space.

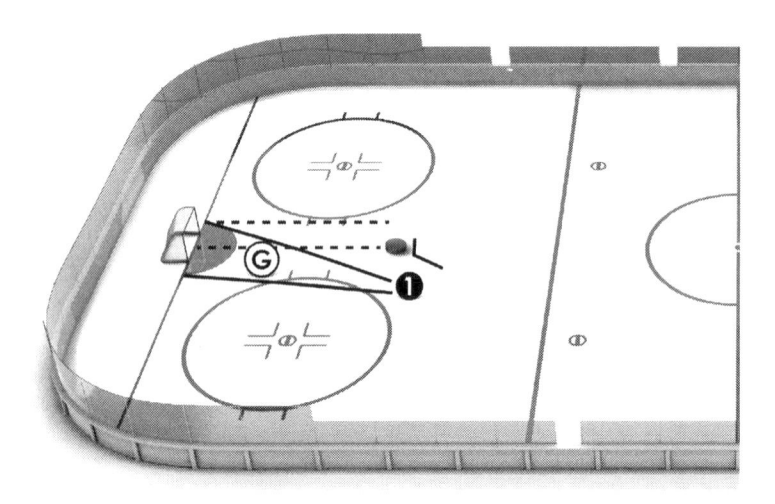

Figure 18: Creating shooting space

When the goalie is off angle and square to the shooter instead of the puck, it opens up net to shoot at:

OFFENSIVE ZONE POSSESSION

b. Expand the area the goalie is concerned about. Establish shooting threats on the opposite side of the midline of the ice. Expanding the distance the goalie would have to travel to make the next save, expands the net. The way I like to term it for the best shot threat (the next play) to align on the backside of the play is staring at an empty net. A pre-shot preparation in expectation of a chance to maximize the shooting surface. Another way of expanding the area the goalie is concerned about is to have a threat on the blind spot net front, just beside the goalie, where a shot pass redirect would be dangerous. This expands the net and surface area the goalie has to defend. A net-front presence who falls into the blind spot would be a great example of expanding the net.

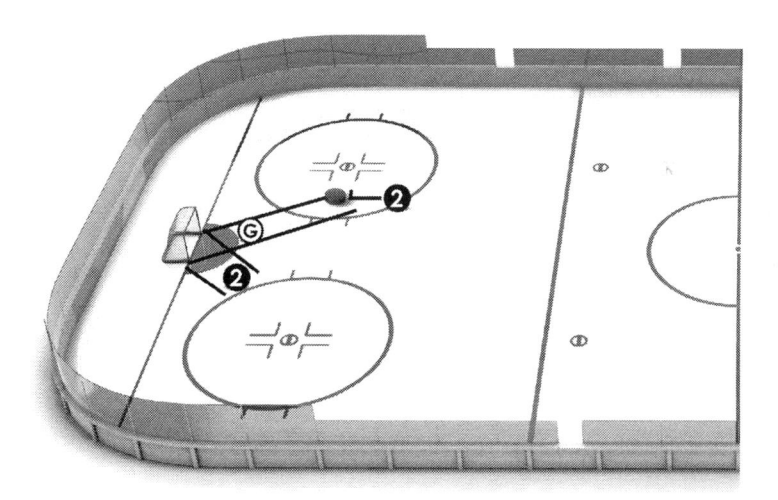

Figure 19: Expand the Net

Here, we have 1 with the puck and ready to shoot. The goalie has a perfect angle. However, 2 being on the backdoor and staring at an empty net expands the net that the goalie has to cover, because if 1 passes to 2, the goalie would have to cover the entire distance of the net. 1, by having 2 as a backdoor threat, has expanded the net.

BELFRY OFFENSE

    c. Panel shots. Panel shots are the inside "panel" of the net. Shooters access the panel by opening those areas through angle change, slant patterns and shooting behind the goalie or against the grain. Panel shooting expands the net for the goalie. Think of a left shot on the right side shooting on an angle above the goalie's pad and below the blocker, or a right shot on the left side shooting on an angle above the pad and below the glove. These are perfect examples of a commonly used panel shot.

    d. Shot placement tight to the body. Goal scorers find the spot just off the goalie's pants, under their arms (or the 6-hole), putting it beside their ears. These spots are difficult for the goalie and many times put the goalie in awkward hand movements to bring their arms back close to their body.

    e. Flatten out their depth. Drive the goalie into their post. If we take the puck below the goal line and drive the goalie into their post, on any pass-out plays, the goalie is working at a depth deficit. Another example would be landing at the net on the edge of the crease, restricting the goalie's ability to gain the depth he would want. Yet another way to flatten out the goalie's depth is to drive them into their post in the dead angle. How about using the game situation as a way to stress the goalie into flattening their depth? When the game is on the line, the sold-out crowd is electric, the tension in the game is rising, and everyone is holding their breath, we can use this tension to score. There is a big difference between "throwing pucks at the net" and using tactics of routes to affect depth and shot placement to create problems for the goalie around the net.

I love the term, "create problems for the goalie around the net." Layer the stress, pass options on the backside, traffic at the net, puck carrier with the puck in the shooting position, expand the net, unsettle his feet by forcing him to move, shot placement, rebound threats ... and as the tension in the game rises, goals can be scored by "creating problems for the goalie," which is very different than "shoot everything at the net. This is the essence of clutch scoring.

I get excited when talking to players about creating problems because it's a way for the players to feel a sense of control of the high stress, high tension times in a game, a season, etc. We have all experienced these moments, either by playing in them and/or as a fan. The building gets tight in anticipation, these are moments where having a repertoire of understanding of how to manufacture problems for the goalie, contributes to clutch scoring in big moments.

Whenever I work in offensive situations, I like to reward the shooter for a shooting process that leads to problems. Many times, the reward is just acknowledging their shot placement created a great rebound, or their timing as the net front gave the shooter a shot-pass option on the heels of the goalie, which expands the net. Or that they preserved the shooting space while still forcing the goalie's feet to unsettle by the route they took. Other times, I'll create competition between the shooters and the goalie, where rebounds in the second layer are scored the same as goals, so the shooters are dialed in on "creating problems for the goalie" and the goalie is focused on rebound control. Quick competitions to three "goals" gives you a chance to build tension of "next play wins."

In scoring situations, I like competitive games to three, I'll sometimes give the shooters a 1-0 lead before we start. I want the games to be 2-2 with the next shot being for the win. Rather than have a single game to 10 goals/saves. I like shorter games to three with best two out of three, so you can maximize the tension.

BELFRY OFFENSE

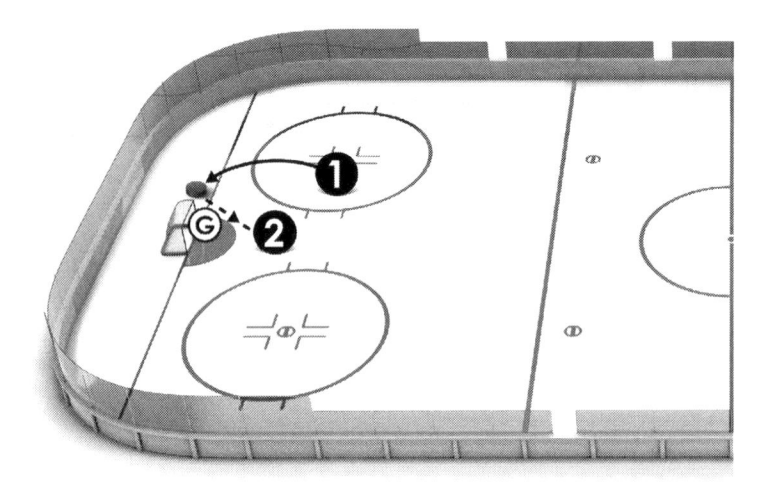

Figure 20:

Drive Goalie into their post by getting below the goal line and then pass it out to affect their depth.

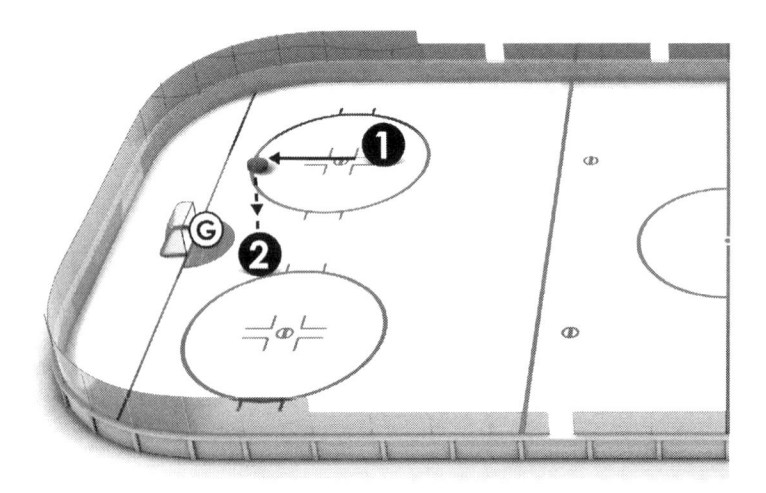

Figure 21:

Drive down into the dead angle and flatten the goalie to their post before centering a pass.

OFFENSIVE ZONE POSSESSION

2. Leverage the Route Tree

In football, the wide receiver has what is referred to as a "Route Tree," which are nine foundational routes.

BUILDING THE ROUTE TREE

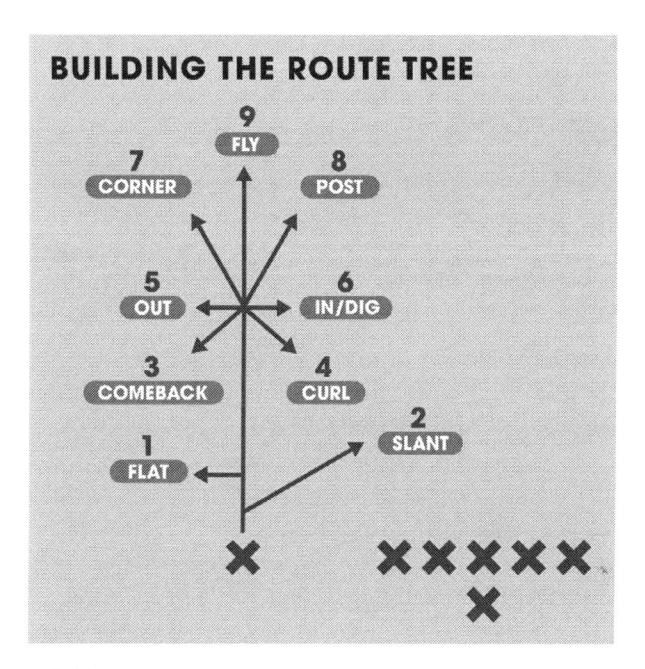

Figure 22: Football Route Tree

In hockey, the puck carrier also has a "Route Tree," in the offensive zone we have six threatening offensive zone routes, which are as follows:

a. Slant
   i. Skating diagonally through the zone.
b. Arc
   i. On a curvilinear route using crossover acceleration.
c. Down
   i. Attacking straight down, usually in the dead angle.

77

d. Drive

   i. Commonly referred to as a net drive, targeting the far post.

e. Inside Cut

   i. Player is moving in any of the other routes but then does a hard 90 degree cut inside.

f. Walkout

   i. Player is below the goal line and comes above the goal line.

The obvious route that is omitted on this tree is the "turn up." The difference with the "turn up," and why I left it off this list, is because the puck carrier turning up is taking himself out of the direct shot threat to manipulate the play for their support players. The threat becomes more singular in the next play, rather than having the puck carrier maintaining his personal shot threat in the route as well as the support player.

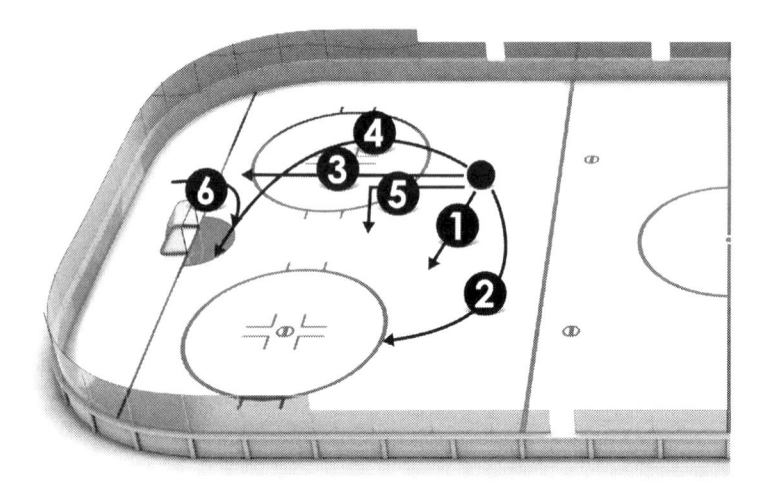

Figure 23: Hockey Route Tree

OFFENSIVE ZONE POSSESSION

Each of these six fundamental attack routes represents different manipulative advantages as it relates to creating scoring chances. The route also speaks to the support needs of the play. When a puck carrier is on a slant route, he'd love to have a linemate cross and slant the opposite way. On an arc route, you'd like someone inside the radius on the opposite side. On a down route, you'd like someone above you. On a net drive, you want someone above you as a passing option to see if you can hold the D just a little to give you the corner. On an inside cut, you want someone either already ahead of you or skating by you to land on the net. On a walkout, you want a backdoor presence. The route tells your linemates where the next play might be, this is the shape and the automated nature of the routes become habit and that elevates our percentages.

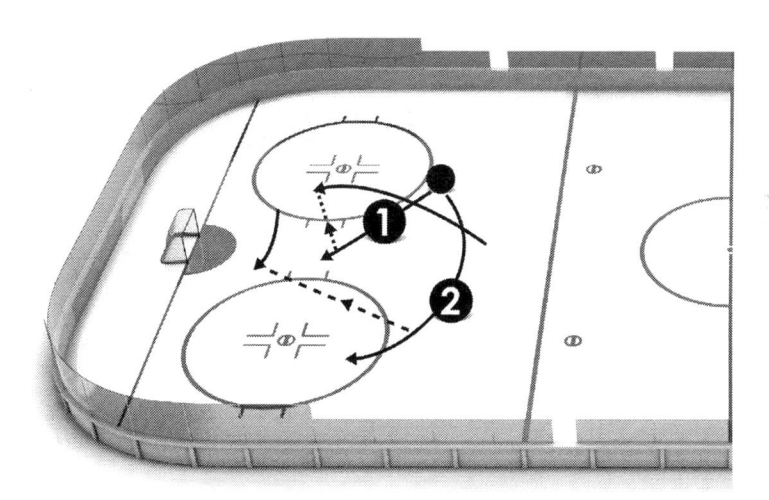

Figure 24: Slant Route

1 slant route love support on the cross and 2 arc route likes a parallel arc route that is trailing their arc.

79

BELFRY OFFENSE

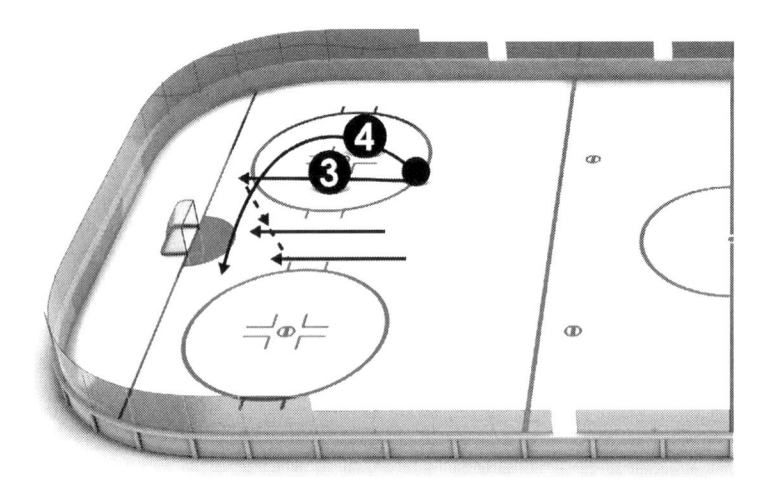

Figure 25: Down Route

3 on the down route likes someone above them, 4 on the net drive wants someone coming down on the net for rebounds.

Now, think of the route tree and build your habits to be outside in and time the routes through the interior of the zone over and over and over again. Going through the interior, landing on the net and working the routes in accordance to the puck carrier, these habits stack the percentages and make it more and more likely you'll get the puck in a scoring area.

3. Unsettle the goalie's feet

We don't want the goalie to be set when we shoot. We'd like him to have to continue to move or to get set and then have to move after being set. The reason is we want the goalie always adjusting to the puck line and depth, force him to continually be adjusting.

    a. Fake shot (freeze him) and move laterally to get him behind the puck and chasing his position. Use the priority of the puck line against the goalie, invite him to the line and set him with a shot threat before changing the line. One of the great skills is "Active Hesitation," an active hesitation is when the shooter

OFFENSIVE ZONE POSSESSION

presents shots moving on a slant or a down route and holds the puck while staying in motion. The hesitation is particularly valuable because the conditions of the shot is changing because the player is traveling and actively changing the conditions, but inside a hesitation.

b. Invite the goalie to the shot line and freeze him with a fake and then move laterally to make him chase the angle. The "active" part of the hesitation is maintaining the shot threat through the hesitation. This is where shot fakes drift into "overhandle" as the puck carrier isn't active in the hesitation.

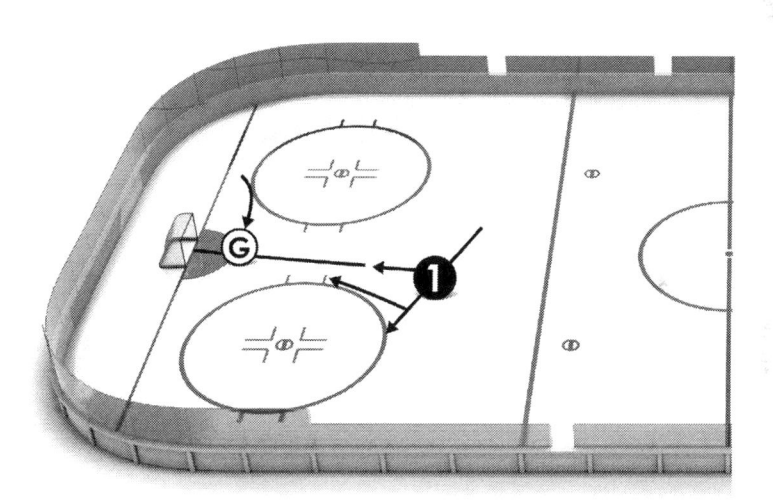

Figure 26:

By moving lateral, we encourage the goalie to hurry to get on the puck line and we can slightly decelerate to get him ahead of the puck and then we can shoot it against the grain. This is a very tough adjustment for the goalie to be moving one way and the shot is going the other way behind your movement.

BELFRY OFFENSE

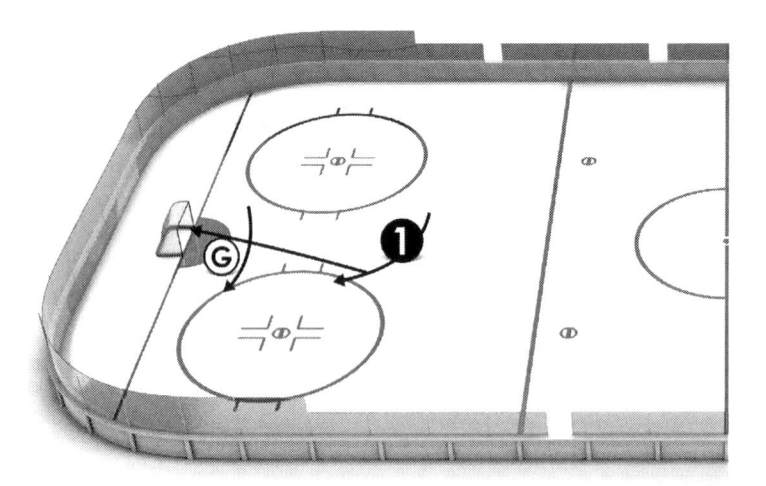

Figure 27:

Moving laterally to get the goalie out in front of the puck and then shoot back the opposite way to shoot it against the grain.

c. Change speeds on the goalie's movement lines when coming down on the net. Goalies have markers in the offensive zone that encourage movement: 1. the top of the circle or ringette line and 2. the end-zone dot. When we are attacking down and we are going to cross these lines, change speeds, accelerate or decelerate. These are lines when the goalie has to move, by changing speeds, we will affect their ability to maintain proper depth. Particularly when we accelerate as we go past the dot, the goalie is going back to their post, this is a great way to use speed change to flatten the goalie's depth and rotate them as they recover to their post. Often times with good speed here, we can get them to overplay the post or overlap it, leaving them in a terrible position to make the next movement.

OFFENSIVE ZONE POSSESSION

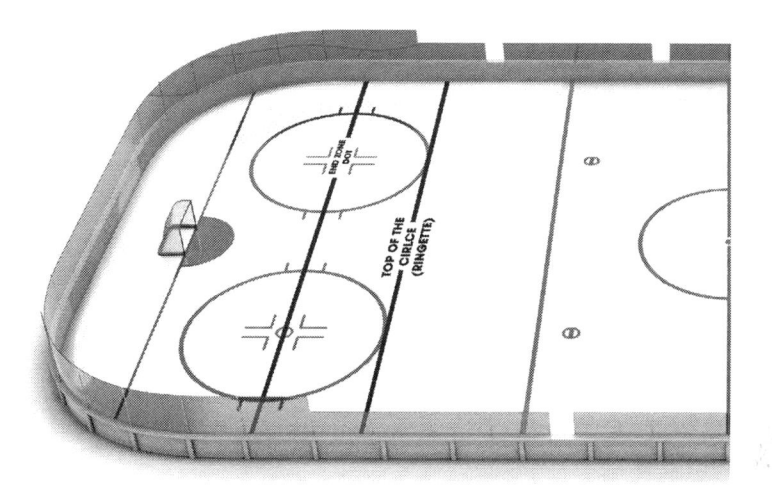

Figure 28:

   d. Change sides, use the back wall and change sides, change sides at the top with the two D, go dot to dot, change sides of the puck. By changing sides, you change the conditions of the play significantly and you turn the strong side into the weak side and you force the goalie/defenders to have to keep track of where everyone is. Not only are you unsettling the feet when you change sides, but you are also unsettling the game conditions, everyone is in a different role and therefore moving different, the goalie needs to know where everyone is. This challenges their awareness and their IQ. Goalies don't just need to track the puck, they also need to track players.

4. Use the goalie as a rebounder.

   Commonly referred to as "pass off pad," although I think the opportunity to pass of the goalie is not limited to just using his pad. The pass off pad can be a great tactic to get the puck to a linemate in a better scoring position than you, staring at an empty net, but the traffic or defensive player is defending the passing lane. We can

83

leverage the goalie's square position on our puck and shoot it off the pad closest to our support in a play that's a pass disguised as a shot.

5. Play in the "gaps."

   When you watch goalies train to move, one of the fundamental movement sequences they train to automation is post to corner of the crease to middle to corner of the crease and back to post. They are most comfortable moving to these spots. From a scoring perspective, we have to learn to recognize and shoot in the gaps. The gaps between these spots. Often we will see shooters skate through these gaps and shoot once the goalie is in their spot. So you see the goalie moving comfortably into their spot, they beat the shooter to the spot, are set upon release and it's a routine save. Now if the shooter shot while they were in the gap ... there is a better chance for a different and much more difficult save for the goalie. When I'm training shooting to score, I refer a lot to the gaps and monitor how frequently we skate through the gap and shoot on the goalie's spot. This is something you can create awareness for in the shooters and develop similar automation the goalie has in their spots they are most comfortable, we can do the same by automating the release in the gaps.

   Now think about the gap in the context of creating problems for the goalie, leveraging routes to unsettle his feet, know when he has to move, know where the gaps are and develop that feel for shot advantage. Forcing the goalie to battle in the problems will create better second pucks.

   When we think of the dead angle gap in combination of using the goalie as a rebounder, this is also a great tactic in tight to get the puck to the other side of the net in a net-area play where we have a backdoor presence but we don't have a direct passing lane. In this case, we can use the goalies shoulder or upper chest on that side of the body to get the puck there. Sometimes we can use the goalie to change sides, where it isn't a scoring situation, rather just send the puck off the goalie for a low-side change. All while shooting while we are in the gap and the goalie is in transit to the post.

When we are moving on a down route on the goalie's glove side, if we shoot it low on the blocker side above the pad and where he needs to use his blocker, we can get him to send the rebound up the middle. This is similar as using the pad, but instead of conceding the shot as a save by purposely passing off the pad, we create a shot that could go in if the goalie misplays it. But if he plays it right, he gives us a second puck chance up the middle, creating a problem for the goalie.

When the forward is attacking down on his strong side and is running out of space and the goalie has done a great job getting back to his post, we can sometimes shoot the puck far side aiming for his ears or shoulder. This becomes a play off the goalie to the weak side. But if the goalie misplays it, it's a goal. Unlike just conceding a save, we shoot the puck where it's tricky and the result is a rebound with a chance of a goal. These plays can lead to scramble plays.

On a side, not for the purpose of unsettling the goalie's feet, but in the family of using the goalie as a rebounder, sometimes we run out of space to make a pass, but we want to keep possession, although the checking pressure is closing. We can shoot the puck to the short side of the net, in which the goalie can routinely rebound it to the corner. We know the puck is going to the corner but the defender does not. If we do it when the defender is not in range of finishing their check, we can use the shot on net with a purposeful rebound to the corner to spin this defender like a top and earn a great first touch in the offensive zone.

6. Use a screen effectively.

The relationship between the shooter and the screen and the responsibility of the net-front player is too often misunderstood. What is the actual responsibility of the net-front player as it relates to being an asset to the shooter? I've asked many of the top NHL goal scorers I work closely with about working with a screen and they often talk about not always wanting a player screening the goalie. When you add the goalie, the net-front forward and the defensemen defending the net-front player, there is a lot of shooting space for the shooter blocked out. They want a net-front presence, but talk about the net-front player starting in the screen and be on top of the crease to affect the depth the goalie can get. In other words, keep him in the net and force the goalie to have to work to look around to locate the puck. Then just before the shooter shoots, fall off the back side of the goalie in an offensive boxout to both re-open net that he was blocking and to offer an off-net redirect option and rebound capacity. That's what top shooters say they want. Now not everyone is a top shooter, so that's not going to be great advice necessarily to someone who is not that level of shooter. In studying the net presence, I've started to settle on a couple ideas that set out to accomplish a wide swath of objectives at the net.

a. Start by establishing position on the top of the crease, to inhibit the depth the goalie can achieve and get in the shot lane to disrupt the vision of the goalie. Goalies when confronted with a guy at the net like this, depending on their height and how far away the puck is, will either stand really tall and try to locate the puck from above, and then once they read the shot is being taken, they'll come down either into their stance or right into the butterfly in anticipation of making a save. If they aren't tall or the shooting situation doesn't allow them to stand tall, they'll look around the screen. I'll refer to this as a "window."

b. So let's say the shot threat is imminent and it isn't a point shot. In this situation, the goalie is likely looking around the screen in a window. Let's say for this example the shooter is a left shot on the right side near the end-zone dot and we have a screen set up at the net, and from the perspective of looking at the goalie, the goalie is looking out of the right-side window. The objective of the shooter then would be to shoot to the left side, which would force the goalie to track the puck blind to that side as they will lose sight of the puck through the screen or will fight to quickly get their head on the other side into the left window. If the screen wants to really help the goal-scoring situation, then in the shooting release would push back toward the right window in an offensive boxout, turning their body with the screen inside the tip attempt, thus opening up more shooting space for the shooter. This approach leaves all the options on the table to maximize the shot threat.

c. The additional skill for the net presence is to know what window the goalie is looking through and know that the shooter is likely wanting to shoot the opposite side. So the shooter should turn with the shot, inside the tipping attempt, but out of the shot line to open shooting space of the shooter.

d. The net presence is important to scoring, however if the net presence in an effort to "take the eyes of the goalie" is also reducing the net and is either blocking the shot himself or forcing the shooter to be too fine with their shot where they miss the net or have a bad shot location choice, then it wastes a strong scoring net-front player. When the net-front presence and the shooter can work together to maximize the impact the net presence has on improving the scoring percentage of the shot situation.

e. More often than not, the shooter and the net presence are not working together. This is one of the key areas I would work on with every team. The value of this adjustment just can't be overstated.

7. Use of the back wall

The use of the back wall is another excellent goalie manipulation tactic to improve our goal-scoring percentages. The value of having the puck on the back wall is it pulls the goalie on their post and looking either through the net, or around the post to locate the puck on the back wall. However, the real shooting threat is in front of the net. The goalie is on the goal line and looking at the back wall, but the next play shot is likely above the gcal line. If the play is made above the goal line to the shooting threat, the goalie has to try to gain depth by coming off the goal line and get the shot line in a split second. Their projection off the goal line has them moving away from the net, often sliding out. If the goalie makes the save and there is a rebound, they're in a compromised position to recover their position quickly. The goalie's ability to see the play and track the threats positioning in front of the net is reduced because they are primarily tracking the puck behind the net. The puck carrier may also try to wrap the puck or walkout, where the goalie temporarily loses sight of the puck as they go post to post. This offers opportunity for the puck carrier to be deceptive and wait for the goalie to turn their head and then change directions or pass it back the opposite way as the goalie turns their head. There is a lot of ways the offensive team can use the back wall to improve goal-scoring percentages and put the goalie at a disadvantage. Puck carriers who are aware of where the goalie is looking and actively try to manipulate their vision and head position will create great chances to score.

8. Dead angle

The dead angle is a term that's bubbled up to the surface in recent years. It refers to this area of the ice:

OFFENSIVE ZONE POSSESSION

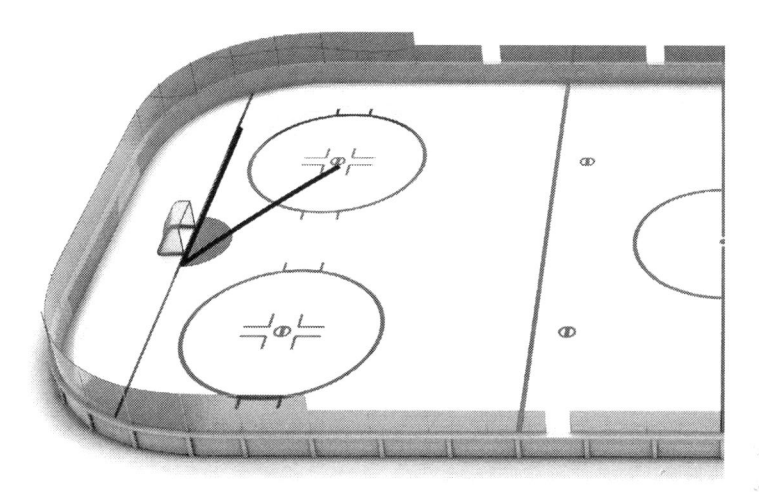

Figure 29: Dead Angle

The dead angle represents opportunity because it's a transition area for the goalie. They are moving between spots and back to their post. The opportunity for the shooter is in the gap or transition movement. As they are going back to their post, this is a great time to put a puck into their feet, or as we've seen from some elite left-hand shooters on the strong side, they'll look to attack the heel of the goalie's stick at this time. We've seen Auston Matthews attack this area with great success in recent years. Sometimes the goalie gets too flat in heading back to their post, which opens up a shot to the far side of the net. Sometimes they overlap the post where they are over-rotated and a wrap-around play or a play to the weak side would be a difficult movement for the goalie. Sometimes we can catch the goalie going down into what goalies refer to as a VH or a reverse VH, and there is an opportunity to go upstairs with the puck. When puck carriers have an attack mentality in the dead angle, they can catch the goalie in movements that make them vulnerable. Creating danger in the dead angle is a scoring skill and needs players to take the time to explore and figure out the timing of movement and the vulnerabilities.

9. Point shooting

   All the way through this book, I'll be referencing my disdain for bad point shots. A bad point shot is one that offers a low percentage to get the puck back and results in an easy exit opportunity for the opponent. Very few things bring an abrupt end to a promising offensive zone sequence more than a bad point shot. Over the years, I've searched for many ways to illustrate the negative effects of bad point shots. I went so far as to say, "If you like to backcheck, shoot point shots." After many years of this campaign against bad point shots, I've left an impression that I don't support ANY point shots, which is not true. There are many point shots that are outstanding to shoot, and there are a lot of point shots that lead to direct goals for and rebound goals for, so I can't really say, NEVER shoot a point shot. What I am really advocating for is to shoot point shots when there is a competitive advantage to do so, and when there clearly isn't, don't.

   When we look at scoring on goalies with point shots, there are a couple things that immediately come to mind:

   a. Tips: The two tips that cause problems are when the tipping player can knock a puck down. The puck is arriving at the tipper around waist high and the tipper can knock the puck down. If the tipper misses the tip, the height of the shot is dangerous if it doesn't hit the goalie in the body. If the goalie has to use their hands, this is a great point shot because the shot height is great for the tipper, and if the tipper misses, it has a chance to go in. The other tip that's dangerous is when the puck redirects upwards. If the tip distance offers the puck a trajectory to get above the pads, this tip can be trouble. The shot along the ice is much more difficult to say it has a good chance to go in if the tipper misses the tip, but a ramped tip effect is dangerous.

   b. Redirects: The high tip is really a redirect, where the point shooter is shooting for a stick in the high slot and the player can alter the direction of travel. This is incredibly difficult for a goalie. The

OFFENSIVE ZONE POSSESSION

other one is when the puck is shot slightly off net and the player redirects it. Sidney Crosby had a stretch where he did this with high frequency and it became an effective scoring tool. The off-net redirect expands the net as the goalie has to be concerned about it, and it can be near impossible for the goalie to track. Point shooters will sometimes shoot off net into a pile of players to redirect off a skate as well. The off-net shot pass is effective at getting the puck to the net around the first layer of shot blocker. When the shot blocker is in the shot lane, rather than blast it into their shin pads, we can shoot off net to still get the puck there.

c. Redirect shaping: The other redirect is when the net-front player can redirect a shot that is going wide and pull it back to the net on a different angle. This is another extremely dangerous play. If the goalie is close to the redirect, the net-front player can redirect it behind the level of the goalie. If the redirect is a little in front of the goalie, the redirect can create dangerous rebound situations. Again, redirecting skills if when the net-front player redirects the puck they turn with the redirect, they can track the puck and find the rebound quickly. I refer to this type of play as "shaping the tip." Shaping the tip is to pull the puck in the tip to the other side, which wreaks havoc on the goalie's ability to track the puck as it rebounds off them.

10. Shooting trajectory and preserving shooting space

An area where goalies have really jumped ahead in the battle between shooting and goaltending is in understanding shot trajectory. Goalies do a great job in their practical solution to shot trajectory. They talk about their head positioning, they bring their hands forward and down depending on the shooting location and can make the net really small. They understand that when the puck is close to them, they are covering the top of the net by having their hands a foot off the ice. Goalies who are really good in tight have great understanding and anticipation of shot trajectory and put the shooter in a lot of small-net situations. As shooters, we haven't always adjusted well. The answer to a goalie projecting their hands forward to shrink the net is to move the puck away from the net to preserve the shooting space and expand the net. Too often, we see shooters in tight and the natural reaction is to go forward with the puck immediately, playing right into the goalie's hands ... literally. As shooters, we have to be aware of shot trajectory and have good net-area shooting habits which include preserving the shooting space, or pulling the puck back before we shoot, to open up the top of the net. Otherwise, these goalies will continue to become more and more difficult to beat in the net area.

If we want to unlock goal scoring as a team, it starts with viewing goal scoring as a group tactical play. This is not to say that individuals don't create offence on their own, of course, they do. It doesn't mean to say that there are players who can create offence independent of the group, and in some cases, in spite of the group. Of course, all this is true. What I am referring to is trying to unlock team creativity and take goal scoring to another level. To do that, we have to approach it differently.

"Creativity" is at the very top of the list of overused, misused and murky terms we coaches and hockey people at every level throw around. Too often, it's used as a catch-all to explain why the team is not organized in the offensive zone and most often play 1v1 hockey. "Well, once in the offensive zone, we let the players be creative." That is not creative in my book. Hockey is a team game, so creativity has to be viewed as a group. If it isn't a group and it's disconnected and disjointed and one player starts being "creative," it's not actually creativity they're expressing, it's selfishness. We see team after team at all levels, including the NHL, whereby creativity is practically expressed by one player skating the puck as far as they can, exhausting all personal attack options before painting themselves in the corner and THEN start looking to make a play. This happens at such regularity throughout the lineup as anyone on the team who fashions themselves as skilled adopts this mentality, so now it's cultural. This culture is reflected in watching the players off the puck when their team has the puck. They don't move. They wait. This isn't creativity. This is cultural selfishness that has just enough instances where every once and a while a player will find a crease to attack and get to the net that we can all accept it and rename it from selfishness to creativity.

The greatest challenge to offence is to get players to play creatively ... with each other. To successfully collectively express when instinct gives way to structure and when structure creates the platform for instinct, where the creativity is found inside the structure, it's not an either or, it's the smooth transition between the two ... as a collective. This is sophisticated offence. Difficulty in offense is finding that sweet spot of instinctual play, creativity and collaboration. If it swings too far the creativity gets stifled through the inability to work with someone because deciphering what the puck carrier is trying to do. When a teammate willfully and unnecessarily engages 1v1 at the puck and others can't read off the puck carrier, they tend to stop moving to support, which stretches out the shape and you lose the puck support you need. In the offensive zone, there are four indicators of unsophisticated offence:

a. Excessive 1v1 play.
b. Point shots without numerical advantage at the net.
c. Unreliable, unfocused and lack of detail in F3.
d. Weak-side D is inactive and is oblivious to how critical they are to the play.

So part of creativity has to be to encourage your teammates to continue active support to keep the shape solid - or moving purposely off the puck. Purposeful movement - what exactly is that?

Purposeful movement is recognizing your role in the play before or as it happens, moving off the puck in support of the puck carrier and in association with the other linemates to maintain the integrity of the shape and doing your part with enthusiasm in your current role. What doesn't get talked enough about is when the puck moves, you have to anticipate your role change and move into the next role with conviction and speed. As you are arriving, you are reading the conditions of the play and anticipate how your role in the play may change and move again (accelerate or decelerate), until the play conditions change again ... and so on ... and so forth, every second of your shift. There is a tactical implication of movement/or the absence of movement throughout the entire shift. Every decision, every step, every relocation, every anticipation, they all either allow you to contribute to the play or degrade it. There are two parts of this that are important to continually develop with all your players:

11. Mental resilience

    You aren't going to get the puck every time you accelerate or are in a threatening position, so learning to mentally shift to the next play is critical. Too many times we see a player who is dialed in to start and makes a great read and play to accelerate into great space at the right time, but doesn't get the puck. Then, does it again, same result, doesn't get the puck. Now, they are frustrated and stops reading the play in advance and stops moving purposefully and with conviction, and sure enough, the moment they stop ... well, that's the moment the puck goes to the right spot and they weren't there. They were too busy feeling sorry they had all that "wasted effort" without reward of the puck. Building mental resilience in all your players to just keep going to the right spot is your job, coach. You must demand it. This is a tenant of developing offensive hockey sense. It stands to reason that if I get frustrated and stop reading the game offensively to move to the next best spot as a habit, then I'll stop moving into good spots ... mental resilience of continuing to move to the next best spot regardless of whether you get the puck or not, that's a major part of developing hockey sense in EVERY player. I believe there are a lot of players who have had the hockey sense knocked

OFFENSIVE ZONE POSSESSION

out of them because they didn't get the puck, or they knew that a teammate just won't pass to them because they aren't confident that they'll do something good with it. So they stop passing to them, if they ever did at all, and the kid sees or feels this lack of confidence in them and stops moving purposefully. That's a wrap on meaningful development of hockey sense, it's over. This is on you, coach. You must demand "best play available" every time, with no executive decisions - deliver the puck.

12. Deliver the puck

    When you see the best play available, you deliver the puck where it's supposed to go. There will be no tolerance of selfish play or making ridiculous assumptions about what the player who is in the best spot to get the puck will do with it. It's not your job to decide who gets the puck in good spots and who doesn't. When the play conditions reveal the play – EXECUTE THE PLAY. This is also coaching. You can't allow excessive 1v1 without purpose to drip into your offensive zone or your offence will be reliant exclusively on hope – hope that you always play a team you are better than, that your best offensive 1v1 players can beat someone and take it to the net, or hope when they unnecessarily paint themselves into the corner and whip the puck at the net, that it bounces off someone. Your offensive chances aren't going to come from people moving off the puck, because they quit moving long time ago. This is, in large part, what happens when a coach does a great job recruiting top offensive talents to their program, but doesn't coach them to deliver the puck. We all recognize these teams loaded with talented individuals whose play continues to perpetuate problem solving with 1v1 and not learn to play with others and learn to play off the puck. If you have a "deliver the puck" philosophy that encourages them to anticipate and move off the puck with these talented offensive players, watch out! If you feel like your job is done after recruiting them, well ... playing in your program with all those top players is probably not going to be enough and could contribute to many of them experiencing a developmental regression.

What is your definition of a scoring chance?

The concept of "best play available" is as tricky as defining "scoring chances." It's been well documented that if you ask 10 coaches for their definition of a scoring chance, you will likely get 10 different definitions. Now can you imagine the variance we would get if we asked about what the "best play available" is? There is no chance for consensus on an open-ended question like that. When I say open-ended, I mean with no baseline of agreement. The exercise is set up for failure and is often structured that way, both intentionally and unintentionally, to push a narrative. Anytime we want to collectively arrive at a definition of something like scoring chances or best play available, we have to first have a discussion of what the parameters are. A great illustrative example of that would be …"is every shot a good shot?" Personally, I absolutely do not think every shot is a good shot. In fact, I think many shots that are taken are what I would consider a bad shot. So, what is a bad shot? A bad shot for me is a shot that is taken without strategic intent. Throwing pucks at the net from all angles wreaks of hope. Hope is not my idea of a good strategy. However, this is not to say that hope shots aren't successful. Sometimes they are. This doesn't make it right for me. I want our players mindful of percentages. This is a big part of Belfry Offense. So I can't on the one hand say percentages matter, and then endorse shooting pucks with low-percentage outcomes (good outcomes: goal, second-chance shot opportunities, puck recovery). If percentages don't really matter, to the degree that we are looking to improve the percentages, then every shot matters. If every shot matters, then shot differential matters. Shot differential doesn't matter to me, it is an irrelevant stat for me. I don't even give it a second thought. I care about interior shots. Now sometimes, a shot from the outside can lead to a shot from the inside, so that outside shot is a good shot, because the difference is the player who shot it was mindful of creating interior shots and using an outside shot to play it off the goalie to create a rebound chance is incredibly valuable. The shooter used the outside shot to effectively pass the puck off the goalie to create the real shot they wanted to create. I have lots of time for that.

In Belfry Offense, we know that the better the shot quality, the more frequent those shots are recovered allowing us to sustain offence. I went on a rant a few years ago, publicly attacking point shots. The reason, point shots have around a 30 percent chance of being recovered by the offensive team. The way I framed it was, "If you like to backcheck, shoot point shots." Does this mean that I don't want any point shots? Of course not, there are many point shots that are excellent. So what's the difference? Well, that's the exact discussion that allows us to arrive at a definition for "scoring chances," or in this case, "best play available." What is a good point shot? For me, it's very clear, a good point shot is one that is taken when we, the offensive team, have a numerical advantage at the net. That, to me, is a good point shot. There is a clear strategic advantage for shooting that puck. The percentages of recovery are stacked in our favor. Now there are many, many point shots that are taken that end in positive outcomes that do not have numerical advantage at the net. Are these bad shots, too? For me, yes. We can win a game without playing well, we can score on a bad shot, and we can have a positive outcome from a poor process. However, I view my job in communicating the game as one that focuses on good habits that stack the deck in our mathematical favor. If the group I'm communicating the game with understands that, then our process should lead to better results more consistently. The question that changed everything for me in this regard was, "If the point shot yields around 30 percent recovery rate and a well under 10 percent goal rate, then what are we potentially giving up by losing possession?" This question made me think deeply about what the value of that would be to offence. What if we taught our players to think in percentages? Does our shape allow us to defend quickly enough to recover failed point shots and therefore we can, in fact, shoot point shots and still maintain offensive zone possession? What would this do to our ability to control the game? What would it do to my perception of what a bad point shot is?

Another breakthrough I had was when I was going to work with a player in the offseason on improving their scoring. The players reported shooting percentage was 7.7 percent. The is a stat I pulled straight off NHL.com. Now what is that stat? Well, that stat is out of 100 shots on goal, the player scores 7.7 times. Now my mind went to, if this player wants to score 30 goals next year, they'd need to shoot over 300 shots on goal. So now I check how many shots on goal they took. While I'm digging this out, I realize this number is all situations - rush, offensive zone, on stick, off the pass, power play, even strength, inside the slot, outside the slot ... this is every shot they took that landed on the net. Then I realized, wait a minute, this isn't every shot the player took. These are just the ones that landed on the net. What is the real shooting percentage then, if I factored in all the shots the player took for the whole year, the ones that were blocked or missed the net? The true shooting percentage isn't good. So, that became my mission, I'm going to take every shot the player takes for the whole season, on net, blocked and missed, and I'm going to chart them so I know where the player is shooting from. The chart had a few layers to it. I wanted to know game situation (5v5, PP, etc.), play type (rush, offensive zone, etc.), contested or uncontested, off the pass or on stick (defined on stick as having the puck for two seconds or longer) and the location. Now I plotted the shots and I had all these layers of data. Once the shots were plotted, I could go into an area of the ice and take a look at what the player's shot profile was from that area.

Now I could see where the high-frequency shots were coming from, whether they were in recurring game situations and play types, and I could dig into shot selection, etc. What I was able to see was a shooting habits fingerprint. The fingerprint also revealed success rates. Once I had all this data, I started to add more data sets to that area of the ice, like "best play available." Was this a good shot to take in the first place? Is there intent to the shot location? Is the player shooting to score, shooting to create a shot, shooting without strategic intent? Needless to say, what

OFFENSIVE ZONE POSSESSION

I learned in this shooting study heavily influenced my thoughts about shooting, chance generation and scoring. I must have done this study over 20 times with many different players just to see what the different fingerprint would reveal. I also did different positions. The original study was on a centerman. After comparing a couple other centermen then I did a couple wingers and then a few D. Every time I did the study, I learned something new and refined my data collection process. Then I took a couple of the more interesting data sets and asked the player about it. The conversation about best play available, shot selection, deception and creating more strategic advantage shots was the most valuable part of the development process. The player, once they were aware and had a chance to look at a few examples, had an entire process rebuilt in their mind before I even had a chance to say anything. Developing a process to invoke thinking in offensive strategy is a direct pathway to improving shot quality and shooting results and ultimately scoring. Especially when the player is inside their own personal offensive shot generation fingerprint. One of the most fascinating pathways to improving deception in players is to illustrate high-frequency shot situations, whereby they shouldn't actually shoot, and when they understand that shooting is not strategic here, they can use the position to improve the shot situation for their teammate. The act of shot deception is, in part, conceding that shot is not the right shot and that a better shooting situation is available in a teammate and I have to deliver the puck. Rather than just pass it, I leverage my newfound recognition of the recurring situation and sell shot to improve the shooting/scoring conditions for the teammate. This is powerful stuff.

Now contrast this thought process with the puck carrier who continually and unnecessarily reverts to 1v1 and is habitually exhibiting the lowest level of offensive sophistication, regardless of their production. Puck carriers who habitually and unnecessarily go 1v1 with high production have a skill set that is above the level of their competition . this doesn't make it right. It's actually a gross misuse of the advantage. Therefore, allowing players whose skill set is above the level of their current league to continually play 1v1 is counterintuitive to good coaching. As a coach, you are indebted to all the players on your team to keep them meaningfully engaged in the game. Demanding the puck carrier make the best play available keeps everyone engaged and trying to move intelligently in advance of the next play. A puck being passed moves so much faster than a puck being skated, but we need players skating off the puck to create the conditions for the pass. A pass is a connection between two people, both are critical in creating the conditions for the pass. What's natural in hockey is that people tend not to move unless there is a reason to move. The longer and the more frequently a puck carrier skates with the puck without passing it, the more time others start to think of all the reasons they shouldn't move. The puck carrier over carries the puck and excessively goes 1v1 when their support is still actively moving with purpose and repetitively delays the play. Now when it happens frequently enough, we know that most players will stop moving. As the puck carrier repeatedly exhausts all their personal options to attack and paints themselves into a corner where there isn't a play, now they look and sees their support players all stopped and watching him. Now they complain no one is open. A classic example of what happens on many teams and the death of sophistication of collective offensive thought.

We need enough structure (shape (roles), habits and percentages), so the group knows how to move in relationship to each other and to the puck and everyone knows how to continually support the play through their role in the shape. Work to teach the group to think the game offensively as a chain sequence. We can also provide a better utility for 1v1 for the player. There are players who have tremendous 1v1 skill that can be leveraged into great team play and keep their teammates moving with purpose and enthusiasm. If there is proficiency in 1v1, then we need to immediately turn it into a "team advantage" not a "me advantage." The team advantage from 1v1 is forced switches. If a player beats someone 1v1, the opponent is forced to make a decision. They either let the player go to the net or they rotate their defensive assignment to cover for the teammate getting beat. So, if it's a corner 1v1 for example, and the

OFFENSIVE ZONE POSSESSION

offensive player walks by the defender, then the opponent has to rotate someone off their responsibility and onto the puck carrier who is now a direct threat to the net. If they rotate their defensive assignments to cover for the teammate, they are leaving a responsibility to do so. That responsibility they leave, well, that represents the best play available as that player is now unchecked. So, if we teach the offensive player to learn how to leverage their 1v1 skills to force switches and they can make plays inside the check change to improve the chance quality, well, that's a great use of 1v1 skill. If, however, the player beats their check and either doesn't see the rotation and therefore doesn't attempt to make the play, rather either shoots themselves or takes on another defender 1v1, well that's unsophisticated offence. Teaching players with strong 1v1 skills how to "break down defenses" and leverage that ability to improve the chance quality for the team ... well, that's sophisticated offence that is projectable to the highest levels of our sport.

One of the most misleading stats on any broadcast is "how much on stick puck time the top players have." In many broadcasts, they'll track a player like Connor McDavid and how much the puck is actually on his stick and it'll come in at just over a minute almost every time. What follows is a diatribe on how important it is to play away from the puck and in emphasizing the play without the puck, indirectly minimizing of how important it is when the puck is on your stick. What is missing in this whole discussion which irks me to no end is, the relationship between the play off the puck and on stick puck possession AND how elite players use both movement and multiple puck sequences in a given possession to control the entire shift. It's not the duration the puck is on the stick, it's the number of times they get it. The player doesn't in fact ONLY need the puck on their stick to completely take control of the shift. The goal is NOT maximizing on-stick possession as the stat implies, or conceding that you don't have it on your stick for such a high percentage of the game and therefore indirectly minimizing its importance. The focus needs to be on how shape, movement, timing and playing the percentages are all tactics used along with on stick possession to completely control shifts.

Knowing full well that the conditions of the puck improve with each possession in the sequence, multiple puck possession sequences are the key to generating offense in the NHL for top players. So rather than belittle actual time of stick-on puck possession in top players, we should be highlighting what makes the player great and how they controlled the entire shift by getting the puck for short durations in different areas of the ice, and as the conditions improved with each successive possession, they found the best conditions to attack, or a brilliant display of "active patience." Multiple puck sequences stitched the control of the entire shift together. This is why I'm not a fan of statistics accumulated in isolation. A statistic is not particularly illuminating unless it is relational. The relationship between on-stick puck possession AND multiple possession sequences to control the shift is fascinating. We have to stop picking one isolated statistic out of the hat and peel back the onion and see what's really going on for players to be great.

The objective of the offensive zone possession is for your best players to get the puck multiple times, and through their process of "active patience," the scoring chance becomes a question of when, not if.

The logic behind where I want to go is as follows:

OFFENSIVE ZONE LOGIC

SHAPE INTEGRITY = HABITS X PERCENTAGES

ROLE CHANGES

ANTICIPATION AUTOMATION

SITUATION

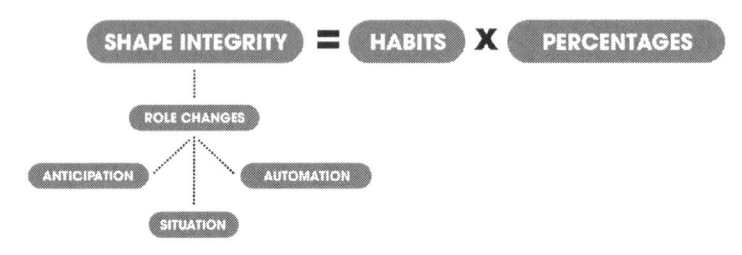

Figure 30: Offensive Zone Logic

The relationship between habits and percentages is the critical understanding for players because this is what unlocks collective

OFFENSIVE ZONE POSSESSION

creativity. As coaches, we focus on developing players game-play habits (board work, entries, body position, etc.) and situational habits (knowing the score of the game, the length of the shifts, the numerical advantage/disadvantage, ice geography and the time on the clock) with an understanding of personal game structure, which is how each individual player leverages their own individual physical/skill/tactical assets to produce a higher success rate and frequency of their habits. This is the heart of player development.

In recent years, there has been more of a push by sections in player development who are endeavoring to settle on a set way to teach hockey. The longer I listen, the more rigidity I hear, and the more sources they cite, the more confirmation bias comes through. Listening to coaches in each of these communities go on about their extensive understanding of the brain and how they know how the use of principles and other similar devices allow them to create automatic reads and responses in two or more players by simply understanding the universal set of "if this, then that" scripts of the principles that they've figured out. This whole mindset reminds me of a famous scene in one of my favorite movies, which captures my take on this attitude brilliantly.

In the movie "Good Will Hunting," there is the bar scene that culminates in Matt Damon's character slapping a scribbled scrap paper phone number on a window and famously asks, "Do you like apples? I got her number, how do you like them apples?" Earlier in the scene, Ben Affleck's character moves down the bar to strike up a conversation with a group of girls. He finds himself in a conversation with an "annoying know-it-all" who quickly recognizes that the Affleck character is not actually a student at Harvard and tries to embarrass him by asking questions that will expose he isn't a student and try to make himself look smart in front of the girls. Damon's character sees all this happening and swoops in to help his friend out of what's escalated into a really embarrassing situation for his friend. What happens next is what I think captures what I'm talking about. In the scene, Damon illustrates the predictable evolution of thought that the "annoying know-it-all" learned while he was in school, as Damon starts, "... as a first-year grad student you just got through reading [a historical perspective], and you'll be convinced of that until next month and you'll read [the next historical perspective], that's going to last until next year and you'll be in here quoting [the next historical perspective]." The "annoying know-it-all" tries to respond by direct quoting a passage in the writing and Damon cuts him off and finishes the sentence, and then asks him if he is going to plagiarize the whole thing, or does he have any thoughts of his own on this matter. This is what I think happens when we get focused on trying to find "a way." Or trying to come up with a shortcut by marrying yourself to a limited and highly-specific method. Then all the reading and discussion points to the same things, similar books, and talk to the same people and spew this propaganda to anyone who will listen looking for a warm blanket in the form of confirmation bias that support pushing it on everyone thereafter seemingly wanting to justify the time you put into acquiring that knowledge. Endeavoring to settle on "a way" would be the exact antithesis of what I am all about. I work under the philosophy that the game is a "live document," and if the game is a live document, then how we communicate it and teach it is also a live document and is ever changing and my job is to keep an open mind to better ideas and constantly evolve. If I'm really doing my job at a high level, I can see trends in the game or traits in individual players and extrapolate those trends and traits into a projection of what can be an advantage and get ahead of it to offer those ideas, trends and traits to my players ... and I do that until ... until I find the next thing, and the next thing. Every new coach that enters the NHL and every new player that enters the NHL has something unique about them that is worth studying, understanding and deducting what aspects are worth exploring with our players. It's never-ending. By the time I finish writing this book and before it even hits the shelves, some part of what I've written here will have already evolved because I've discovered something better. [16]

---

[16] Good Will Hunting clip: *https://www.youtube.com/watch?v=nWoFPcdcA1E*

At the root of the problem I have of the rigidity of these scripts, there is never any real mention of how individual assets are accommodated in the script. This is not to say that I don't believe in philosophy pyramids, cognition development, small game theories, CLA and any other teaching approaches that any of you have uncovered to communicate the game to your athletes. All of them have great value, none of them are the exclusive answer. However all of them done in various combinations or at different times in the players development is where the most value comes from. No different than the players we teach, the more background knowledge, depth of skill and awareness you have, the more effective a teacher of the game you will be and the more players you'll be able to reach. If you settle on "a way," you will head in a spiral of confirmation bias and stop learning and challenging yourself to use new tools. The learning never stops, the combination of tool you use is ever changing. You have to keep pushing forward.

When we talk about habits and percentages in the offensive zone, I like to start with the recurring team tactical situations that the puck ends up in. In an NHL game, around 80 percent of the plays are within three feet of the boards. When we project our offence, so much of it is building playmaking capacity in our players to make plays from the wall to "good ice" or interior ice. It is also a situation where we have to be able to get the puck back in this area. So much of where we will go in our offensive development work both from a team perspective and individual originate from the three feet to the wall out. Defense is "inside-out" and offence is "outside-in." The objective in offensive zone offence is to create scoring chances ... in bunches.

BELFRY OFFENSE

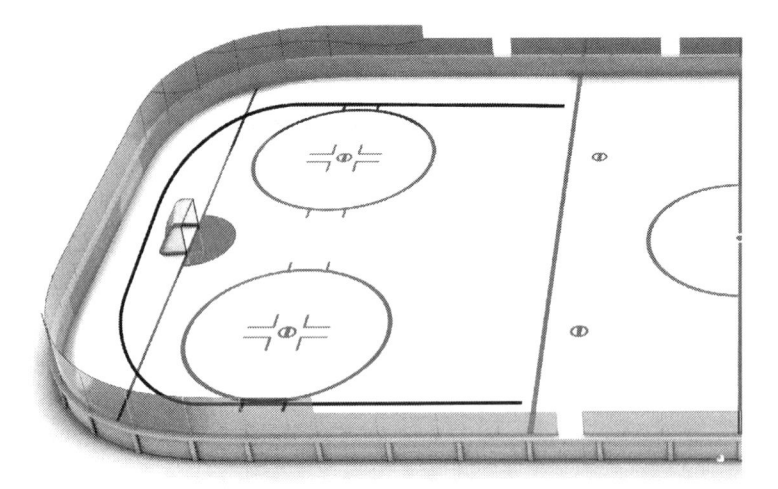

Figure 31: Three feet from the wall

The backwall

There was a great interview years ago with Jaromir Jagr who was describing how he wanted his teammates to support him when we had possession in the offensive zone. Jagr wanted 1v1 isolations where he could leverage his assets of being able to work a defensemen off his back and beat him off the wall to create walkouts. He wanted his teammates to leave him in the 1v1 and not over support the corner to draw more defenders into that space. He wanted his teammates to clear the space and allow the 1v1. Once Jagr beat his check, the opponent would have to rotate their defensive support and that would be how his teammates would get open. This is a player with a clear understanding of who he is as a player and how he can create competitive advantage. He leveraged his assets and his teammates had clear reads they could make to support. It was a clear asset-driven approach to the offensive zone.

OFFENSIVE ZONE POSSESSION

BELFRY OFFENSIVE ZONE

ZONE CONTROL = **ELEVATED SPEED OF SHAPE** X **HABITS + PERCENTAGES**

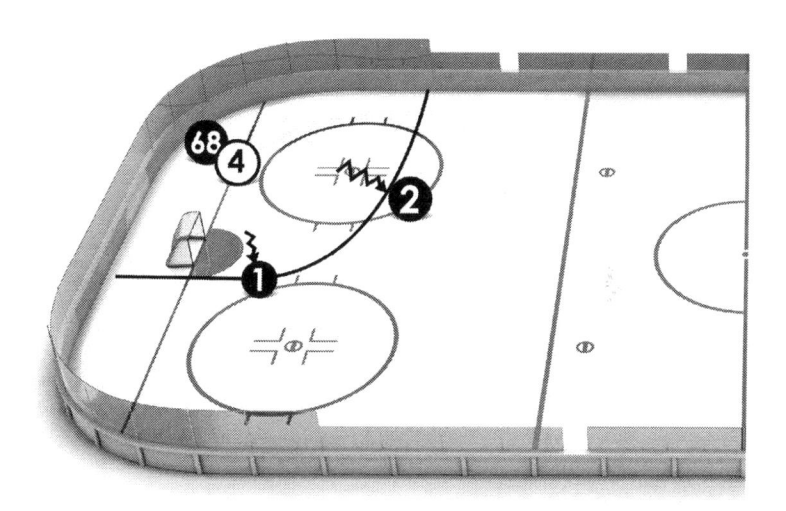

Figure 32: Jagr Isolation

Jagr (68) - Puck control deep in the zone, in the corner or back wall, he used puck protection skills with support players moving off the puck to pull defenders away from him. Jagr would work his skill habits to beat the player off the wall forcing a need for a rotation. If the opponent doesn't rotate quick enough or at all, Jagr walks to the net for a grade A. If they rotate to defend Jagr's path to the net, he passes inside the rotation to the newly-open player for a grade A. In Jagr's case, he slowed the offensive zone down into the 1v1 and then sped it up once he beat the player off the wall.

If you are playing with Jagr, it would be pretty clear what you'd need to do when he got the puck in his spot. Your role in the shape is clear and your movement once Jagr worked off the wall was clear. This is what great players do; they bend the game into their assets and they are so consistent with their habits that their teammates have a fair understanding of what might happen, making it easier for them to support. If they don't know, this level of player will probably tell you without mincing many words. Jagr may have been one of the best "forced switch" players in NHL history, his ability to beat people 1v1 and force check-change decisions and then be able to make the right read to make the best offensive play available. The ability to leverage individual assets to consistently improve chance quality tends to lead to a lot of offence ... and in Jagr's case a Hall of Fame career with multiple Stanley Cup wins and individually being the second most prolific offensive producing player in NHL history.

Now this is an example of an approach from one of the best players to ever do it. How does this apply to players who are near the median of the league or just battling to stay in the league? How does it work for these players? It's the same as Jagr in objective, but expressed with different habits and utility of assets to improve the percentages. The creativity comes from how the player leverages their individual habits and assets to create advantage. When you have a team of players, every player is a little different in how they should create advantage. We need to offer the players the equation and insight into understanding their teammates so we can make decisions on how to support them. I don't want the team to have to memorize a bunch of "if this, then that principles." Rather, I want them to know their teammates and how they create advantages. This is where skill development is a great bridge between coaching and the players. A top player development thinker will know how to study each player to determine their success habits and both develop a plan for that player to further develop their habits, and highlight to other players how they can play with a player with this habit/skill set. Here's an example:

1. I worked with a player who was a big player with good hands and could make plays all over the rink, but on the back wall, he really struggled. The issue was because he was so big and rangy that when the defender used the boards as another defender, this player would get pushed into the wall and it would restrict his movement and range. The player's normally best asset was now a weakness. The goal

OFFENSIVE ZONE POSSESSION

was to develop solutions to ensure that the player could leverage his best assets in this area of the ice. The plan included the following strategy:

a. Play off the wall far enough that his outside skate could turn without hitting the boards. This would allow him the space to move if he gets pushed in. The goal of pushing someone into the wall is to reduce the space for their skates to move, limiting movement capacity. By preserving the turning space between him and the wall, he could always maintain movement, or the defender would push him into movement. When you are close to the boards, the stick blade gets further separated from your feet and you can't protect the space between your stick blade and your body. This is the space defenders will attack for defensive body position to separate you from the puck. By preserving the space between him and the wall, he could hide the space between his stick blade and his body allowing him to protect the puck.

b. Keep his shoulders perpendicular to the wall, don't turn his back to the play. By playing with his shoulders perpendicular to the wall, he could see the play and he could see where the space was. Being perpendicular also allows him to protect the puck and invite defensive reaches offering him the trap-door escape on the other side.

These two strategies combined with rim-collection skills of being able to control the rim both going with the direction of the puck and going counter into the puck - catching the puck in a protection position. This allowed him to field a larger percentage of pucks in motion which started stacking percentages.

Once the spacing was established (off the wall far enough the outside skate had full radius to turn), the body position (being perpendicular to the wall) and he became fluent in rim collections, he now had the habits to stack the percentages and become a much more effective player on the back wall.

BELFRY OFFENSE

Now let's explore the back wall and where the offensive opportunities are:

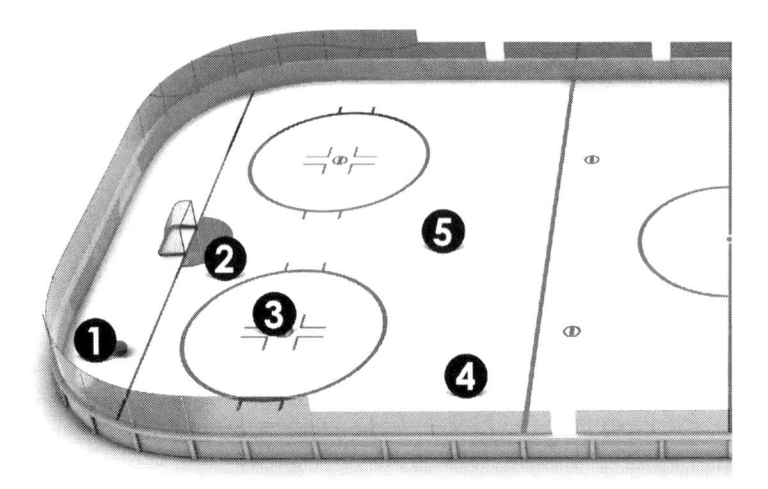

Figure 33: Basic Shape

PLEASE NOTE: I'll use this shape as the starting point for many of my illustrations throughout the book, I've kept it common on purpose, but, of course, there are many, many different shapes you can use. This is by no means the only shape. I just thought by keeping it common throughout the book, the illustrations would be easier to follow.

The basic shape when the puck is on the back wall is a player at the net, a player at the puck and a player on the dot with the two players at the point. The shape will move based on the movement of the puck and transition response. Depending on the time of the game, the score and the players on the ice, we could see the shape shift a little to adjust to the new conditions.

Shape also to where the high forward is on the weak side and becomes the weak-side change option and the strong-side D is the strong-side top option. The idea is to have two long outs that stretch the defensive shape and start movement. This is where we first saw Patrick Kane and Artemi Panarin start doing this regularly. One would play one side on the dot and

OFFENSIVE ZONE POSSESSION

the other would play the other side on the dot, and they would use each other for side change. Since they did this in Chicago, many top lines will use this. I'm sure you can picture Nikita Kucherov in this spot.

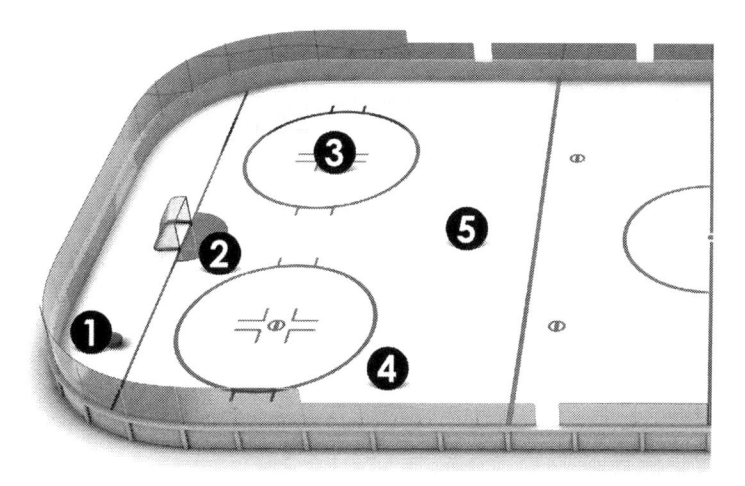

Figure 34: Weakside Dot

Or the shape could be that the D play wide and the weak-side D is responsible for the hard rim.

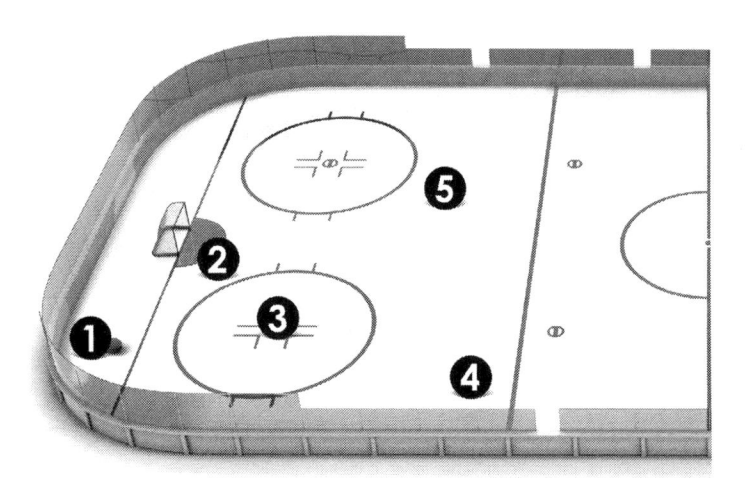

Figure 35: D Wide Shape

111

BELFRY OFFENSE

Shape could also shift to where the high F3 forward moves between the D to be a true 3, like Nathan MacKinnon started to do regularly. This leaves both D very active to take care of the side changes and the use of the low to high.

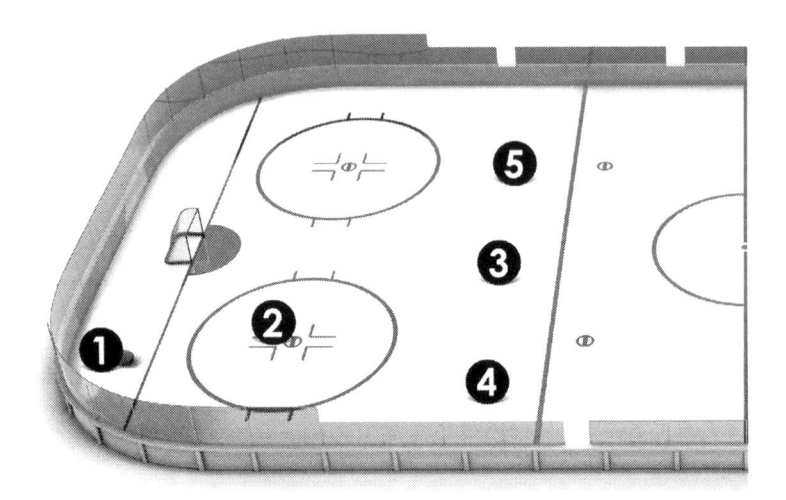

Figure 36:

2. Habits
    a. The objective is to get the puck off the wall and keep it moving. Don't let it come to a stop as offence is movement and defense is stopping movement
    b. Skill Habits are related to direction of the puck and the percentages are to read how to keep the puck in motion. Go with the direction of the puck, go into the puck or counter pickup .
    c. Gain seal-contact body position to maintain the puck in motion, build spacing off the wall, preserve space to turn. Trap door to extend possession as long as necessary.
    d. Skills of weight shift, cut off, seals, Kane push, cutbacks, spins, chucks, playmaking between checks, walkouts.

OFFENSIVE ZONE POSSESSION

3. Walkouts

    A walkout is the term I use to describe a player bringing the puck from below the goal line to above the goal line for a personal scoring chance or to create a chance for someone else. The act of bringing the puck from below the goal line to above the goal line is a walkout.

4. Wraps

    A wrap is when the player's feet are still below the goal line and they try to stuff the puck in by bringing the puck above the goal line and quickly shoot it. The distinction of the wrap is the feet are still below the goal line when the shot is taken.

5. Forcing switch decision

    A forced switch is when the puck carrier separates from their check forcing a different defender to pick up the puck carrier as their new defensive responsibility. The value of the forced switch is there is a moment in the switch when neither of the two defenders are in good defensive position and are in fact chasing their position. Making a play inside the changing of checks can lead to uncontested scoring chances. Forcing a switch decision is creating separation from the check and becoming an immediate threat to the net, forcing the opposition to make a decision to allow the threat to attack the net or to switch checking responsibilities. There are often chances to score created by merely forcing the decision.

6. Flatten out the support

    In the offensive zone corner, the defensive team will often defend in layers. To flatten out the support means to invite the defensive player to the corner and then pass the puck to your support, inviting the defensive support player to the wall to defend. Now if the original puck carrier beats his check off the wall, they can take advantage of the moment where the defensive support is flat.

BELFRY OFFENSE

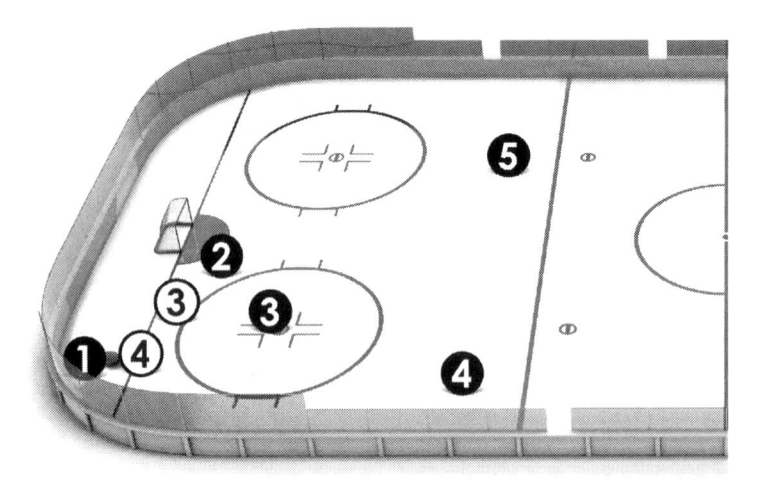

Figure 37

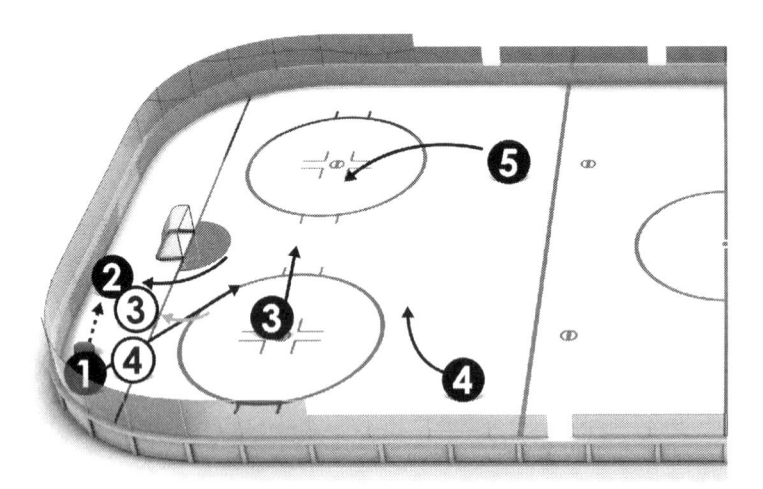

Figure 38

In the first diagram, the white defenders have the defender at the puck White 4 and a layer of defensive support in White 3. Now in the second diagram, the net-front Black 2 moves to support and Black 1 passes to him to draw the support to the wall, then jumps past his check when the support is flat.

OFFENSIVE ZONE POSSESSION

7. Isolating the defensive forward down low

    There are times when the puck carrier is being defended by the low defensive forward. In these situations, it can be an offensive advantage to isolate that defensive forward and force him to defend, to challenge the defensive forward to dig in and defend. This is not only a more favorable matchup as very few defensive forwards defend as well as defensemen, but also puts miles on the defensive forward which can be an excellent investment later in the shift, the period, the game or the series.

8. Contact Habits

    a. Seals

    A seal is when you position your body completely on one side of the opponent, thus creating a physical seal to that side of your body. This offers a natural escape route the sealed opponent wouldn't be able to properly defend.

    i. Rolls

    A roll is when the opponent is about to take a contact and uses a soft shoulder technique where they go with the contact and roll on the opposite side of the contact.

    ii. Offensive stick check

    An offensive stick check is when the puck carrier or an offensive player without the puck pops or grabs the defensive players stick with their stick. A puck carrier would leave the puck and pop the defenders stick in an effort to preemptively eliminate the stick check opportunity of the defender.

    iii. Use of the net

    The offensive player will use the net as a shield from a pursuing check. They will sometimes "peel" the checker off the net to create separation.

BELFRY OFFENSE

Being from Toronto, being a lifelong Toronto Maple Leafs fan and having worked for the Leafs for so long, I naturally became a Toronto Raptors fan. When the Raptors won the NBA championship for the first time in 2019, they brought in superstar Kawhi Leonard to spearhead the run, and did he ever. One of Kawhi's famous media interview quotes was "the Boardman gets paid." [17] He was referring to rebounding the ball at both ends of the floor helps you win games. Limiting the opposition to one shot, or extending possessions on the offensive end. He talked about how this became a motto as he was coming up to get to the league. In the 2023 Stanley Cup Playoffs, former head coach of the Anaheim Ducks Dallas Eakins, highlighted that close to 80 percent of the puck time in the NHL happens three feet from the boards, [18] and guys like Kucherov taking a missed shot whipping around the wall, and in one motion, pulling that puck off the wall and making a play to the slot or to the weak side on the money for scoring chances, you can say, "Boardman gets paid" in hockey, too. In the NHL, if you aren't good on the wall, you won't play in the league.

The Half-wall

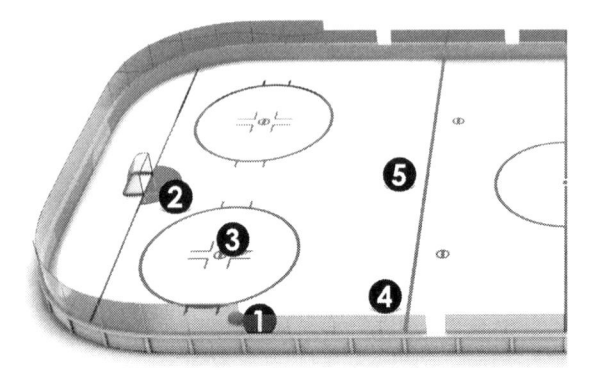

Figure 39:

---

[17] *https://www.espn.com/video/clip/_/id/26908855*
[18] *https://twitter.com/Mitch_Giguere/status/1653971934000955392*

116

OFFENSIVE ZONE POSSESSION

The half-wall has become an increasingly more difficult place to make plays from. It's become defended much better. Not so long ago, you could bring the defensemen up the wall to the hash marks and he would pass you off to the strong-side defensive forward, who would then be caught in a 2v1 with the strong-side offensive D. With this one movement, a ton of offensive plays would open up.

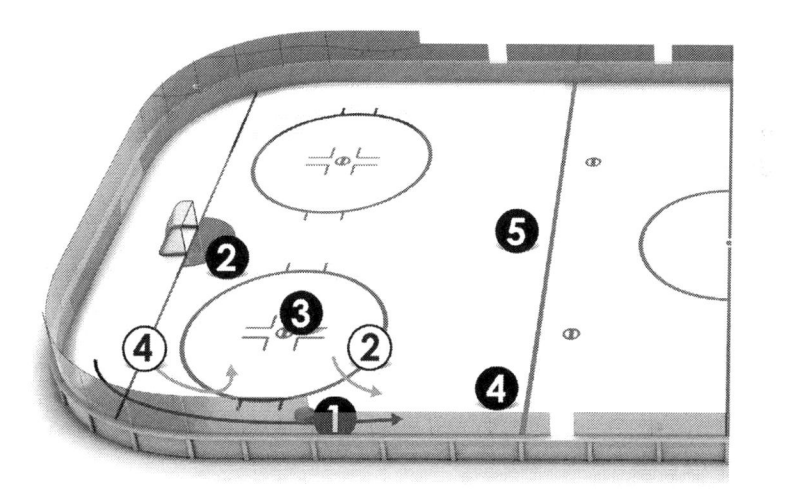

Figure 40:

9. Continue on the elbow into the high 3v2 and work the 2v1 with the D, whether it's a high scissor (where the strong-side offensive defensemen would come down the wall as the puck carrier rolled over the elbow. The puck carrier (1) rolls over the top of the elbow and (4) jumps down the boards. The idea is to have a counter play between 1 and 4 and a go with the puck play with 1 and 5 available.

BELFRY OFFENSE

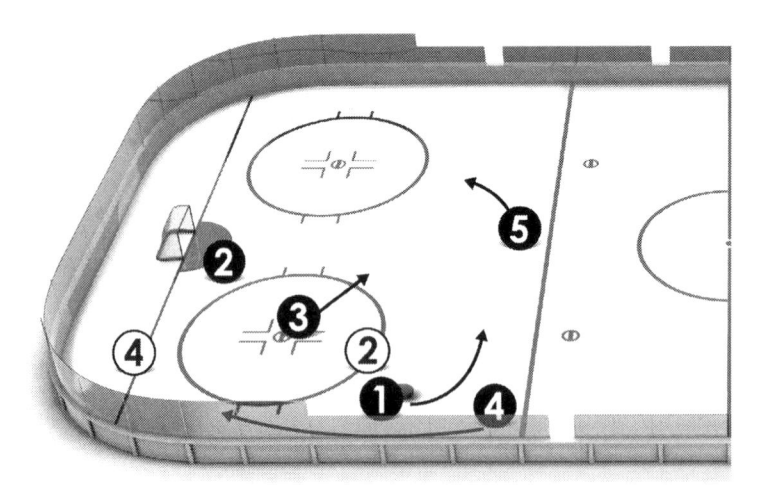

Figure 41:

10. The strong-side D could rotate to the middle and now work the 2v1 vs the high forward. Now they can accelerate the speed of the play with everyone going with the direction of the puck. Or (3) could go back to the half-wall to offer a counter option inside the shape acceleration.

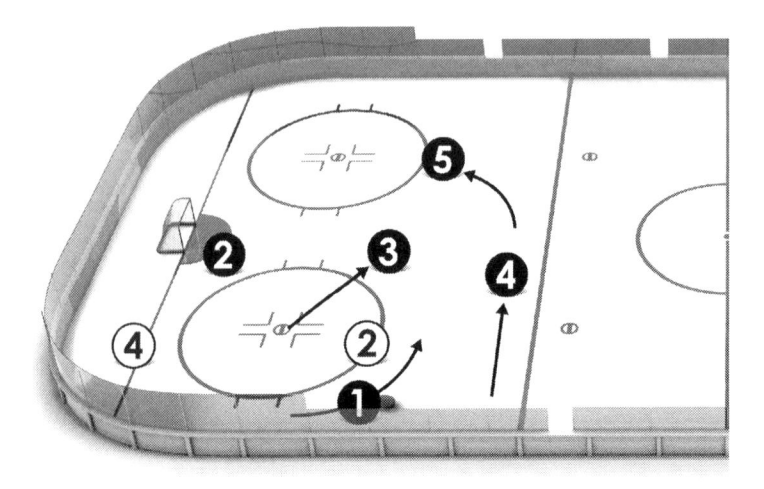

Figure 42:

118

OFFENSIVE ZONE POSSESSION

11. If the spacing isn't exactly right between the pursuing D and the strong-side defensive forward, the puck carrier could personally attack interior using that space and leave them both on the wall.

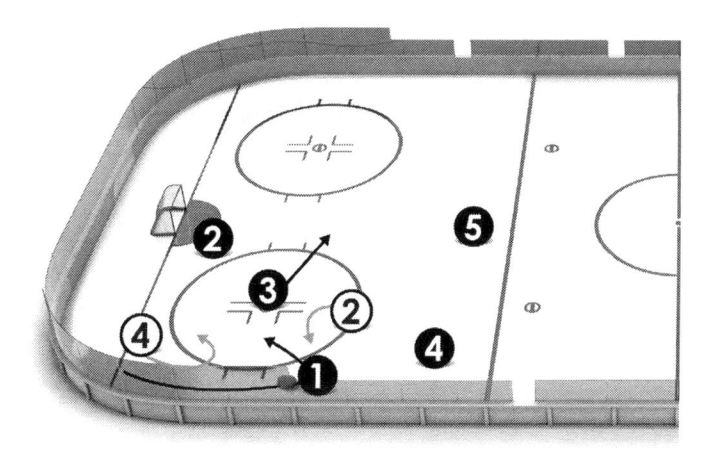

Figure 43:

a. The puck carrier can also pass the puck to the weak-side offensive D using this passing lane.

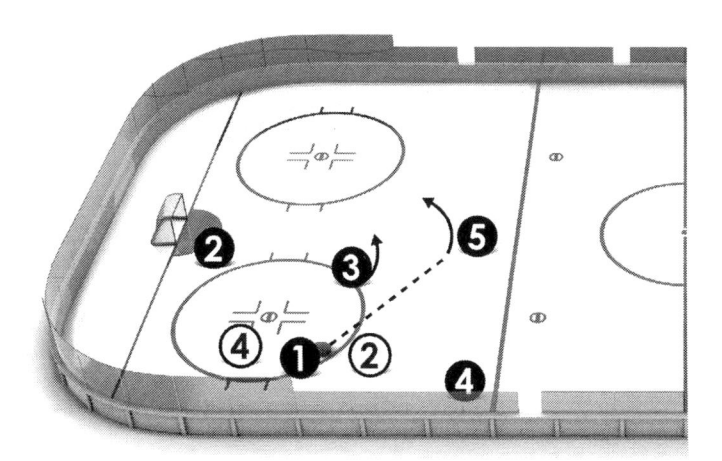

Figure 44:

119

BELFRY OFFENSE

12. Time it so you turn down (cutback) as you feel/see the defender falling back after the hash mark pass off. Now the defender is retreating while you are turning, so you have the defender in an awkward defensive angle as he is backing up while you are attacking.

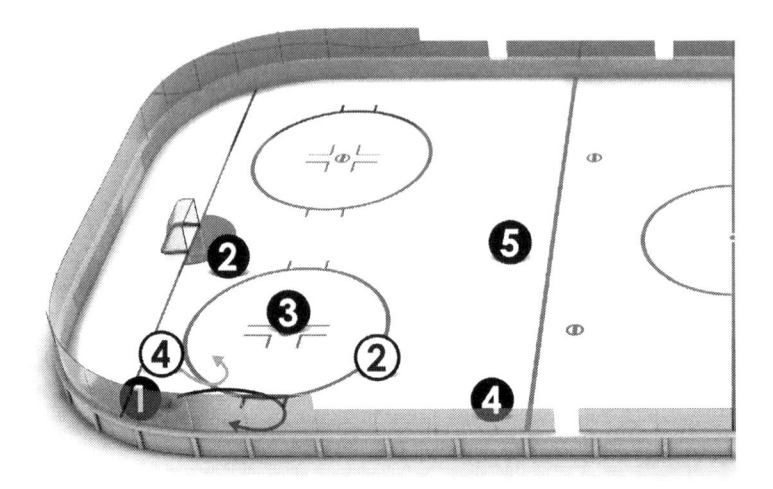

Figure 45: Cutback

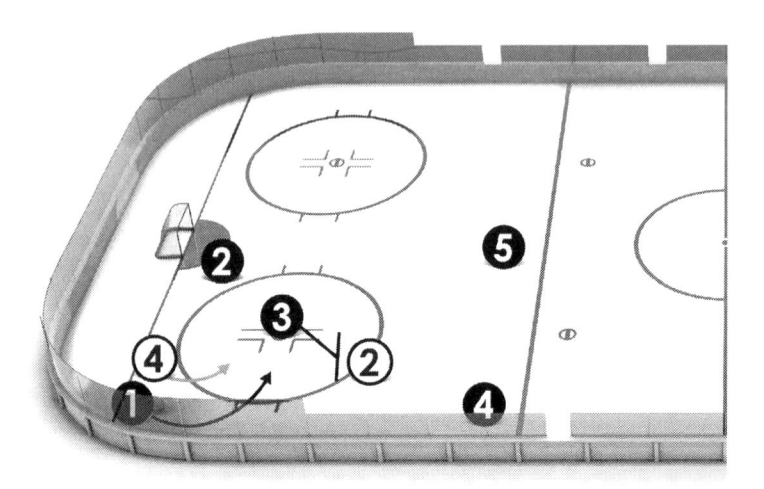

Figure 46:

OFFENSIVE ZONE POSSESSION

13. Take the dot release (F3) and have him set a pick on the defensemen as he's climbing the wall to open up the interior.

    a. The dot-release player F3 could let you go past and then go to the half-wall as the pursuing D (4) passes the check off and pulls back. As he pulls back, F3 jumps to the half-wall and the puck carrier passes it to him and then both attack interior.

14. Skating on first touch from the strong-side offensive D is a great way to get the jump on the defender, improve your offensive spacing and create lanes and space for playmaking up the wall. Playmaking up the wall is an offensive tactic whereby you are making interior threatening plays or plays to the weak side of the ice while skating away from the net. Passing the puck on a back diagonal into space or leading the offensive player downhill is a tough skill to learn. It's a different passing movement as you need to be able to separate your upper body from your lower body to clear your hands around your body to execute the play.

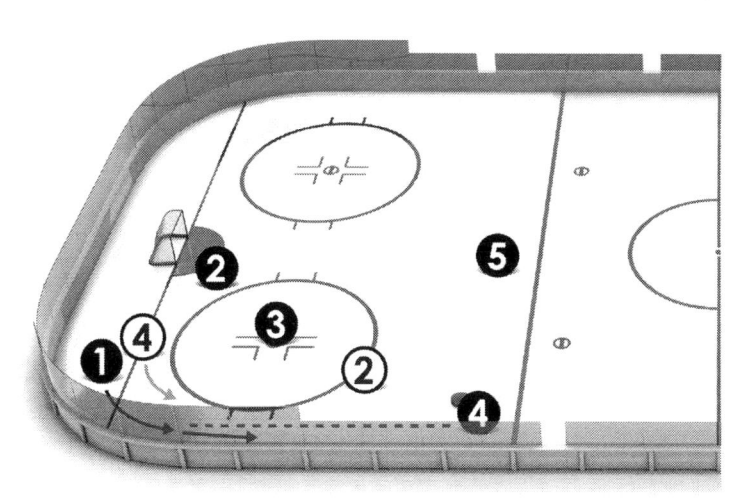

Figure 47:

BELFRY OFFENSE

As you can see, the number of opportunities an offensive team has to attack off the half-wall were extensive, and because it was such a problem, team defences put some real thought into how to better defend the half-wall and they do a much better job of cutting off the top, closing the puck carrier off before he gets to the hash marks, encouraging their pursuit D to stay with the original puck carrier and eliminating the engagement rules of having to fall back or pass the check off to the player at the top. They'll now come up with him and make it a 3v3 at the top and not allow it to move into the high 3v2, where the defensive problems can compound.

For a few years, the half-wall became a graveyard for offence. Even the special half-wall thinkers and creators had trouble with the defensive scheming. Once the defensive adjustments had a smothering effect, it fell on the offensive players to figure out new pathways to open the half-wall back up. So now you see the strategies look like this.

15. Weak-side net release, where the net-front player will pop out to the weak side dot as the play comes over the top. This opens up the half-wall for either immediate shot attempts off the pass or movement down or up the zone.

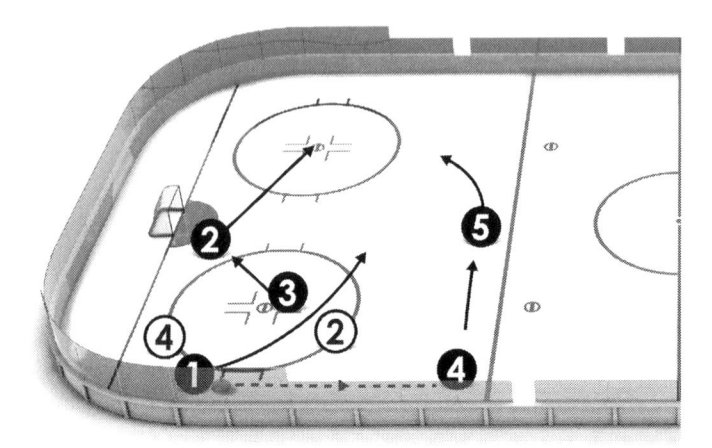

Figure 48: Weakside Net Release

122

OFFENSIVE ZONE POSSESSION

16. D turn up: So on rimmed pucks, the pinching D will invite the weak-side defensive forward into that foot race and then turn up on him opening up the forward to move differently.

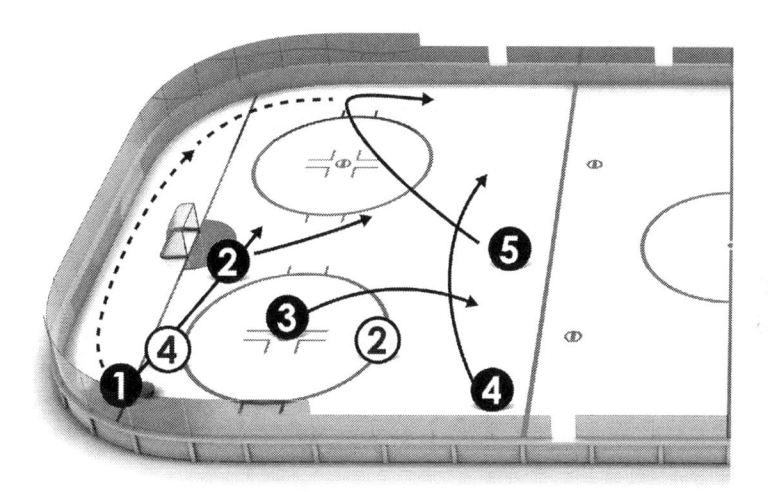

Figure 49:

17. Weak side release to accel up the wall. This first came about through Panarin and Kane when they played in Chicago. Each player would primarily stay on their side and they'd use the back wall to change sides to each other. When they did, the new puck carrier could skate on this touch and accelerate up the wall, way before the defensive group could get over to defend. The defensive group was likely in some kind of compressed defensive structure, like a swarm or something like it, making it really difficult for them to quickly defend that area of the ice.

BELFRY OFFENSE

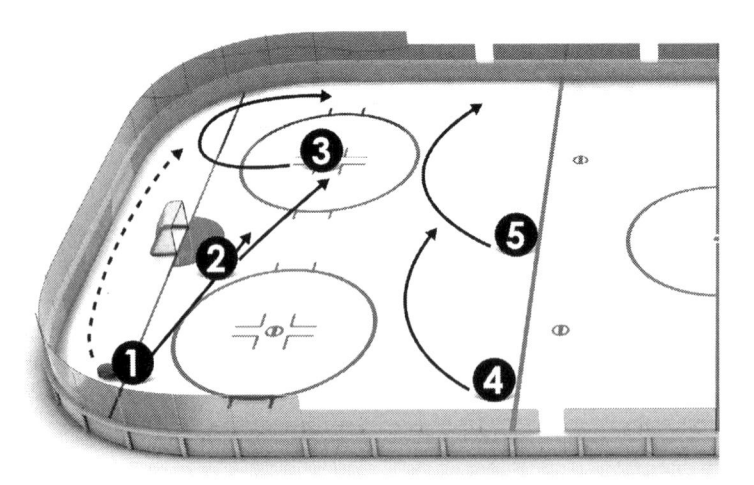

Figure 50:

a. Weak-side Dot availability. Different from the weak-side net release, this is now the offensive player just holding position on the weak-side dot while the puck is on the other side of the ice.

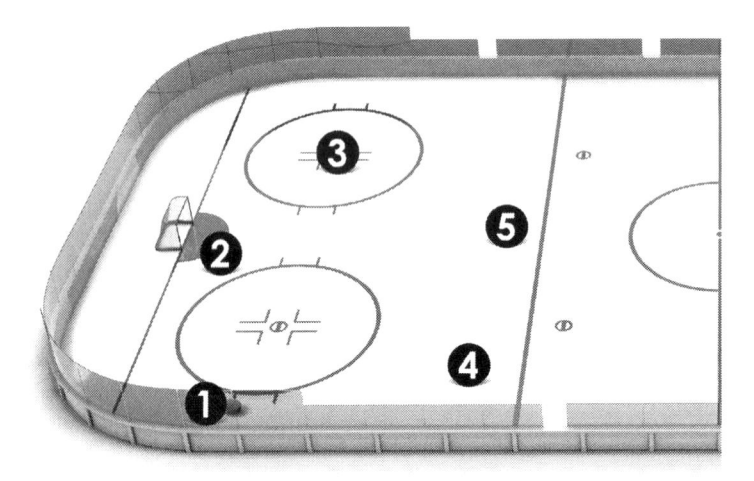

Figure 51:

What is the difference between how the half-wall was previously played and how it has been adapted? Well, the half-wall used to be able to be created from the strong side. However, with defensive structures going to more compressed defensive shapes and schemes designed to force the offence to play 3vs5, they've compressed that area of the ice so much that there just isn't a lot of room to create off the half-wall on the strong side. The answer to bringing back the half-wall offence then became to use the weak side of the ice. Now in using the weak side the half-wall is no longer a play on the wall. Now it's a player on the dot, which is very different. Rather than invite the defensive player to you on the strong side and leave him and hopefully another defensive player on the wall, we now invite the defensive group to a compressed defensive zone coverage on one side of the ice and then quickly change sides to find attack angles and opportunities.

Now how has teaching offensive on the half-wall changed? Well, those of us who have been around for longer than we'd like to admit, all remember teaching the cycle. Three players bringing the puck from the corner to the half-wall and repeatedly bumping it back to the next player swinging from the net to the corner. With three spots in the OZ, each player is rotating into ... the net, the corner and the high F3. Spending practice after practice trying to get the timing, the spacing and the weight (how hard you pass it) of the puck. Then trying to teach the defenders how to be good dummy defenders, so they don't ruin it. Many of us taught this extensively.

BELFRY OFFENSE

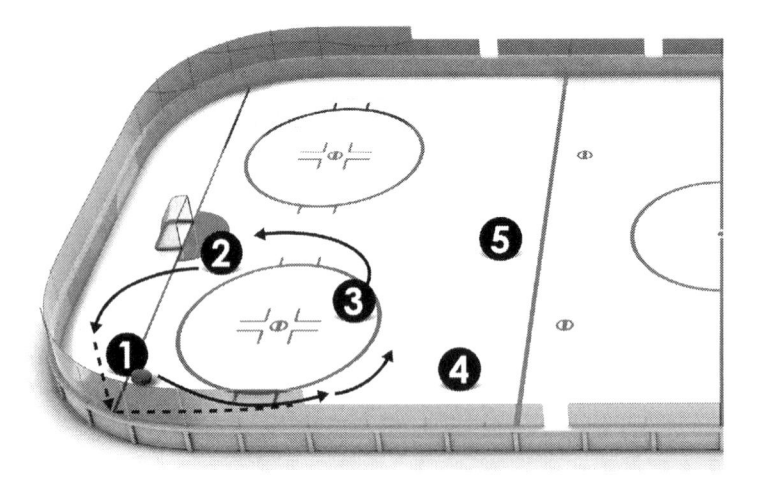

Figure 52: The Cycle

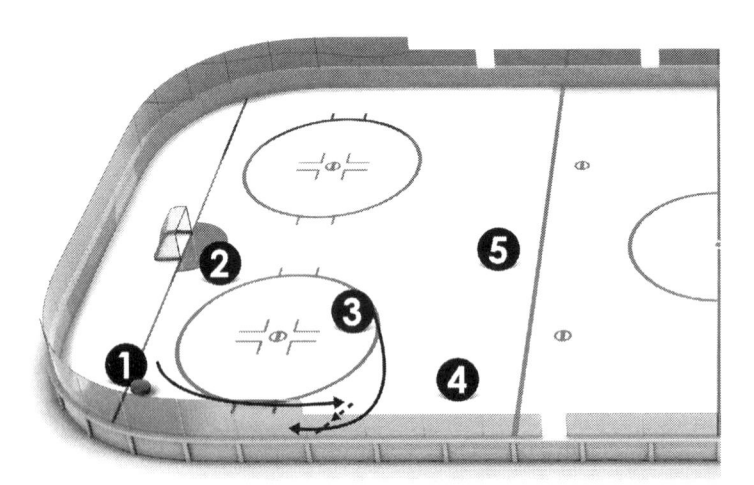

Figure 53: Scissor Cycle

The next part was to introduce the scissor cycle, which now rather than have all three players moving in the same direction, the F3 would move down the wall in the opposite direction of the puck carrier and try to create confusion amongst the defenders with the

126

OFFENSIVE ZONE POSSESSION

switch. Now we are again focused on timing and spacing, but also the need for the puck carrier to build space off the wall for F3, so now it's a little different responsibility on the puck carrier. There was also a different way to move the puck now. Rather than bump it back to the corner, you want the puck carrier to leave it for the hard-charging F3 coming down the wall. So the puck carrier now had to build space off the wall, lean into their check and leave the puck. I remember someone used the term "European pick" to describe this handoff. So for years, we now had the corner cycle that worked into the half-wall and the options were:

a. Bring your check up the wall to the hash marks and bump it back down to the corner for the next guy and then reload as F3, before continuing your route to the net and jumping back to the corner to pick up the bump, but don't leave the net until the puck is bumped. I mean this isn't "Ring Around the Rosie."

b. The puck carrier could fake the bump back and cut off the wall into the interior. A little brazen, but a lot of skilled players made a living off this exchange.

c. F3 could choose not to continue in the same direction as the cycle movement. Rather they could go the other way and come down the boards to the corner, in which the puck carrier would build space off the wall and execute the exchange.

d. Of course, the puck carrier could also fake the handoff and cut to the middle and attack the net himself or pass to the F3 who is rounding the bottom and heading to the net.

e. Next we could do the "high cycle" using the D, where we could bring everyone up into the high elbow and start working both directional cycle options with the strong-side offensive defensemen.

BELFRY OFFENSE

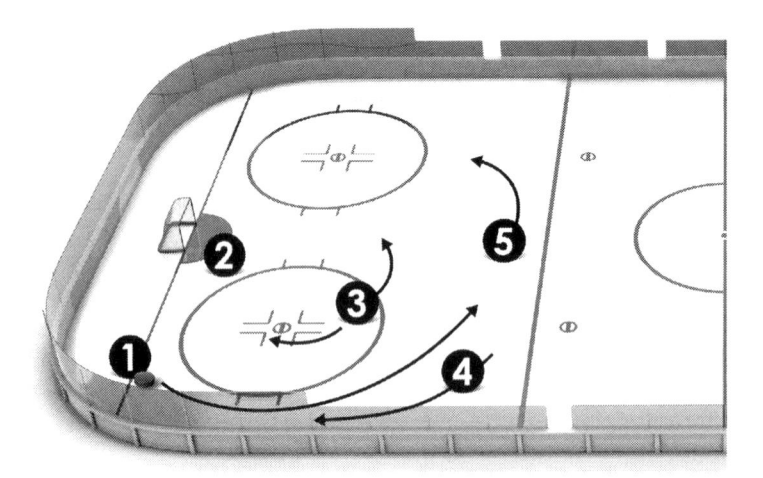

Figure 54: High Cycle

Then we started to use the guy at the net to change sides, so we could open up the other side of the ice. We could maybe do a normal cycle a couple times and then the puck carrier would hard rim the puck behind the net before they got above the goal line. The net-front person, who learned the discipline of holding the net until the puck was sent down, would then seal their check at the net and go with the direction of the puck on the back wall. This then opened up some shot attempts for the weak-side D coming downhill.

OFFENSIVE ZONE POSSESSION

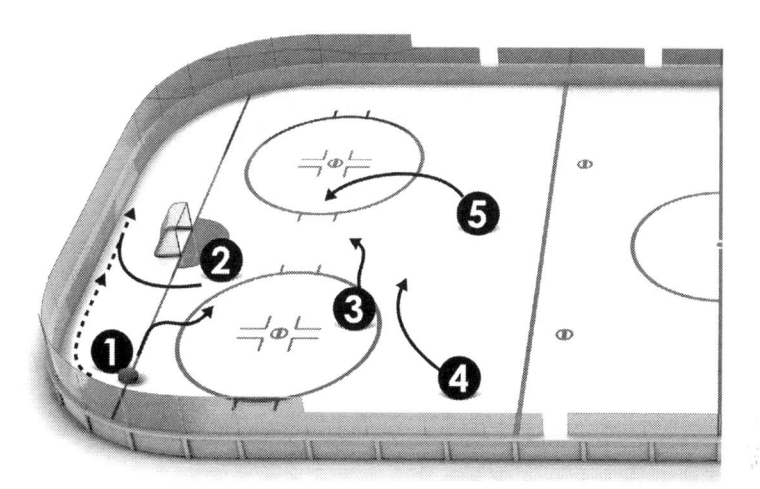

Figure 55: Net-Front Side Change

Then we started to use F3 on the side change, where the puck carrier would send the puck again on a hard rim. This time, it would beat the person at the net and go to the other side of the ice, F3 would sprint down on the puck in the corner and now we have a side change with movement.

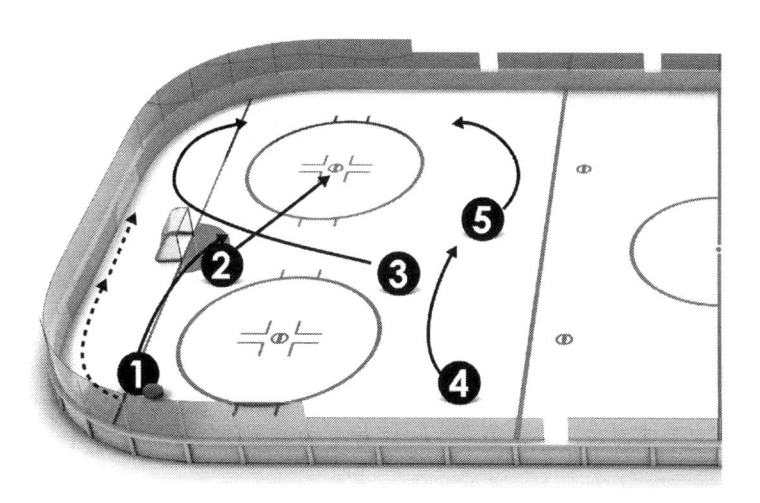

Figure 56: F3 Side Change

129

BELFRY OFFENSE

Then we see situations where the rim is even harder and the weakside D becomes the first touch on the weak side engaging in a scissor cycle on the first touch.

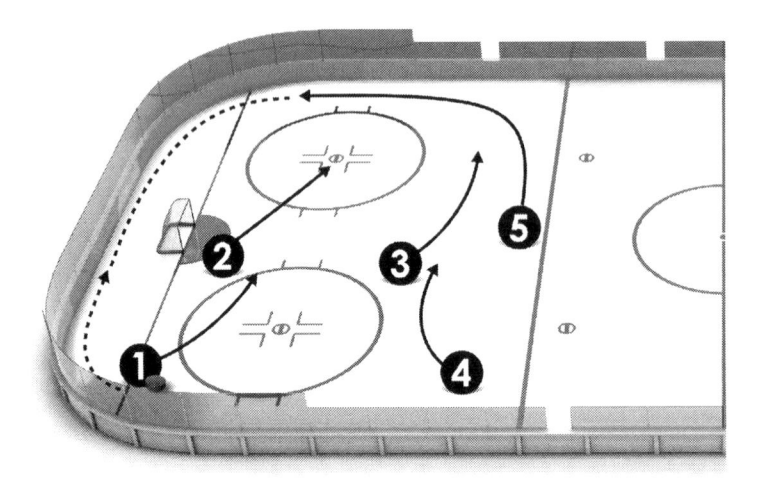

Figure 57: Rim to Weakside D

Now you look at all these diagrams and plays that look like a football playbook, it is far from it. It's a movement map of recurring patterns that groups often do depending on the location of the puck, the pressure, the condition surrounding the puck, the score, the time in the period, etc. So how do the players know when to do what? How to "read" off each other? What is the logic that they work off of? Are there principles or rules to abide by? Does every player have to memorize all these play options? No, none of that. You coach them in accordance to our equation. This one equation governs all of it. Once each player knows the roles of the shape and how those roles change depending on where the puck is and they know the equation, the only decision to make is whether or not to go with the direction of the puck or counter, and where possible, have both directions present in the play. This equation produces those plays I diagramed and 100s more that they create on their own. This is how you produce collective offensive creativity.

BELFRY OFFENSIVE ZONE

(ZONE CONTROL) = (ELEVATED SPEED OF SHAPE) X (HABITS + PERCENTAGES)

I used to talk about ice balance a lot in working in the offensive zone. I had a whole thing that I called "2 up and 2 down." It referred to the number of players who should be up in the top of the zone and down in the bottom of the zone at all times, and the movement of the players worked in accordance to maintaining that ice balance. I do not mention ice balance anymore. Ice balance falls in the category of principles of play. If you are talking principles, you are at least one generation of the advancement of the offensive zone behind. If you have a hardened set of principles that you work off of and have built for yourself, then you have some catching up to do. Now you have set a way. As soon as you settle on "a way," your development will be frozen in time. Any new idea will be evaluated against your way and you will accept the ideas that lend themselves to your way and are confirming and you will reject the ones that don't. You become fixed. So when I was talking about ice balance, I was fixed. I had this whole thing that was ice balance and rules of engagement, a lot of "if this, then that" type of rules. The list of principles and rules for those principles and reads and all that became as long as my arm. If you are still deep in principles, rules and reads, you have built a good foundation for yourself in understanding how the game moves and works, however, it's time to evolve to the next generation. To get there, you have to be willing to unlearn and to move off of ideas that you held so tightly before in favor of exploring new ones. If you don't and you tightly hold onto that pyramid, you'll gradually fade in the rearview mirror. That's just the nature of our sport. It's always advancing, whether you like it or not. Every new exciting player entering the league will bring assets and creative expressions of those assets that shake the game up. Embrace it, no sense fighting it. There is a ton of fun in evolving and exploring the next generation.

Or ... we can just let the kids play games and they'll just figure it out on their own. I mean, come on, I say this facetiously, but it does speak to the ridiculousness of that entire rhetoric. They will all not figure it out on their own. What will happen is the kids above the achievement gap will assert themselves individually. But learning to play as a group of five, that only comes from a sequence or progression of ideas moving from group development through to the competitive teaching process. A process that starts only when the coach commits to undertaking a personal education process to push their knowledge to the tipping point where their understanding allows them to communicate complexity, simply. I hope that process takes a big step for you with this book.

In recent years, players have been encouraged to use cutback in the offensive zone. A cutback is when the puck carrier walks up the wall and takes a defender with them. Prior to when they want to cut back, the attacker aggressively cuts in front of the defender, through their hands and stick. The more aggressive that the attacker drives through the defender, the more they can turn the defender's feet to the inside to both manipulate the feet and build turning space off the wall. Now the attacker knows when they want to cut back, so they force the defender at a double disadvantage; a) They turn their feet counter to the direction they're going in next; b) They know when they're turning and force the defender into reaction. When the attacking player pushes the defender in and builds the turning space, the attacker can create separation needed to make the next play. The objective of the cutback is to pull the defender close to the attacking player and then quickly create separation. This particular play became a long study of mine because the cutback is not just a half-wall skating escape tactic, it can be used in many areas of the ice and in many situations. The skills and tactics have excellent transferability. To truly understand the cutback is to start with the tactical advantage it's supposed to create: the manipulation of the defender to create separation to make the next play. To manipulate the defender is to strategically move them where you want him to go. In the cutback, we want to turn the defender's feet to the interior to both increase the turning space between the defender and the wall and to put the defender in a position where they are forced to recover their

OFFENSIVE ZONE POSSESSION

position. Now that we know what it is and what we are trying to achieve from the movement, how do we teach it? The first part is puck acquisition depth of skill. How many ways can the player get the puck? Off a good pass is a given, then we have rim collections going into the puck and going with the puck, seal-contact takeaways, loose-puck escapes and board passes. The reason why puck acquisition depth of skill is so important is because the cutback is reliant upon the player being comfortable handling the puck under physical contact. Players who struggle in acquisition will take longer to get the puck into a good position, if ever. The extra time taken to get the puck organized will also extend the time they take to get into good position prior to the confrontation with the defender. There is no sense digging into cutbacks until the player feels confident in a multitude of acquisitions. Once the player can field the puck cleanly and get it quickly into a good position, then we can move to getting off the wall. Now, this eventually will become simultaneous with acquisition, but for illustration of development process, we will need to next get the player off the wall. The reason we want the player to get off the wall right away is to build the trap door (the space to turn into). The earlier the player gets off the wall, the more space the threat of the cutback will aid in controlling the defender. To get off the wall, there are really four skating skills to get off the wall that players should become proficient in: 1) crossover, 2) weight shift, 3) side push and 4) hook turn. The really good players employ these in all different combinations, not just in isolation. This means they should be trained together. Crossover pick up on first touch, hook turn to get into the defender's space and weight shift to present a strong wall (shoulder, hip) to drive through on a counter lean. Side push is a sneaky way to take more space in front of the defender, and the hook turn is a rare combination of subtle and nasty turn to cut the space. While the goal is to have players be able to use these, either all together or two or three at a time at minimum, they can first be introduced one by one, then combined in different combinations. The crossover is a key element that often gets overlooked because of the tight spacing on the original acquisition on the wall, but is so important because it helps the attacker get a little ahead of the defender right away. This sets up the hook turn to get into their hands. These two pieces are what separate good from great.

Once the player has fluency in acquisition and body position, now it's about the manipulation of the defender to set up the cutback. Once the attacker is inside the space, they need to push inside to pull the defenders feet to the interior, then the situation is primed for the cutback. Now going back to the footwork on the cutback. When the attacker uses the hook turn, they are using their outside foot to initiate this movement. Then, the hook turn becomes a violent weight shift as the weight transfers from the outside-foot hook turn to the inside-foot weight shift. Now that the weight is on the inside foot, when the player wants to cutback, they initiate the turn with another hook-turn weight shift into the turn going the other way, with a crossover finish to separate into the space. So the footwork is crossover to hook turn to weight shift to gain entry, to hook turn to weight shift to crossover to exit into space.

We haven't talked about hand-fighting skills, like nudges and chucks or how to use the push you typically get from the defender when you get position.

The next area is puck placement. Puck placement is critical in every movement because it can really help or hinder skating. Puck placement on a cutback is to have the puck come last on the way in and first on the way out.

Back to the half-wall cycle … now it's pretty much evolved from a three-man corner cycle to a four-man cycle with the strong-side D to now a five-man cycle where everyone is involved and every inch of the offensive zone is potentially in play. These are adaptations to defenders who have learned how to stop the cycle and now the offensive group has to figure something else out and level up. It's also individual players leveraging their assets into the play differently and opening our eyes to different approaches and options. It doesn't matter how it evolved; the fact is that it has.

Now when we look at this, all of these plays described happen in

OFFENSIVE ZONE POSSESSION

virtually every NHL game. How do they know when to do what? How do they read off each other? How do they know what to do? The options are based on the shape. The shape moves in accordance to the positioning of F3, the pressure at the puck and the movement direction of the puck.

What are the skill habits?

We spoke about the details surrounding the cutback. Now let's dig into the other ones:

1. Playmaking up the wall

The offensive zone play whereby the puck carrier skates the puck up the wall toward the offensive blue line. While skating the puck up the wall, the puck carrier evaluates their pressure restrictions (time, space, support) before deciding to make a threatening interior play, change sides (through the dot line, using the weak-side D or cross-corner dump), extend possession in the high elbow or send the puck back to the bottom, either to the corner to continue a cycle or hard rim to change sides.

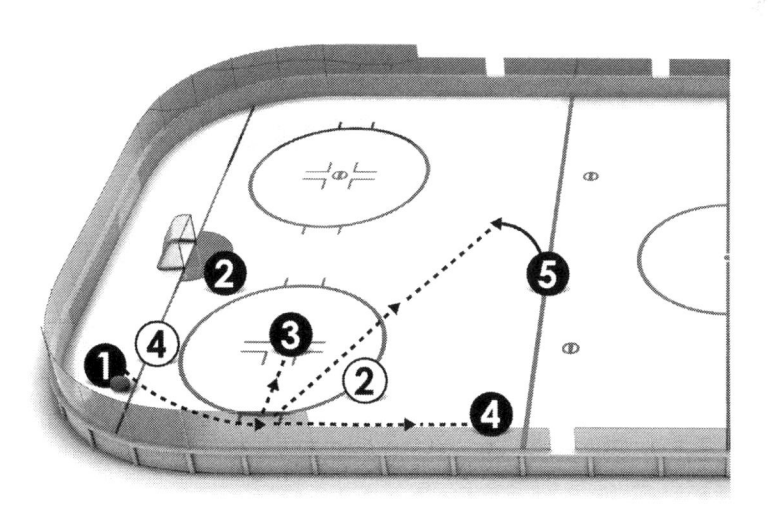

Figure 58:

BELFRY OFFENSE

As more and more players carried the puck up the wall, coaches began looking to mitigate the natural transition risk against as the player moved closer and closer to the blue line. Some started to implement geographical "decision-line markers," the goal line, the hash marks and the top of the circle. Each of these decision lines was designed to offer the player a window to make a play, and if the play wasn't there, then to send it to the top (goal line decision line), or to the bottom (corner for the hash marks and top of the circle) to reduce the natural turnover risk of making plays moving away from the net. This was part of the reason the cutback became more and more of a thing to mitigate risk and get the puck back to the bottom.

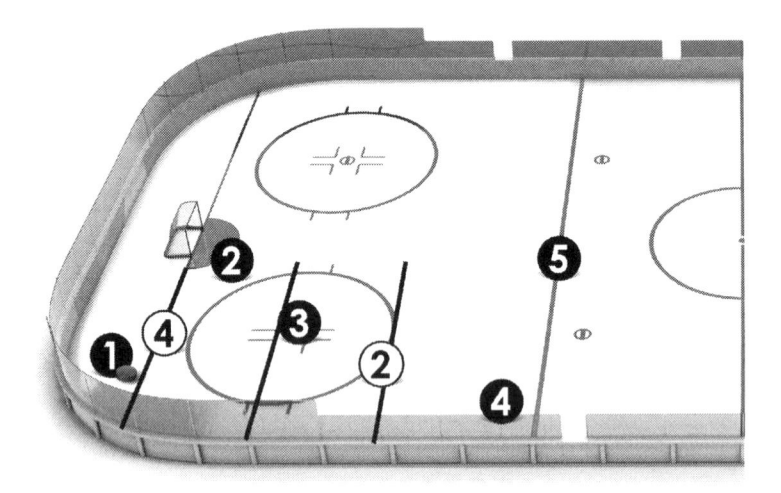

Figure 59: Decision Lines

For the longest time, there was a great group of playmaking forwards who would constantly generate offensive chances consistently in playmaking up the wall. When they paired this offensive zone skill set and options with rush delay plays, they were constantly working away from the net and finding dangerous plays to the interior and on the weak side. They started to activate the weak side of the ice more with D looking to

OFFENSIVE ZONE POSSESSION

slide down the weak side or with F3 working different interior routes. The playmaking forward climbing the wall becomes F3, so options of engagement come alive as the playmaking puck carrier climbing the wall rotates a D or F3 to engage moving toward the net.

Playmaking players who could really pass could create passing lanes or open a lane based on moving up the wall and back-diagonal passing and slip and hook passes through defensemen's triangles (space between their stick blade and their skates), and between two checks and leading players into passes going towards the net became a particularly deadly arsenal. However, the most important skill that players working to play-make working up the wall was their pre-touch position between two checks. One of the main constants that offered these players a significant advantage over defenders was moving stealthily to catch the puck in motion and between two checks, not allowing a check to be clearly attached, where being between two checks creates momentary confusion and immediate ice to threaten upon first touch.

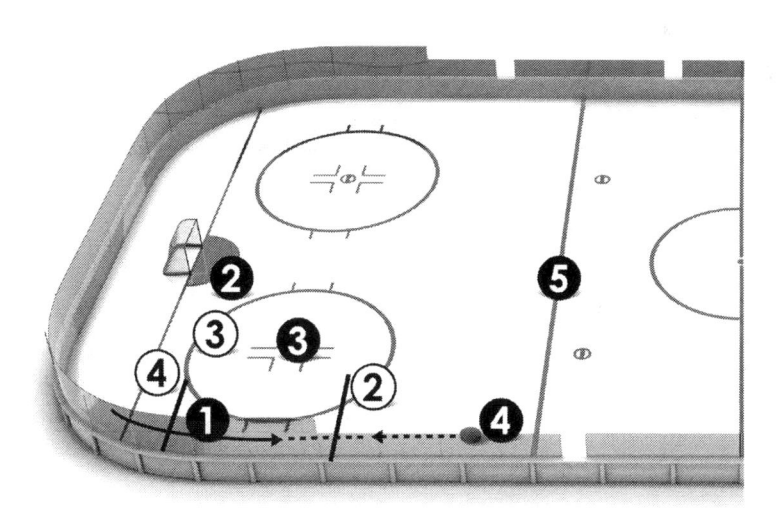

Figure 60:

BELFRY OFFENSE

2. Flatten the support

One of my favorite things to teach over the years is the art of flattening the defensive support. This originated from teaching low layers in defensive zone coverage. When in the defensive zone, the idea was to have a defenseman defending at the puck in the corner, with a low forward positioned as a layer directly behind them, and the weak-side defensemen playing the front post at the net.

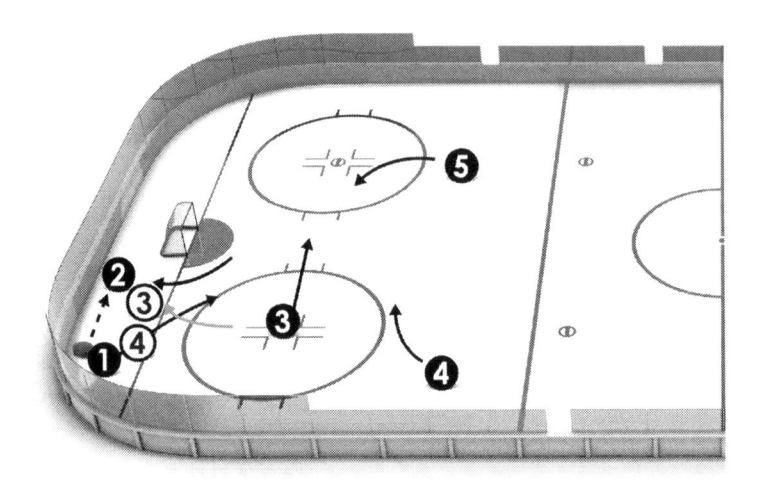

Figure 61: Flatten the Support

This is pretty standard layered defensive zone coverage. Now the offensive advantage comes from the way they rotate to maintain pressure on the puck. So if the attacking puck carrier passes the puck to their corner or half-wall support, then the low defensive center jumps to the wall to defend that player, and the primary defender pulls back into the support layer space. That's how it's supposed to go for defenders. Now the defenders learn how to interchange these two roles to maintain both pressure at the puck and a layer of support regardless of the puck moving and changing responsibilities. So not really a man-on-man situation, but rather layers. In teaching the defensive zone coverage aspects of the low

OFFENSIVE ZONE POSSESSION

(back wall, corner and half-wall) defending, one of the biggest challenges is rotating the pressure player at the puck into the support layer quickly and effectively to maintain the pressure and support layers.

For the offensive group, you can learn to take advantage of this defensive zone coverage by inviting the switch, anticipating the rotation and beating your check off the wall after you have flattened the support. Flattening the support means to have to invite D1 on the puck carrier, make a play to your offensive support player which engages their low forward to come to the wall, and the original puck carrier beats D1 off the wall when the support is flat. This allows you to create offence by working together to beat the rotation and capitalize on the moment where they are in between rotations and we can attack the vacated space where the layer is momentarily undefended.

3. Dot Release

Dot release is the utility of F3 when the puck is in the corner or the half-wall and the opponent is in a defensive zone shrink, which compresses the space available for the offensive team to move and move the puck. In this situation, F3 slides to the dot, which is a soft ice area of the offensive zone that isn't specifically defended, and the idea is for the offensive team to be able to automatically pop the puck to the dot and release the pressure.

BELFRY OFFENSE

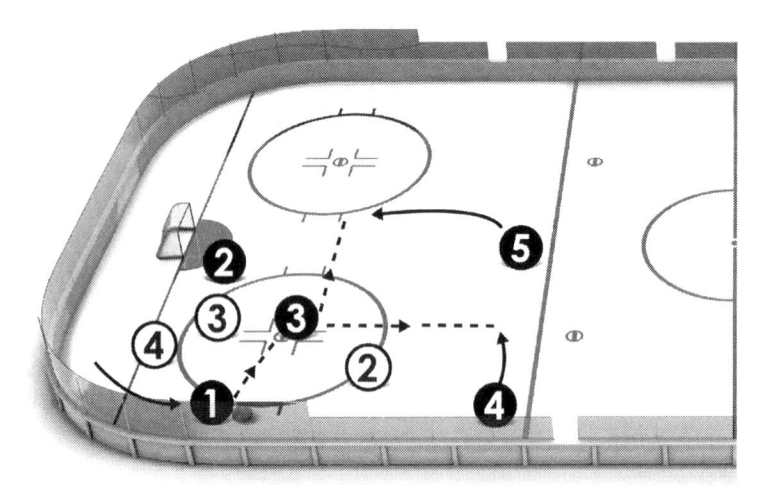

Figure 62: Dot Releases

The dot-release player can shoot the puck, can relay it to the top or use that dot seam to change sides to the weak-side D who can engage into that space.

The High 3v2

The high 3v2 has evolved in recent years. As more and more players started to play-make coming up the wall, the D started to activate more and in different routes. The interaction between F3 and both defensemen moved past pinch support and into three interchangeable positions.

OFFENSIVE ZONE POSSESSION

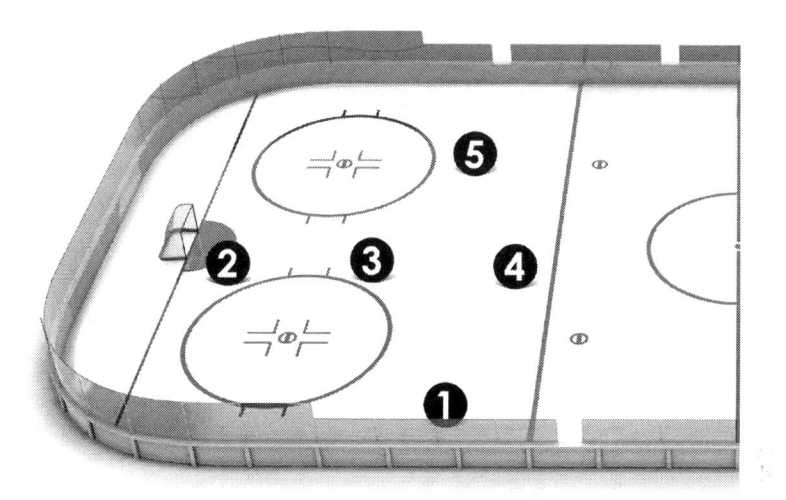

Figure 63: High F3

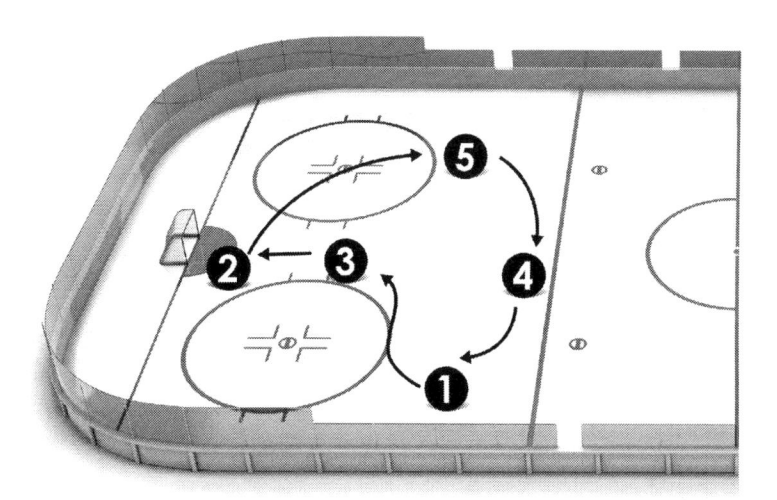

Figure 64:

One of the best and most innovative approaches to the high 3v2 was Nathan MacKinnon's. He would set up near the blue line between the two D and play alongside them. When he started consistently coming into that area, he created a lot of different looks and attack advantages for Colorado.

BELFRY OFFENSE

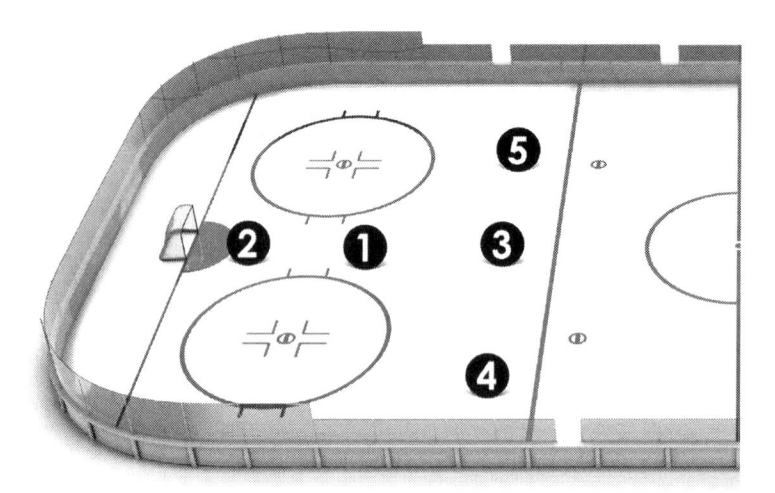

Figure 65: MacKinnon F3

1. When the puck would come up to the top, he was a shooting option from the middle which was difficult to defend because there were three players up at the blueline with just two defenders. With MacKinnon in the middle, he was shooting right down main street, and if you over-committed to the middle to get in his shot lane, he would pass to the open D (Cale Makar) who was now attacking downhill.

2. If the defender had to race to get into that shot lane, MacKinnon would take advantage by attacking the defensive forward 1v1 with the defensive forward moving in awkward defensive angles and routes that he could take advantage of. With a player as electrifying 1v1 as he is, especially when the defensive forward is in vulnerable positions, this led to a lot of interesting offensive situations and chances created.

3. The consistency of his presence up between the two D was freeing for the two D to aggressively activate both in pinch situations and in attacking down. Therefore, extending possession in the offensive zone through exit kill, loose puck recoveries and shot recoveries.

4. When the D pinched down, he would assume their point position and with the strong-side defensive forward tied up with the pinching D. When the puck got to MacKinnon at the top, he could attack the interior space and work with the weak-side defensemen vs. the opposition's weak-side defensive forward in a 2v1 going downhill.
5. When he was in this position with his speed, he was also able to contribute to exit kills, force icings and sustain either offensive zone pressure or recover chip outs for re-entry chances.

Nathan MacKinnon invented this version of the high 3v2. We hadn't seen anyone consistently play in this spot before he started to do it. Every year since, he's continued to evolve the tactics surrounding his utility of this position, and it continues to be a source of a lot of offensive zone time, offensive chances and sustained game control.

One of the best versions of the high 3v2 which changed defensive zone coverages was when the defensive zone prioritized "cutting off the top." This meant the strong-side defensive forward would play lower in the zone, near the hash marks and try to block both players and the puck from getting to the top. When the puck did beat the cut off, and the strong-side offensive defensemen didn't just shoot it right away, they had the strong-side defensive forward trapped on the wall, which offered a tremendous opportunity to attack that space and use the weak-side D in a short downhill 2v1 vs. the opponent's weak-side defensive forward.

Teams also evolved the routes that the three players would use in the high ice. We saw teams use the three players like a shell game, where they moved fluidly interchanging positions in the high ice. The puck would move from one side to the other. These were no longer players standing still at the offensive blue line. These were players in constant movement, reading off each other, trying to create or find a crease to attack in.

It became very hard to defend the high ice with just two players. The movement and the inherent 2v1s created a lot of challenges to defending the middle. Defenses were giving up more quality chances from middle distance. In response, the defensive group started bringing a third defender right into the high ice in more of a 1v1 defensive strategy to eliminate the 2v1s and protect the interior of the ice.

When the defenses started bringing the third defender up, then the space opened up at the bottom for the offence to draw three defenders into the high ice and then send the puck down to the bottom quickly and jump past the check, opening downhill shooting chances off the pass that were uncontested.

Some offensive players, in response to the three defenders coming into the high ice, would leave the offensive zone when they didn't have the puck and then re-enter with speed or at a different angle or entry point. This created differentials that were difficult to defend.

The high 3v2 continues to evolve as teams look to utilize more square footage of the offensive zone to create scoring chances and work their way around the various defensive adjustments. The leap-frog effect - the offensive team creates an advantage, the defensive group figures out an adjustment to mitigate the advantage, forcing the offensive group to try to create another advantage. When this repeats and repeats, you have a leap-frog effect.

When I see the high 3v2 now, it's very similar to the half-wall in that you can and will see all the different tactics we've explored here all in a single game. Once that leap-frog effect takes hold, it expands the toolkit of everyone through the adaptations, evolving and holding a variety of different attack options.

The Highway

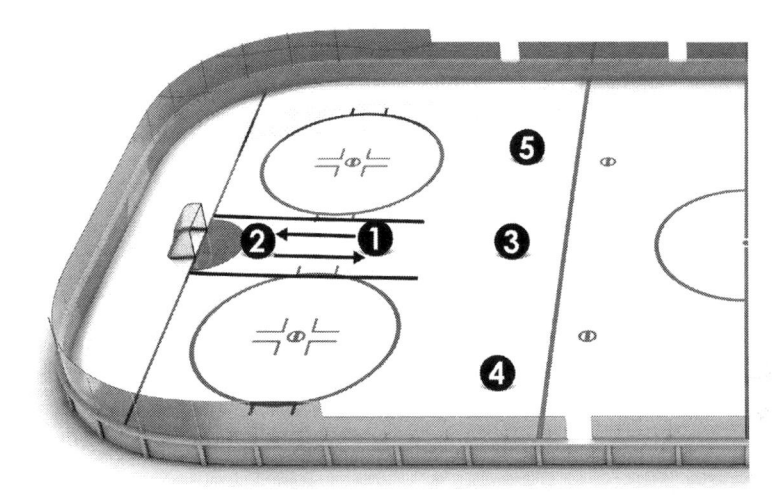

Figure 66:

I refer to the interior area of the offensive zone as "the highway." I don't think I'm alone in the evolution of my thoughts on this area seemingly changing in some way every year. At this moment in time, I refer to it as the highway because I view it like there is two-way traffic with movement coming from the net out and from the top down. The highway is the best descriptive word for how I view the movement of that area, which is largely why I've settled on that term ... for now.

Most of the terms for this area aren't descriptive, that's been largely my issue. I prefer terms that describe the area and describe the movement or actions that I want to see there. I like to evolve all the terms that aren't descriptive to become descriptive. Terms I've adopted before have included home plate, the house, the slot, the scoring area, the funnel and the interior. None of these capture the movement I want in this area.

In recent years, the biggest change to my attitude in how I like to see players approach this area is the connection I'm making with the net front and the high F3. I now see that these two spots are not only connected but interdependent upon each other. They became connected when I evolved my thinking from having a "constant net presence," which implies once you get to the net, you stay there, to wanting a constant net presence but not from the same player, to that this spot is rotated in and out of. The player is continually replaced. I don't want a player stationed on the net, rather I want the players continually landing on the net. This makes the net -ront presence much more dynamic in the overall context of offensive zone play. A surprisingly large number of net-front goals from the top scorers come from finding themselves alone, temporarily unguarded, or with perfect seal-body position on the defender giving them exclusive access to the puck, largely coming from rotation situations that create opportunity. The net-front presence has more responsibility than taking the eyes of the goalie. While that is important, it's not the only responsibility that they have. The responsibility profile of the net-front player for me includes:

- Taking the eyes of the goalie
- Compressing the space of the goalie to the crease
- Tip, deflections and rebounds
- Seal-body position
- Puck recovery
- F2 tracking
- Pop-out shot availability
- Side change using the back of the net
- Side change weak-side dot availability
- Set net-front picks
- Backwall contact and puck support

OFFENSIVE ZONE POSSESSION

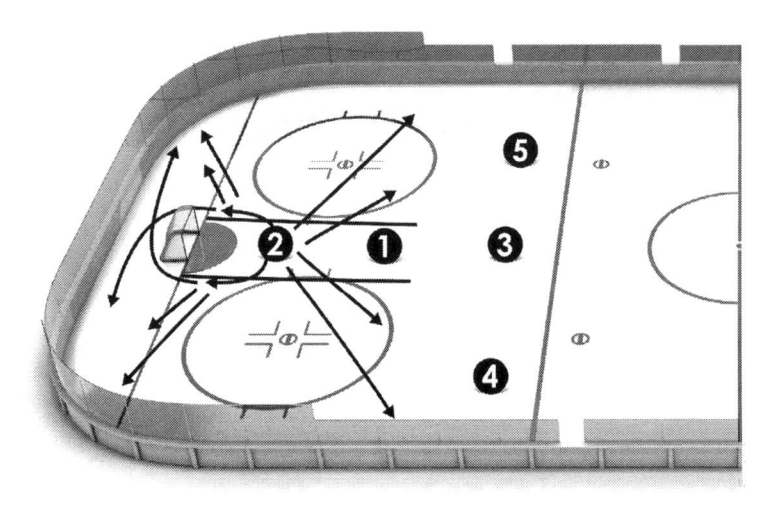

Figure 67:

Needless to say, with this evolved role profile, a lot more has been added to the plate of the net-front presence. This is difficult because the net-front was a specialized art form with the player just stationed there for a screen, deflection, tip and rebound. The net-front spot has to evolve because they have to contribute to team possession. The key to net-front presence is understanding the timing of positioning. There are three main positioning situations that the net-front player has to be aware of and adjust as the conditions change.

1. Screen, tip and deflection positioning

The consideration is the relationship between the goalie's eyes and the shot threat. Forcing the goalie to look around you creates scoring opportunity on the other side of where the goalie is looking. It's harder for the goalie to pick the puck up as the puck goes on the other side and the goalie has to try to pick up the shot on the other side of the screen. There is a moment where the goalie's vision is obstructed.

When it's done effectively, the net-front player is directly in the shot line (in line with the shot threat and directly in the shot lane for the

BELFRY OFFENSE

goalie's vision.) When the puck is shot, the shooter turns with the puck through the tip attempt and turning into tracking the rebound. The net-front player also seals the defender on their back in the turn to the net to gain exclusive access to any rebounds on the seal.

The hardest thing about being at the net is getting there in the first place and establishing position first before the defender occupies the space. So, fighting through a boxout from a predictable route to the net, battling to establish position on the defensemen and then trying to hold your position while keeping your stick free is a tall ask for anyone. The more locked in and embattled the player is at the net, the less available they are for other key possession and support responsibilities. We need a net-front presence, but we want to be rotating in and out and potentially coming from different angles, making it challenging for the net-front D to manage the number of rotations and the amount of threatening space.

What I love about the highway is the net-front player and the F3 will often exchange positions. When the puck goes from high to low, the net-front forward should be popping out into shooting space, while the F3 should be coming down on the net. Both are moving passing options and difficult to defend. The net-front defender has a net-front forward who is popping out into space and now a player coming down the highway onto the net. They are faced with a decision. Do they flex out onto the popping net front forward to defend the pop out? If they do and they vacate the net too far, they may not be able to properly defend a cross-crease pass to the F3 who is driving the back post. If they hold their position at the net, there is a moment in time, they aren't really checking anyone. Yet, two offensive players are moving purposefully in the 15-feet area around their net.

OFFENSIVE ZONE POSSESSION

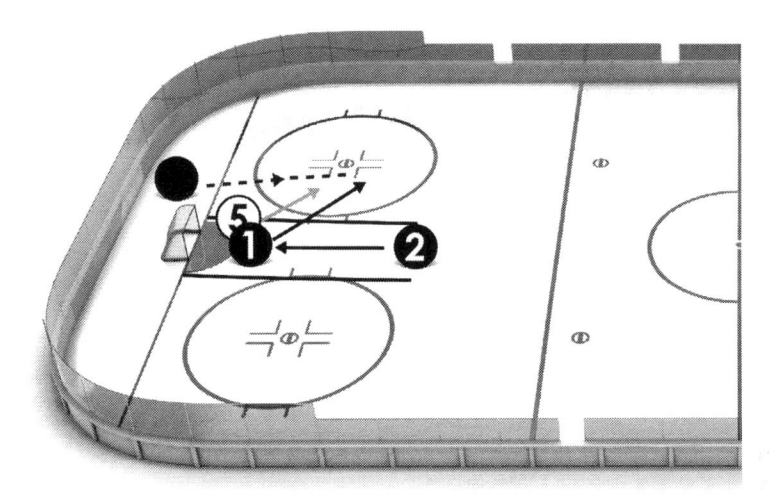

Figure 68:

If they let the net-front player pop out and absorb the F3 (2 in this diagram) driving down the highway to the net and look to get body position, the F3 has speed and can and usually will spin down on they getting under they at the net. F3 has to learn how to read the top hand of the defender so they can spin down on the top hand to get underneath the D. The top hand is harder for the defender to defend with two hands without turning their upper body and ultimately their body to go with the spinning forward. If you spin towards their bottom hand, you are spinning into their strength and into their stick. The defender will have an easier time defending the spin without having to rotate his upper body. Defending the net-front becomes a hard position to be in all of a sudden with decisions. This is great insight into how movement and rotation creates decision making that can often put defenders in awkward positions. If they aren't able to do it just right with their spacing, stick position and body position offensive chances are going to be created in the most dangerous area of the ice.

BELFRY OFFENSE

2. Release and Replace

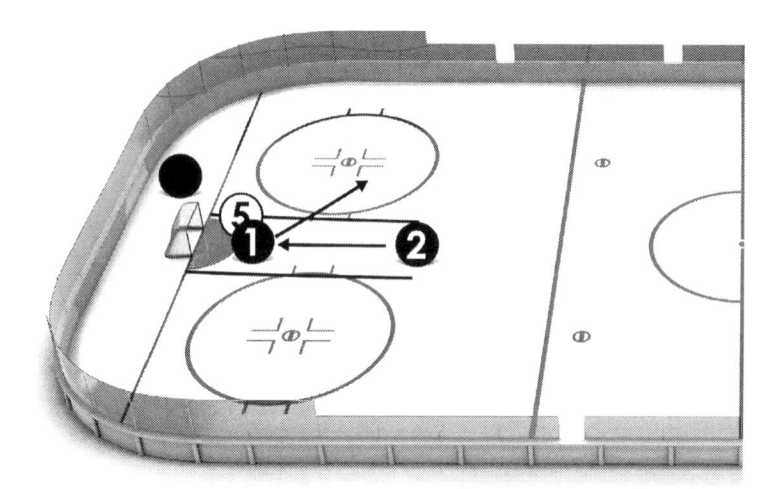

Figure 69: Release and Replace

Now what if the play is going low to high and the net-front forward rather than hold they position at the net, they pop out to the weak-side dot availability, and the F3 comes down on the net, able to easily back down into the net-front picking their line directly in line with the puck? The passer is a playmaker coming up the wall and becomes the new F3, now I have so much more movement and options. I refer to this play as "release and replace." This is a core habit of effective net-front play. The player at the top with the puck can pass to the dot now for catch and shoot and one-timer options, depending on handedness of the net-front pop-out player. The dot player who gets the puck could then fake a shot and shot pass to the backdoor to the new net-front player who was the F3 coming down. If the net-front D flexes to defend the shot threat, they're leaving the new net-front player momentarily unattended. If the net-front guy has good scoring habits from the net front, they will fall of the heels of the goalie for a tap in chance at the net. These scenarios force decisions from the defensive team that are a departure from what's normal behaviour from a net-front player. Most net-front players they play against, well, they go low to high with the puck in the corner and battle through the box out to get to the net, then look to outwork and out-determine the net-front defender who has to be knocked off the best defensive positioning. They dish out a few well-placed cross-checks for good measure, and just before the sifter arrives from the point, they either front it and block the sifter to initiate the offence going the other way, or they tie up the stick of the offensive player with good body position to prevent the player from doing much of anything. That's what they are used to. Now, you have players coming from different routes landing and leaving at the net, and there are decisions to be made as to whose check is whose. The challenge with the net-front is you can't choose the physical matchup, and often time, the players are at a positional disadvantage to begin with and have a lot to overcome to get into good position. Not every player is physically capable of pushing their way into the right position. By rotating people in and out, as a team, we can realistically use a larger percentage of our team to land at the net. We can now create utility and more effective tools for undersized forwards, we can also use activating D, we don't necessarily need to have the bigger and more predisposed players have to do this work. We can use everyone because we aren't asking for extended physicality at the net. We are getting in, getting great position and rotating out. This alone makes it a worthwhile venture. Everyone learns to play at the net using their best assets.

The best-net front player in the NHL in 2023 is Matthew Tkachuk of the Florida Panthers. His intelligence and feel for when to be where is what separates him. One of the interesting habits he has is his attachment to the front post (post closest to the puck). He uses this as a bit of a home base and a lot of his support decisions originate from being around this area. He falls off the post into the backwall and has outstanding passing and scoring touch from anywhere in this area. Definitely a player to study.

BELFRY OFFENSE

3. Backwall possession

What's most important is that you don't allow the puck or your body to get stopped. Backwall effectiveness comes from finding a way to get in the leverage the strongest position to stay in motion. Over the years, I've spent a lot of time researching effective play on the back wall and approached it from many different ways. The most effective starting position to manage the backwall is to start under the D at the net. This is not to say, in any way, that being under the D at the net is the ONLY way to be at the net, and players should always be under the D. There are circumstances that being in front of the D at the net is advantageous, like scope tips (projecting out toward the puck to tip moving away from the goal), or when you are timing a shot to arrive at the net and you start in front of the D to pull they up closer to the hash marks to set they up for a spin down.

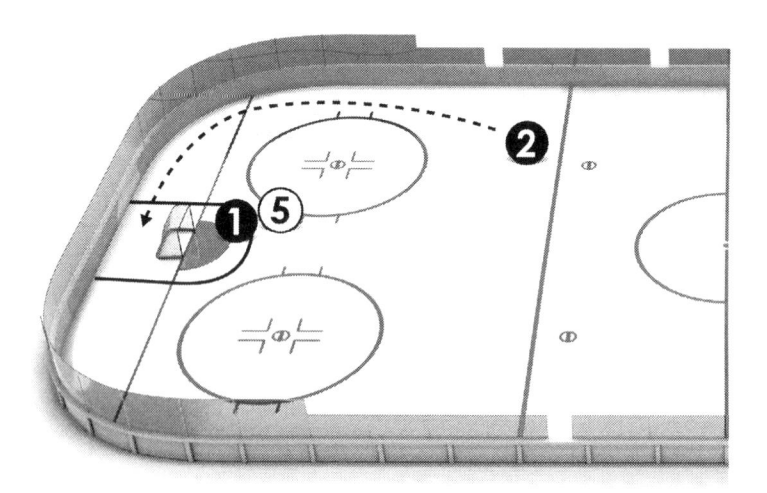

Figure 70: Backwall Possession

By being under the D at the net, the advantage is in controlling plays to the backwall. The position allows you to physically control the spacing between the defender and the wall. The most critical aspect of this is understanding the value of first touch and being able to create movement

OFFENSIVE ZONE POSSESSION

on first touch. Movement is reliant upon spacing and reading the weight of the puck. When you are under the D at the net and the puck rims down to the bottom, you have to first push off on the defender. If you read the rim and just go to the wall to collect the puck without first pushing off or physically engaging with the net-front defender, you are, in effect, inviting the defender to the wall with you to time his contact and push you in.

The mentality has to first preserve collection space and protect yourself from contact. If the mentality is to preserve collection space, then the player will initiate contact prior to leaving the net and not be in a rush to touch the puck. We want first touch, but it's more important to be able to control when. To position yourself where you have "exclusive access." This requires a push off and a read of the weight of the puck (speed the puck is coming around). Once you push off and have read the weight of the puck, the next piece is to read the escape space. This requires a shoulder check, whereby you look beyond the pressure to read the space and support while the puck is on its way, the look has to be as the puck is on the wall. Next, we want you to collect the puck in motion, sometimes that means going with the puck and other times that means meeting the puck and going counter the direction. Regardless of which direction you pick the puck up in, you need to position your shoulders perpendicular to the wall. Of all the things I've learned about the back-wall that has had the most impact, emphasizing the player prioritizing maintaining their shoulders perpendicular to the wall may be the most pivotal. Shoulders being perpendicular to the wall accomplishes a wide swath of important execution elements.

- Not trusting exposing your back to the defender. Not presenting your back as the first point of contact. This is a very important to protecting the player in contact.

This is a shift from convention as puck protection has been previously associated with turning your back to the defender. When along the wall, this approach is very dangerous, so I've completely changed my approach to now demand players prioritize being perpendicular and only expose their back briefly in turns and spins in change of direction.

- Maintains sight to the interior. Dramatically expands playmaking vision while directly seeing the defender.
- Encourages movement and players are more inclined to work themselves off the wall. Players with perpendicular shoulders are much harder to push in. When they get pushed in on the outside hip or outside shoulder, they are naturally inclined to spin or turn with the contact. Therefore, the contact they take is more absorbed and less physically jarring.
- They can control the feet of the defender, they use more weight shifts and earn leverage in body position.
- Maintain the duality of protection and playmaking. They also are more capable of playing interior plays with direct sight to the play. As opposed to blind pop plays through their legs or hope plays. They'll also shovel the puck down the wall and transfer the problem to a teammate much less. Players who face the glass and are stopped on the backwall will create chains of board battles and transfer their puck problem to a teammate, rather than solve the puck play. Players who prioritize maintaining the duality of protection and playmaking give themselves a much better chance to problem solve heavy backwall pressure.

Once you read the space available and determine the collection direction, we need deception at the puck. Hide your intentions and try to control the feet of the defender. Stick fakes and last-second direction changes are key here. Both stick fakes and last-second direction changes are reliant upon weight shift. Also key is a well-timed offensive stick check (where the offensive player lifts the defensive player's stick prior to the puck arriving to eliminate the defensive stick upon collection) on the defender's stick. This will take one of the many control factors off the immense challenge. Timing and feel with escapes takes a long time to learn to do well. This is an area where you need a lot of reps and the reps need to have variance of conditions. The same rep, with the same weight of the puck, the same pressure and so on is not going to be helpful. Varying the pressure, the weight of the puck, the support, etc. is what's going to help with learning the feel for spacing and pressure.

Now the actual collection. Rim collection is a very tricky business. What makes it especially hard is the puck is often spinning really fast as it comes around the wall and is often travelling buttoned up tight to the wall. The combination of the puck being tight to the wall, the spinning puck and defensive stick and contact pressure makes collection a real challenge. To collect the puck efficiently, you have to get a good quality first touch. A quality first touch has three elements to it:

1. The pre-touch body position and preparation
2. The physical control of the defender
3. Receiving the puck (first touch)

The first touch is usually a soft catch that deadens the puck and pulls it off the wall to make it easier to handle and make the next play. The body position is an opposite weight shift. The player leans counter to the wall. If the player is a right-handed shot and in a rim collection going to their left or a backhand rim collection, their weight would be primarily on their left skate. Their shoulders and hips would be stacked in a direct line on the left hip.

The challenge is in one touch, the player has to get in motion at the right time with the right spacing, establish strong opposite weight-shift body positioning, preserve space, control the stick of the defender, read the weight of the puck, read the escape space, deceive the defender, get a good first touch that deadens the puck and pull the puck off the wall. The pull is an absorb-catch toe-drag movement. Regardless of whether or not the player is collecting the puck on the forehand or the backhand, the player looks to execute the absorb toe drag to get the puck off the wall and into protection.

BELFRY OFFENSE

Yes, I'd say it's a real challenge with a lot of pieces that have to come together at once. It is incredibly difficult, which makes it important that players get a lot of meaningful reps and opportunity to expand their understanding of the key execution elements. Now you combine all this, and that gives you an average collection execution. The execution quality shifts to elite when the rim collection is inside a crossover on first touch. The player in the moment of first-touch toe drag off the wall is simultaneously crossing off the wall in a speed change maximizing their positioning on the defender. Another elite execution of the collection is inside the first touch the player cuts back on the immediate touch.

The collection is just the half of this challenge. The other half is controlling the defender to extend the possession. To control the defender, you have to get body position and expand the movement options. One of the key elements to expanding the movement options is the spacing of the outside skate in relationship to the boards. The outside skate spacing is what opens up the spin into the trapdoor. The closer the outside skate is to the wall, the more restricted the turning radius is which reduces the escapability options. Getting a feel for the turning radius impacts of the outside skate is an extremely valuable process for expanding capacity on the backwall. When the spacing of the outside skate is coupled with weight shift to cut through the hands of the defender and take control of the space. That outside skate is key to driving through the stick space of the defender.

Once the player executes the collection, earns space off the wall through pulling the puck, managing the distance of the outside skate and cutting through the hands of the defender, the puck carrier is now in a position to extend the possession. Determining the puck plays available, extending possession leveraging the defender on your back, or controlling the feet of the defender and working on the cutback, if needed to extend the possession.

I know, you read this and you see the number of elements that have to snap together with perfect timing to execute and it's hard not to

OFFENSIVE ZONE POSSESSION

become overwhelmed. I don't want to leave this section in a mental pretzel and you worried about the number of elements, thinking how am I going to teach all this? All of these elements are equally important, so how do you not have to teach each of the items? I've approached the backwall a number of different ways, and here's what I've uncovered as best practices.

1. There is a lot of chunking that can be done where, if you focus your attention in one area, you can create a domino effect on other areas automatically. Those key areas are as follows: preserving space tactics prior to touch, opposite weight shift positioning and absorb pull catch. Focusing on these individual chucks in sections will allow you to snap many of the other pieces together naturally.

2. In the event that through the chunking process some players still struggle, customize your instruction for those players to highlight the skill gap that they are personally struggling with, keeping in mind that often the struggle can be related to restrictions in their assets.

3. Start with defensive pressure right away. Now you can control and scale the pressure in terms of how intent they are from the beginning and as the players get better, but developing a feel for the physical presence is so important that it needs to be an element that you introduce from the beginning.

4. Vary the weight of the puck. The understated skill is executing the collection under physical pressure WITH good timing. However, no two collection pucks are going to be the same in terms of the weight of the puck, the intensity of the pressure or the quality of the support. It is imperative then that a major part of the early development strategy must be forcing the player to constantly adjust, initially adjusting to the weight of the puck and then adjusting to the intensity of physical contact. Varying the situation and forcing continual adaptation to improve consistency of timing is something that dramatically improved and fast-forwarded development once I started utilizing this development practice. When we try to make it

BELFRY OFFENSE

easier by reducing the number of variables the player has to manage, while this approach makes logical sense, it elongates development.

OFFENSIVE ZONE LOGIC

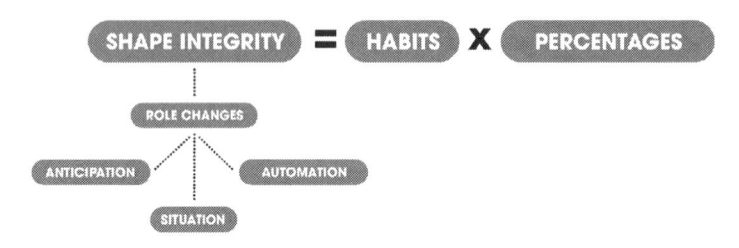

(SHAPE INTEGRITY) = (HABITS) X (PERCENTAGES)

(ROLE CHANGES)

(ANTICIPATION)   (AUTOMATION)

(SITUATION)

What is the impact of the backwall in relationship to our process?

The impact of our shape when the puck is on the backwall is the conditions of the puck. If the puck gets stopped, then we need to move to support for puck recovery vs compressed coverage.

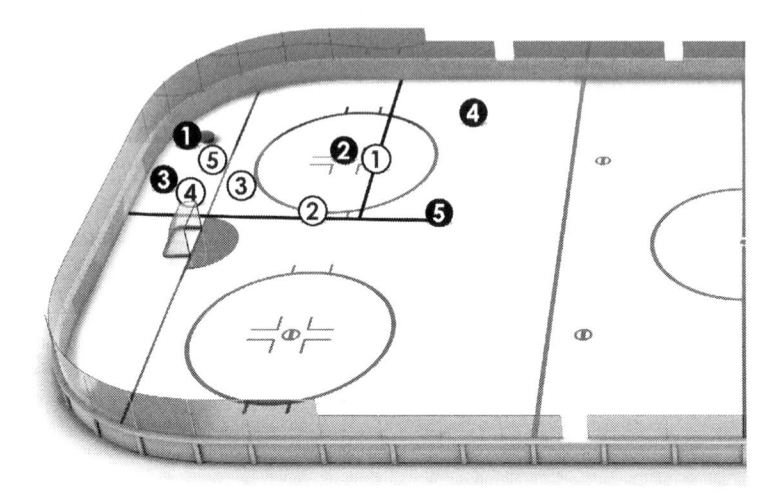

Figure 71:

If we can change sides on the backwall, we want to elevate speed of the shape and stretch the defensive structure in the side change. If we go into the puck on the backwall, we have to initiate movement vs. compressed coverage. The effect of our response from the backwall is to "attack the backside of the coverage." This is similar to what we have all termed as the "accordion effect." The accordion effect is when you collapse the defensive group and then stretch them out. I've evolved the accordion effect concept to now be "attacking the backside of the coverage" because I prefer terms that direct the player into specific action. In this case, attacking the backside of the coverage implies accordion effect, but specifically describes where the opportunity is.

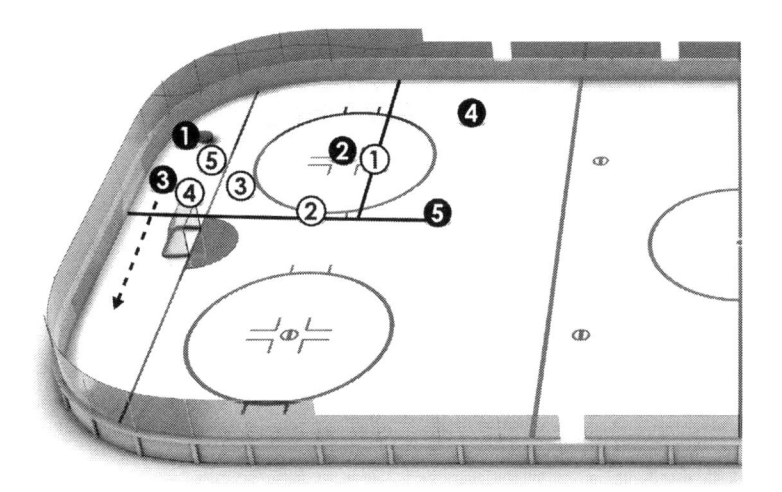

Figure 72:

The shape integrity of the offensive zone is directly impacted by the direction of the puck and the conditions surrounding it. The execution habits of the players to activate and sustain possession at the puck is what helps us tilt the percentages. The players off the puck read the direction of the puck and move to organize an attack on the backside of the coverage, the possession habits of the player at the puck and the

BELFRY OFFENSE

pressure conditions surrounding the puck to make decisions of how to support the play in either continued collective puck possession or in reacting quickly to anticipated loose pucks or changes of possession where they can quickly leverage the active shape to get the puck right back.

The opportunity to create offensive advantage often involves a play to the player who is furthest away from the puck on the backside of the coverage. That player is also critical to puck recovery, so a big part of maintaining the integrity of the shape in the offensive zone is the shift of responsibility of the player who is the furthest from the puck on the backside of the play. The integral part of it is that this player is unchecked and can freely choose their route. When they are on the backside of the play, they have a chance to "hide in the weeds."

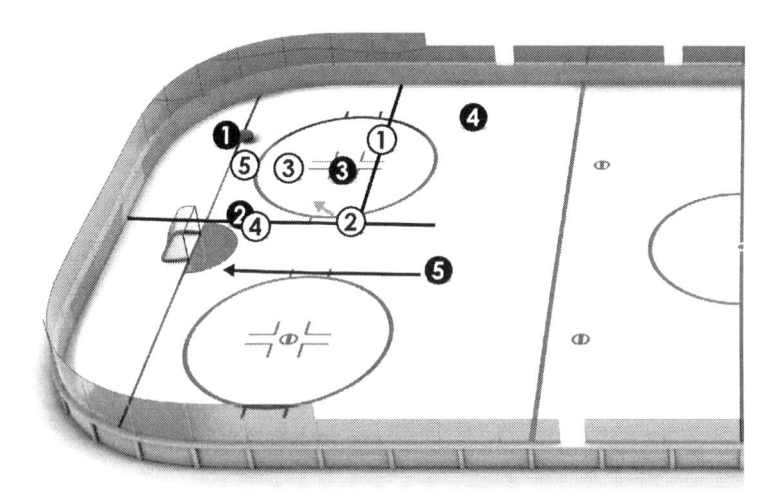

Figure 73: Backside

This is something we see with elite offensive thinkers, they are incredibly intelligent in the routes they take when they are furthest from the puck, and the routes they take before the play is made tend to make the play. The routes are linked to their habits that put them consistently

160

in position to make these plays. The weak-side D, for example, watches their weak-side defender, and when they turn their back or their eyes are off them, they can now move unchecked and focus just on timing. However, they should already be surfing the top of the circle, if they don't have the surfing habit, now when they do want to slide down, it's much easier for the weak-side defender to detect them. If their habit is to surf, they're always in position and now it's just watching the eyes of the weak-side defensive forward. When they turns their back, you jump by them to the net.

Players who aren't elite offensive thinkers tend to be inactive in purposeful routes or move with any sense of arrival timing. Offensive thinkers are well aware of "arrival timing." You have great timing when you satisfy three elements:

1. Arrive at the right place
2. Arrive at the right time
3. Arrive with the right amount of speed

Arrival timing is critical to offence, and players who recognize the advantages of being the furthest from the puck on the backside of the play, are active in determining attack routes and have a keen sense of timing are extremely dangerous. From an offensive development perspective, we can get caught sleeping on arrival timing, and it's a disservice as many more players could become very good at it once they have the awareness and understanding of what their responsibility is.

The best part about having a five-man offense in the offensive zone that prioritizes elevated shape speed is that it promotes a mental engagement of players furthest away from the puck in a dual read dramatically enhancing the threat of the offense and the ability to disrupt an exit attempt.

"Getting Goalie'd"

We've all been in games when the goalie is standing on his head and you can just feel the energy for the offensive team draining with every missed scoring chance and every shot the goalie saves. This happens more and more frequently at every level that it's becoming a normal expectation from the goaltending fraternity. They expect to "goalie" you. We all recognize that feeling that you just aren't going to score when it sets in. What's worse is when this gets coupled with one team dominating possession, zone time, shot share, scoring chances, interior shots and shot recoveries, with one wave of chances after another only to see the opponent come down once with a grade-A scoring chance and score. This is incredibly frustrating.

When you are "getting goalie's," what do you do?

We hear the usual strategies that feel more like hope than a strategy, that work just frequently enough to keep us bringing them up, but not well enough to actually become a reliable scoring strategy. These include: throw everything at the net, crash the crease and bump him, create traffic in front so they can't see the shots, throw pucks at their feet to create scrambles, stick to your process … wait what? What process?

On most teams, the offence is rooted in 1v1 play. We hope we have recruited enough "skill sticks" (highly-skilled offensive threats for the league), that when the game is going on, we have a few different players who could break the game with one play that get them a clean look. This is our process? It is for more teams than we all would like to acknowledge. When you are "getting goalie'd" if your answer is a combination of throwing pucks at the net, getting traffic at the net and hoping a skill stick beats someone to get to the net, you are more likely to continue "getting goalie'd" rather than get to the goalie and turn the offensive tide.

Again, this isn't to say that it's not good to have skill sticks who can break a game, of course, it is. I'd hardly say that that is a process, though. That's good recruiting practice for the league, try to have more skill sticks on your team than the opponent has on their team.

OFFENSIVE ZONE LOGIC

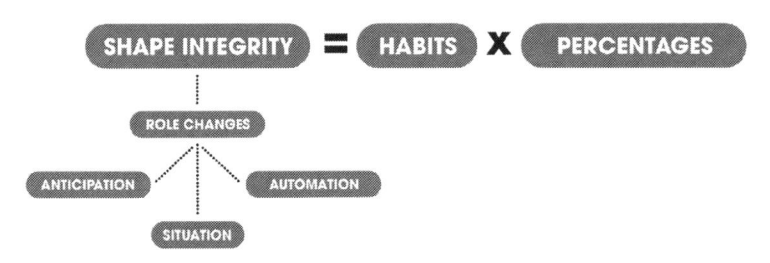

SHAPE INTEGRITY = HABITS X PERCENTAGES

ROLE CHANGES
ANTICIPATION
AUTOMATION
SITUATION

Coaching and player development, though, would be an actual group-oriented strategy to generate scoring chances and score goals.

The answer for me is an actual strategy.

A strategy that include elevate shape speed + good habits to improve the percentages. So, what does that look like in trying to solve the "goalie'd" riddle? Well, we are going to stack our shifts and leverage our zone time and create a cumulative shift effect, then we are going to elevate our speed vs. a tired defensive group, then we are going to focus on creating interior chances. However, we are going to do things that we know will affect the goalie, and what we should expect an unnatural commitment to shot blocking by the opposition, all of a sudden, making it even more difficult.

Our mindset has to go to both expand the net and challenge the shot blockers off the puck by a commitment to shoot off the pass. We are going to do as many things as we can to affect the goalie's ability to gain proper depth. We are going to drive him into their post. We are going to work the backwall. We are going to establish a constant redirect threat off the side of the net. We are going to work our skating routes and make plays while we are affecting the goalie's depth and ability to stay square. We are going to rotate someone in and out of the net front all the time to take the goalie's eyes and disrupt their vision. Perhaps most importantly, we are going to play a five-man offense and reload hard and have a reliable F3, so we don't give up any easy odd-man breaks against. Murphy's Law is they are scoring on those straight away, so let's not give them any easy chances. This understanding of logic is not a departure from what we've been saying we want to do in the offensive zone anyways. Now it's about being patient, expand the net and stack the shifts and chances. The key to overcoming "getting goalie'd" is group. It's a sharper commitment to good offense and being patient not to overreact to brilliant saves and improbable shot blocks. It's sticking to our good habits, but looking to dive into the ways we can improve the percentages. It's a very relatable situation to show how all this fits together and how our offense works.

BELFRY OFFENSIVE ZONE

ZONE CONTROL = ELEVATED SPEED OF SHAPE X HABITS + PERCENTAGES

Belfry Offense

My approach to the offensive zone is to leverage our equation of elevated shape (habits and percentages) to relentlessly "attack the backside" of the ice. I want to use the entirety of the offensive zone. I am looking to stretch the opponent's shape with speed and puck movement. For me, the hardest place to defend is the space behind you and the net front when you don't have body position first. By attacking the backside of the ice, I can consistently get my players in position to challenge these two pressure points. Generally, I'd like my team to work the offensive zone and create situations where they can change sides in an "over and in" mentality. Over - side change and in - interior shot chance. The stress of constantly having to defend the backside inherently opens the middle of the ice. It also provides conditions for our rotating net-front presence to have better body positions.

OFFENSIVE ZONE POSSESSION

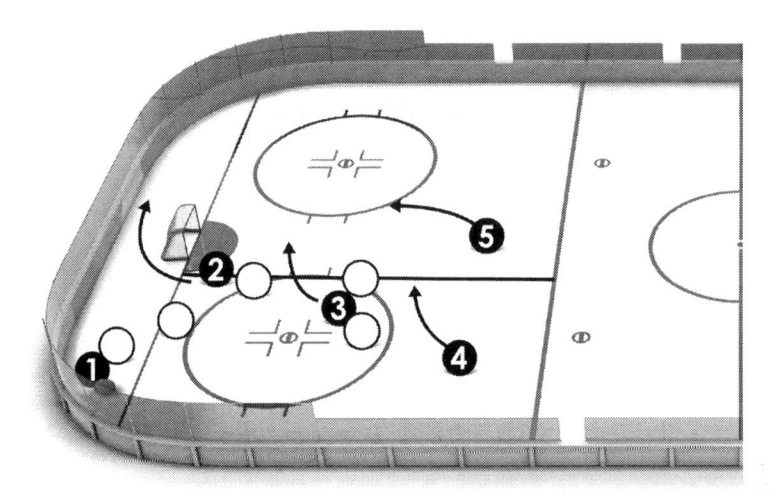

Figure 74:

By changing sides, we can get more players on the "inside."

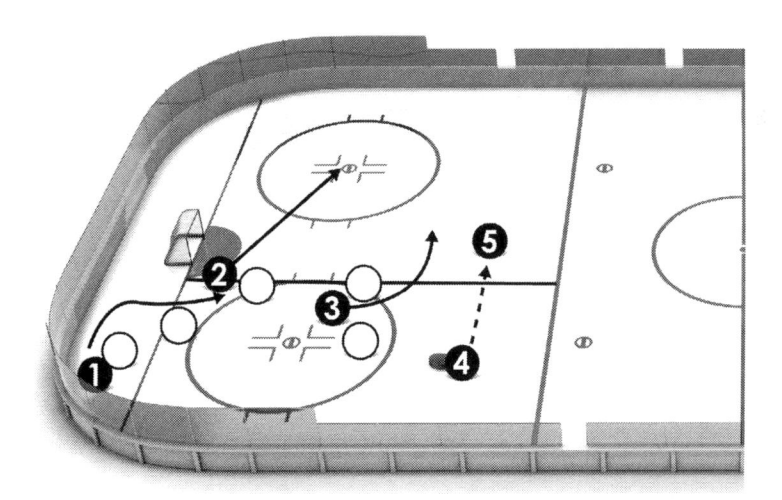

Figure 75:

We can do it from the bottom or the top.

165

BELFRY OFFENSE

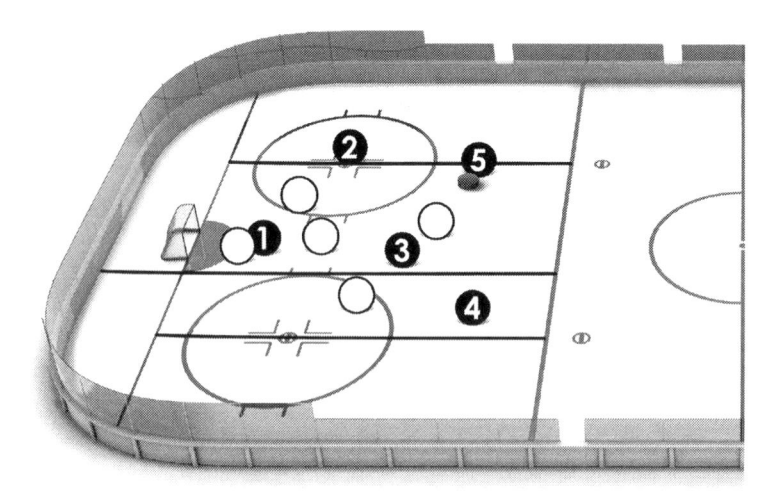

Figure 76:

In the end, when we go over and in, we want five players inside. This sets us up for our shot recovery and exit kill. When you reflect on this offensive zone section, you'll notice that I've been working my way to get to this. All of what we've outlined leads us right here.

At the core of our style of play, I favor a spread offense that converges on the middle with numbers and inside routes and leverage the numbers and speed to create chances and recover shots to sustain the offense. This is a much more patient and methodical offensive zone with an emphasis on game control. My metrics on this model is a stark departure from the shot-differential proxy we worked off of with the advent of "advanced analytics" or now moving toward "expected goals." Neither of these metrics satisfy what I really want to know about my offensive zone. My metrics model is based on game sequence and statistical relationships that offer me direct insight into my process. I've left isolated stat collection.

POSSESSION LINE CHANGE

When I started shooting the episodes for my podcast in 2022, I did so because I was looking for a platform to work on improving my communication skills. More specifically, I wanted to learn how to become more descriptive in the way I communicate the game. In the Belfry Hockey podcast, the premise was to study a specific player, determine their game habits, decide on a narrative and describe clips in a way that painted a picture to the listener so they could imagine the plays I was describing and follow the details of the narrative. This is incredibly challenging. The podcast was inspired by research I was doing on storytelling. In my reading on presenting, I came across storytelling as an under-valued communication tool in most walks of life, but specifically in teaching and presenting. There is too much value not to try to become really good at it. The storytelling rabbit hole has a lot of fascinating tunnels to it. I found myself researching stand=up comedy. Endless hours of interviews of comics on YouTube describing their process on joke writing, evolving jokes, layering, tie-backs, the science behind laughs per minute, the difference between styles and then I found myself listening to comic after comic trying to recognize how they stitch the stories together. This led me to Charlie Chaplin and the silent movies era. Imagine producing an entire movie, a comedy at that, without saying a single word? Talk about an extraordinary ability to tell a story. That led me to mimes and their ability to convey emotion through movement and gestures without saying a word. How about songwriting? How do the storytellers create stories in songs? In just a couple verses, they relate to something in your life and attach their song to that moment and take you immediately back to that time in your life. Powerful way to communicate. Next, I was onto the great sports radio announcers, Foster Hewitt, Vin Scully, Howard Cosell and the ability to describe a game/sporting event on the radio to the listeners and pull the drama of the game through their voice and into their listeners' imagination. To articulate the game so brilliantly that the listener could feel like they were there. Then trial lawyers presenting a case, and then finally famous interviewers, like Oprah Winfrey, Barbara Walters, Diane Sawyer and Howard Stern who could brilliantly string questions together, use set ups and backstory to lead their guest in their questions. All different ways of using storytelling to communicate. It's a rabbit hole I don't think I'll ever emerge from ... I love what I'm learning too much. Storytelling to communicate the game, to present ideas, to illustrate opportunities, it's a skill I am compelled to continue to invest time and energy to. I think it's particularly important when detailing ideas such as a concept like possession changes.

There seems to always be a correlation between teams who generate a lot of offence and teams who are exceptional with their changes. There is more to changes than energy management and matchups. The importance of line changes is in that I call the "cumulative shift effect." The cumulative shift effect is the "story." It is a platform that drives the narrative of stacking good shifts on top of each other. To have one line improve the game conditions for the next line.

When you have a shift, there is a starting point for the shift and an ending point for the shift. Now as a line, you could have started in a defensive zone faceoff, and during the course of your shift, gained control of the puck, transported it through the neutral zone and into the offensive zone and after taking a shot on goal, you earn a whistle that improves the game circumstances for the next line. Your shift resulted in a positive game effect for the next line. Now if the next line isn't able to gain possession after the offensive zone faceoff and the opponent marches out of their zone and through the neutral zone before maintaining offensive zone time on your line before you finally get control, chip it out and race for a change. In this shift description, you have degraded the shift effect. Your line was net-negative in terms of game control. Game control, and more importantly, momentum can be reflected in cumulative shift effect. The following is a grading metric for shifts. It works as a priority list:

1. Goal scored

    The line advances the puck into the offensive zone and their shift ends by scoring a goal.

2. Offensive zone possession change

    The line advances the puck into the offensive zone and sustains pressure before initiating a change, offering the next line a chance to play with an energy advantage (against a tired defensive group) and start with the prime territorial advantage in the offensive zone.

3. NZ re-entry possession change

    The line is in the offensive zone and forces the opponent to chip out, we change on re-entry without allowing the opponent to change. We offer the new line the chance to play with an energy advantage and a re-entry into the offensive zone.

4. Sustained pressure followed by a forced icing

    The line has sustained pressure in the offensive zone and forces the opponent into an icing, now they can change and offer the oncoming line an energy advantage and a chance to win a draw and continue with the offensive pressure.

5. OZFO

    The line advances into the offensive zone and creates an offensive zone faceoff, allowing the next line to start in the offensive zone. There is no real energy advantage, the advantage is territorial.

6. NZ possession change

    The line has the puck in the NZ either from the offensive zone or from the defensive zone and rather than dump it and change, they turn it back into a deep and slow regroup and change with possession. This may not have an energy advantage for the oncoming line, but certainly territorial.

BELFRY OFFENSE

7. OZ no possession

    The preceding line concedes possession, but forces the opponent to start in their own end. The oncoming line has no energy or possession advantage, just a territorial start to try to get the puck back from.

8. NZ no possession

    The line gets the puck into the NZ conceding possession and gets the change. The oncoming line is at a disadvantage as it has no energy advantage, no possession and territorially the puck is coming back into their defensive zone.

9. DZ FO

    The preceding line conceded a defensive zone faceoff, the oncoming line must first win the puck in the DZ.

10. DZ FO following possession against

    The preceding line conceded a defensive zone faceoff after a possession stretch against. The oncoming line has to win the puck first in the DZ vs. a team with momentum.

These are the "shift starts" and "shift ends." As a line, your objective has to be to sustain a positive shift from the line before to contribute to stacking shifts. To sustain the momentum earned from the line before. If the shift start wasn't an advantage, then your job is to improve the shift start for the next line, therefore improving your shift ending point and improving the shift conditions for the next line.

This is a big part of how a team can influence game control and ultimately game momentum is sustaining advantage shift starts.

Cumulative shift effect is the bedrock understanding of what we are trying to accomplish with our shift changes. It's not just about managing your individual energy and being able to recover between shifts. While that is part of it, that's not what we are really doing. What we are really doing is using line changes to contribute to game control. Shift changes is a unique part of our sport that represents many different opportunities for advantage.

Shifts are fascinating because as the period goes along, there are so many shifts where there is a competitive imbalance. One team is at a shift deficit, through either energy disadvantage, starting without the puck, starting in the defensive zone or talent mismatches. The shifts have staggered start times, there are many situations where they aren't changed at the same time. There are moments in the game where the change situation IS the competitive advantage. Recognizing and knowing how to take advantage of these change situations.

In extended OZ possession situations, where we can initiate a possession change, we can disable the opponent's willingness to counter. When the opponent has been trapped defending in the defensive zone and needs a change, when they do get the puck, they are more interested in changing than they are in mounting a rush attack. This is another major competitive advantage that we have to recognize. When the counter is disabled, this is a time to attack their net. Obviously when the opponent is tired, we can stretch their shape and open interior chances. We can force more switch situations and stress their communication, their check handoffs and their defensive zone discipline. In attacking their net, we also force them into more net-front defending as a collapsed coverage, now shot recovery situations and foot races favor us because their position is more compressed, and they are stopped at the net while we are in motion. This allows us both to pepper their net through multiple puck recoveries, the compressed coverage makes their possession exits much more challenging and increases the likelihood of icing the puck, or chip clears we can counter on. It isn't quite a free shot, but it's as close as it gets. Applying pressure on the opponent when they are in need of a change is an investment.

A big part of winning the change game is recognizing when you have an advantage and when you are at a disadvantage. This changes the shift objectives. Shift objectives are more easily identified in the Stanley Cup Playoffs. In the playoffs, you can see the shifts fall into three buckets:

- Bucket 1: Investment Shift

  An investment shift is when you have the clear advantage and you invest in sustained offensive zone time and leverage the investment to game control.

- Bucket 2: Push Shift

  A push shift is when you just push the game forward, you don't have an advantage or your opponent doesn't have an advantage. The shift is a push.

- Bucket 3: Transport Shift

  A transport shift is when you start at a disadvantage and you have to win the puck back and then transport it to improve the conditions for the next line.

This team approach to shifts offers a chance for coaches, lines and individual players to think differently about the process and metric to evaluate winning shifts and their role in game control over a section of multiple minutes in a period. The practical utility of this model is that it allows coaches and players to talk about how shifts relate to other shifts, which is the key to how we want our players to think and the language that they use.

Faceoffs

When you track raw faceoff data, there is no direct correlation to winning. Early in the analytics movement, when they were scrapping data from NHL.com and they take the immediate results of the faceoff, it is difficult to find data to support any assertion that faceoffs matter. That is until you dig a little deeper than just the raw data. When you go through the faceoff video, one of the things that jumps out is faceoffs that are originally lost, but the puck is quickly won back. Or faceoffs that were originally won, but possession is lost quickly thereafter. Now when you change your lens and expand the faceoff determination of won or loss to include 10 seconds after the puck is dropped. What we really care about is game control. If we lose the offensive zone draw, and inside 10 seconds we have the puck and are still in the offensive zone, that slides to the game control win column. We could technically win the faceoff, but inside 10 seconds we lose control of the puck and the opposition exits, that slides to game control loss column. Now the ledger has four columns that detail result of the actual draw and who had the puck after 10 seconds following the draw which we term zone control:

1. Faceoff win and zone control
2. Faceoff loss and zone control
3. Faceoff win and lost zone control
4. Faceoff win and lost zone control

By expanding the metric of what's really important in faceoffs, it changes how we approach teaching faceoffs and the importance we place in achieving game control. Immediately, we need a faceoff loss plan that launches us into a scheme to win the puck back quickly. When we approach a faceoff, we used to just set up in hopes we would win, or set up in the event that we lose, all depending on the game situation. Now when we approach teaching a faceoff, we teach it with a dual purpose, the win routes and the loss routes sync to automating movement on the draw. We don't want "if this, then that" reads, as players will either hesitate for a second to see where the puck ends up or they'll cheat to one approach or the other.

The approach now is for the faceoff win route and the loss route are the same, so we get a jump on possession. The more identical the routes, the quicker we can move off the puck drop and the faster we can get to possession or get to pursuit.

When you combine this approach to the draw and with cumulative shift effect, that perspective may encourage you to think differently about

BELFRY OFFENSE

the personnel configurations you may use in certain situations. If you are down a goal, with an investment shift that preceded and the opponent is tired and has iced the puck, this scenario may inspire you to have a four-forward-and-one-defenseman package or a five-forward package.

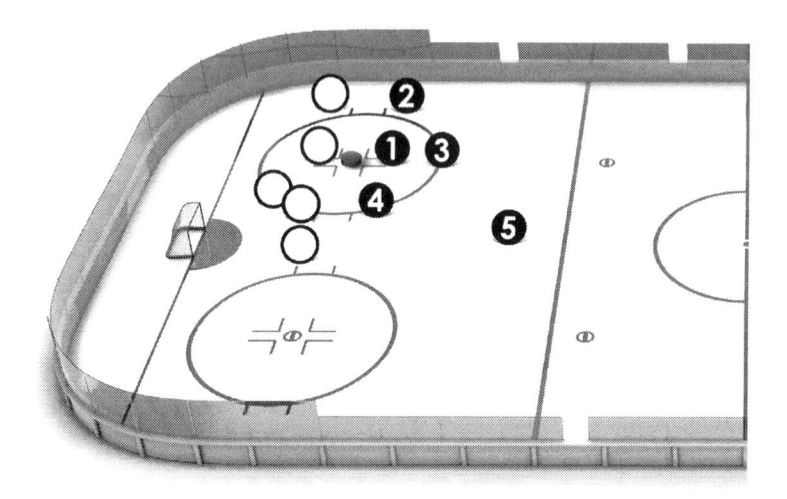

Figure 77:

When you think about it with this perspective and these considerations regarding the inequity of shifts and knowing the skill set configuration of your team, you may see different recurring scenarios present themselves where it may make sense to have a faceoff package to capitalize on the advantage and one that includes a recovery plan for 10 seconds after the puck drops. This could lead to the opportunity for more offense.

Second period

Now if we take what we now know about cumulative shift effect and our attitude toward game control through line changes, the second period,

POSSESSION LINE CHANGE

all of a sudden, comes directly into focus. In the second period, your bench, at least a portion of it, is actually inside the offensive zone. Your entire bench is on the offensive side of the ice. Moreover, the opponent's bench is in your defensive side of the ice. The utility of second periods based on the configuration of the benches has to have some inherent competitive advantages upon deeper inspection. For me, also not having heard much in terms of second period specific tactics, makes it even more alluring for me to find some of my own.

What about a situation whereby we have a lead in the game in the second period, we also have full control of the puck and have had significant zone time, enough to execute a full offensive zone line change? The opponent is on an extended defensive zone shift and their counter willingness has been severely compromised. With their bench so far away, they can't easily change. The opponent has packed it in a compressed defensive zone coverage at the net front and is blocking shots.

We have all seen situations where the puck finally just gets out of the zone, but it is still in the neutral zone, and as soon as the puck comes out, the opponent will try to get as many players as they can changed on the re-entry and will leave counter-entry exposure that often opens up quick odd man situations. The quality of the re-entry chance is often better than the combined zone control chances. We have also all seen a desperation clear by the opposition that goes the length of the ice, the goalie of the offensive team races out to negate the icing and snaps the puck right back to the offensive blue line providing opportunity for re-entry chances before the players changing can get in position.

With the game in the second period, an idea may be to strategically pull the puck out of the offensive zone and invite the defensive team to change, and when they start to go for the change, we, of course, have maintained full possession of the puck. Now we organize a re-entry designed specifically to take advantage of numerical advantages due to the line change.

BELFRY OFFENSE

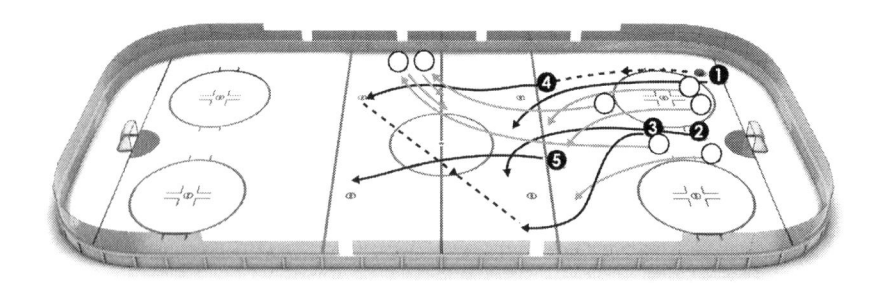

Figure 78:

We've seen the goalie quickly snap a pass on a cleared puck to catch the opponent changing, we've seen the opponent try to change on a puck that gets into the neutral zone. What we haven't seen is an offensive team take the puck outside the blue line purposely to invite or bait the opponent into trying to execute a change and we capitalize on the incomplete change and players so far out of defending positions. Moreover, with the length of zone time adding up the defensive team naturally packs it in close to their net, moving to a re-entry rush situation, pulls the opponent away from that packed in defensive zone structure, even if they don't take the bait and try to change. We still open up their shape and continue to stress the opponent with offensive zone time.

To take this idea a step further. In situations where we have extended offensive zone time, again have disabled the oppositions counter and packed them in at the net in the defensive zone, but haven't yet executed an OZ change, it may make sense to pull the puck into the neutral zone to both get a couple players changed and in working inside our change, we inherently are inviting the opposition to change. This hides our re-entry intentions and may be enough to expose the defensive team to a re-entry chance against while they are in the midst of a change.

These two related ideas carry a lot more weight because of the location of the benches.

Another idea in the second period to control the opposition's changes is to play long and fast by stretching in the neutral zone in any re-entry situations to control the ability of the opposition's defensemen to get

POSSESSION LINE CHANGE

changes in without exposure. Playing long is to try to keep the D pair on the ice in extended shifts as much as possible. This is an investment in the game. To stress the fitness of the defensemen by making the play defense for extended periods of time in the second period and to control their changes as much as possible through how we manage the puck.

Sometimes we see these ideas in NHL overtime 3v3 where we see the puck carrier purposely pull the puck out of the offensive zone with control to re-attack in re-entry.

Another idea is to use side change away from the bench to initiate changes. Normal side change using the F3 or the net-front or using a cross dump in the offensive zone to initiate changes with the players closest to the bench. We can disguise the offensive zone line change by using side change to disguise the change. Now the players coming off the bench are not initially checked or accounted for, leaving them free to reengage in the play. This moment in the offensive zone where there are players on the backside of the play who are unaccounted for, that's a momentary competitive advantage.

These are just a couple ideas. How many more ideas are there really? Once you start studying it, the number of ways you can create little advantages is endless. How about a second period power play, knowing that you have the defensemen's bench so close to you. Is this a time where you can play five forwards on the power play, knowing that you have an easy change as the clock winds down or maybe you have two defensemen on the second unit? Now you can devise a PP scheme in zone taking advantage of the proximity of the bench. Perhaps you start with two D on the PP, and upon recovery you quickly change both D to forwards and run a five-forward PP until you get to the time when your second unit is to come on the ice or the PP is about to expire. You then execute a possession change while you have possession on the PP. This may represent all the special teams' advantage you need to extend a lead or to get back into the game.

In my study of second periods, I view it as a game within the game. It is its own entity for me and a major part of sustained winning can come from decisively winning second periods. Moreover, you don't have to even drive the score out of reach in the second to decisively win. The accumulation of investment shifts stacked upon each other may empty the opponent's gas tank enough that it opens the door to have the energy advantage in the third period. Now you win the third period on the scoreboard on the strength of the possession, investment shifts and line changes in the second.

I am a lifelong fan of documentary films. I am a chronic binge-watcher of the "ESPN 30 for 30" documentary franchise and any other sports documentary that I can watch. I was all in on *The Last Dance* when it came out and then was riveted to *The Defiant Ones*, the documentary chronicling the partnership of Dr. Dre and Jimmy Levine which shattered all the barriers. On my flight home from Italy, I watched another great one: *Hans Zimmer - Hollywood Rebel*. Zimmer is a Hollywood film score and music producer. His films include *The Lion King*, *Gladiator*, *Pirates of the Caribbean* and *The Dark Knight* franchises along with 150 other ones. The documentary *Hollywood Rebel* details his life, and, more importantly, the brilliance of his approach.[19] I loved the documentary because it details all the rules he broke to create his sounds. He looked at convention, the rules that surround it and proceeded to break them. This documentary reminded me of one of my favorite interviews of all time, the Eminem *60 Minutes* interview with Anderson Cooper.[20] In this interview, Eminem details his approach to rhyming and word bending.

When you look at offensive zone possession, one of the restricting rules is offsides and the blueline. What if you paired the offensive zone with re-entry? No one wants to come out of the offensive zone once you are in it, to take it out of the zone purposely would fly in the face of convention … which is the exact reason why it's an idea worth exploring.

---

[19] *https://en.wikipedia.org/wiki/Hans_Zimmer*
[20] Eminem 60 Minutes *https://www.youtube.com/watch?v=zJg2PgpKRQc*

Possession penalty kill

One area of "possession" that I've been all about for the last number of years has been possession penalty kill. A possession penalty kill is when you win the puck from the power play and rather than automatically clear it down the ice every single time, there may be conditions surrounding the puck where you can possess it. Situations where when you win it, there is an easy pass to a teammate who has time and space, or where you can skate it a couple steps to change the possession conditions and make them even more favorable for possession. With the knowledge that the option to clear the puck down the ice is always there for you, there may be situations in a game where it may make more sense to hang onto the puck. Situations where we are down in the game and you want to use possession to create scoring chances for during the penalty kill and you use your possession penalty kill to open the ice up for chances, or the opponent has an excellent power play and we want to limit their power play time by evaporating the time through puck possession.

The premise is that in many penalty kill situations there are favorable opportunities to possess the puck. If our team become fluent in these situations and began making plays and extended their possessions before clearing, we could yield a number of opportunities we wouldn't otherwise have:

1. Evaporate valuable power play time against.
2. Frustrate the power play, force them to work to get the puck back.
3. Short-handed shot generation situations may present themselves.
4. Opportunity to target a forward who is playing the point on the power play and go after him directly offensively.
5. Influence the way teams play the power play against our team.

I've identified four stages of implementation to gradually begin adding this capacity to our penalty kill repertoire:

BELFRY OFFENSE

Stage 1: Situation identification

1. We have to start with the recognition of the game conditions where we can possess the puck.
    a. Favorable game conditions
    b. Uncontested loose pucks
    c. Immediate passing outlets
    d. Time and space to skate the puck
    e. Faceoff wins

Stage 2: "One more pass"

The is to create awareness and a commitment to try to make one more play. The impact of making just one more play will open the ice for the new puck carrier to skate and perhaps make another play.

Stage 3: "Four-corner spread"

An idea of possessing the puck on exit, forcing the defending team to defend us and we turn the puck back and pass back to our D who continue to possess the puck. This is incredibly frustrating for the power play and create momentum for our penalty kill group as they kill the penalty this way.

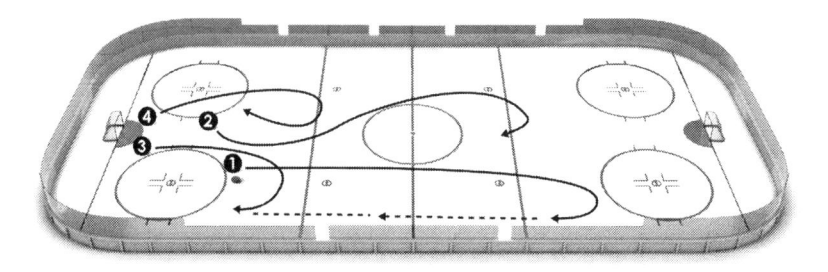

Figure 79: Four-corner Spread

Stage 4: "Possess to break them down"

In this stage, the group has confidence in its ability to recognize opportunities to possess the puck, now we are looking to extend the time the power play doesn't have the puck and look for opportunities to attack offensively.

The opportunity

The opportunity is most power plays when they lose possession of the puck are expecting the penalty kill to automatically clear the puck. They aren't expecting to dig in and win the puck back or defend rushes and chances against. By possessing the puck, we turn what should be a momentum builder for them in the game to the opposite, where penalty kill situations give our team a massive emotional boost.

When we have the puck, the penalty kill is not shooting on ours, therefore our penalty kill percentage should jump. We may disrupt the power play rhythm and timing so they frustrate the lack execution.

This is not to say that we shouldn't clear the puck, or that we should force plays when they aren't there.

If you are coaching a junior team or lower level, what a great tool to teach players puck poise and improve their hockey IQ. Every time your players are killing a penalty and they get a chance at the puck, they assess the conditions surrounding the puck and decide whether or not they can possess the puck or if they should clear it. Once they start making one more play, now see if they can use the four-corner spread and see if you can generate some chances to score, all the while evaporating power play time against. This fits in line with the entire philosophy.

OFFENSIVE ZONE EXIT KILL

An exit kill is an offensive zone defensive tactic to quickly regain control of the puck and get back on offense It is when you are in the offensive zone and the opponent has or is about to gain control of the puck. The objective of an exit kill is to win the puck back before they are able to exit the zone. The ability to exit kill is reliant upon both your shape discipline when you are on offense to be in position to react quickly to the change of possession, your reload speed and your pursuit intensity. It's about flipping from being on offense, which is outside in to defending, which is inside-out. This, again, is the duality of offense and defense, whereby the players who are on the "inside" offensively are then responsible for activating quickly from the inside position to work defensively to get the puck back. The offensive players who are working offensively from the "outside in" have to quickly recover their positioning defensively. Teams who play on the perimeter in the offensive zone when they have the puck and their puck support habits are on the outside will struggle with exit kill because they don't have the players on the inside to defend when the puck turns over. The duality of offense and defense is that the better and the more players playing on the inside offensively, the faster we will be able to react defensively to get the puck back. Our defensive players are already ready to defend from the inside out.

OFFENSIVE ZONE EXIT KILL

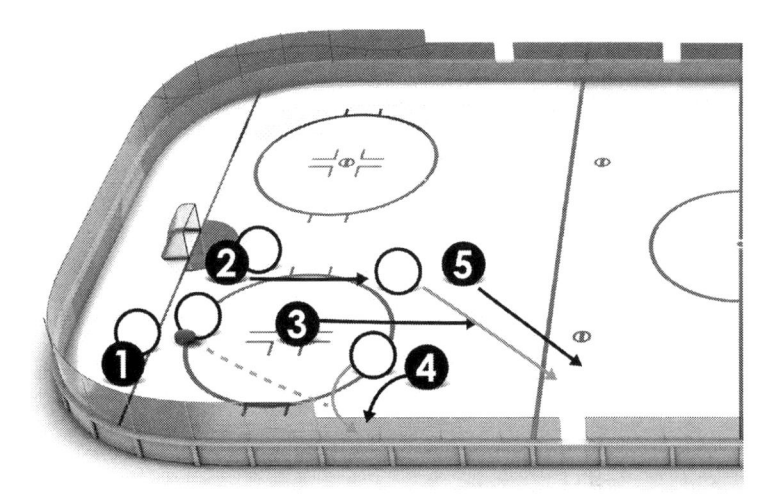

Figure 80:

A good exit kill has three phases:

- Phase 1: The shape we are in when we have the puck in the offensive zone. How many players do we have on the inside?
- Phase 2: The moment we win the puck back.
- Phase 3: The speed at which we can get back on offense.

Each of the three phases is reliant upon how well the shape of the group moves together. The more coordinated the movements of all five guys, the more pucks we can win back and the quicker we can create opportunities in extended offense.

There are four primary roles in an exit kill:

4. Pinching defensemen and the high 3v2

This is what we are most familiar with as it relates to exit kill. The defensemen pinching down the wall to collapse on top of the breakout winger and break up the breakout and keep the puck in the offensive zone. We used to instruct the defensemen to check and make sure they had a

BELFRY OFFENSE

high F3 who could cover for their pinch before going. Now we don't need to do that because a high F3 is no longer something we need to check for; they will be there. We can count on them. The entire offensive zone is reliant upon having an F3 and sprinting reloading. There is an interchangeable positional relationship between F3 and the two defensemen work together to pinch down.

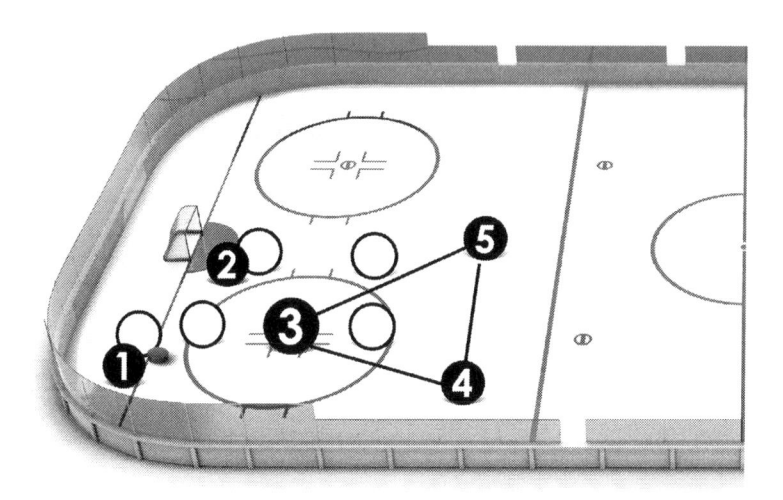

Figure 81:

5. F3 Track

F3 has two tracking responsibilities; the first is to interchange with the D in pinching situations and the second is in the F3 track. This track is when the D are not interchanging with F3, rather F3 starts their route above their speed and tracks the puck from above to contain the exit. F3 is responsible for ensuring that the play doesn't change sides.

OFFENSIVE ZONE EXIT KILL

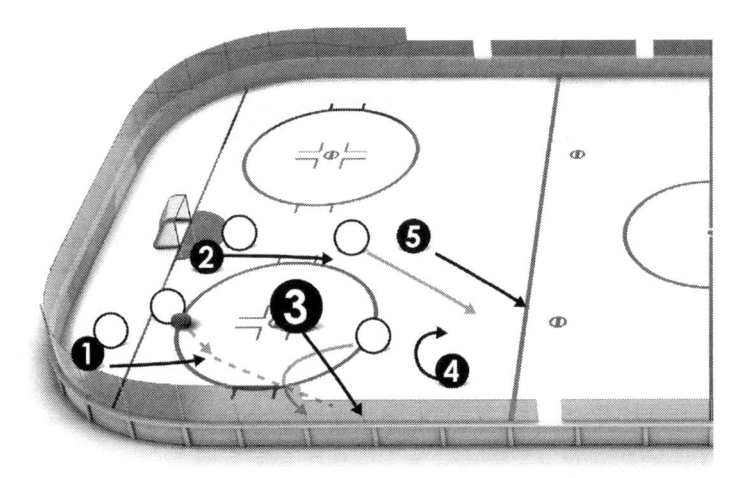

Figure 82:

6. F2 Track

F2 is usually at the net front or on the half-wall and this player tracks the puck, usually from behind to pressure the play. F2 is looking to gain steals or sprint to get above the puck. F2 is sprinting off the puck to back pressure the play.

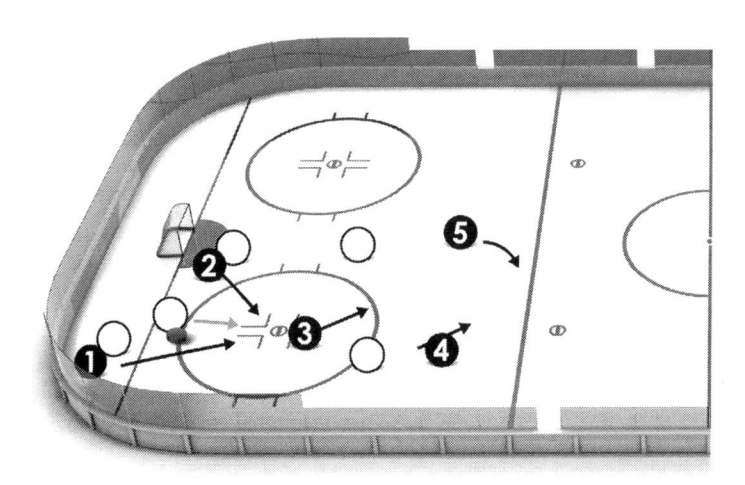

Figure 83:

185

BELFRY OFFENSE

7. F1 Strip

The F1 strip is another key piece to the exit kill. F1 is usually the last puck carrier deepest in the OZ prior to the puck turning over. This player needs to sprint to either pressure the puck on the strip or begin backchecking to close space and tighten our defensive spacing.

The most important part of exit kill is to get as many players above the puck and above and attached to speed as quickly as possible. This is the duality of offense and defense, the faster we play on offense, the more speed our players are playing with, the more they have a head start to both get above their check and attach to speed. The more players we have above their checks and attached to speed, the more aggressive our defense can play in the offensive zone.

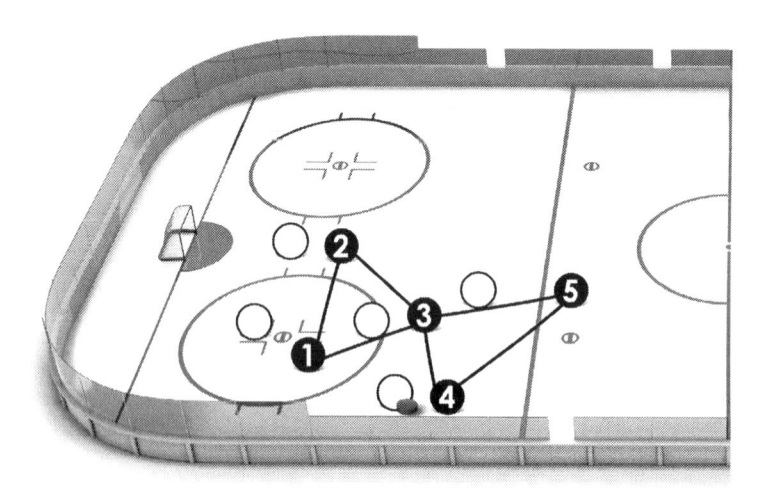

Figure 84:

The offensive term for getting back above checks in the offensive zone is "reloading." Teams who excel in exit kill, have excellent discipline and energy in their reloads. They are constantly working back up high in the offensive zone. The most important part of an exit kill is killing the exit before it has a chance to get started. Once the exit players are

OFFENSIVE ZONE EXIT KILL

organized, in position and in motion, it's much harder to kill the exit. Exits are killed before they get started. Get to the speed before it gets fast. If your team is going to become proficient in exit kill, they will clearly and consistently execute their offense while maintaining good transition shape.

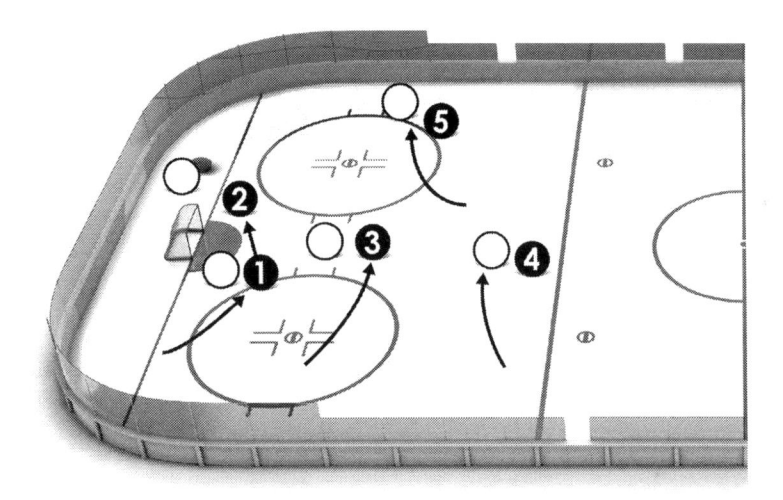

Figure 85:

The legendary women's basketball coach Geno Aurriema of UConn tells a great anecdote that perfectly describes the urgency you need your players to play with in F1 Strip, F2 Track and F3 Track. He talks about it from a practice perceptive and says, "Kids want to come to practice and they want to play at their pace." He has something that he does at clinics to illustrate the difference between the pace the player wants to play at and the pace he wants them to play at.

"...And you say to a kid ... I want you to run to from here to the end line and back."

"The kid, says ok?"

"Now you say, ok go, and they come back."

"Then I reach out into my pocket and I go alright look ...

I've got a $100 ... If you can get from here to there and back in 10 seconds, I'll give you 100 dollars. "

"Ready. Now the kid gets in his stance like this."

"Go! Like they are shot out of a cannon, they go flying down there and come flying back, and I'm counting and when they get right to where you are (a short distance away), I go, 10!"

"And they just get so upset that they don't get the $100, because they are like I ran as fast as I could. I said, I know you did."

"The only problem is the only reason you did it is because I offered you $100. When I said the first time go there and back you went at your pace. Now you went at the pace I want you to go at."

This great anecdote by Coach Aurriema depicts the relationship between motivation and habits. How do you create consistency in the motivation to have great effort habits when we need it the most? Or as Coach Aurriema says, play at the pace I want you to play at? The answer lies in the puck. This is why I think effort habits start in the offensive zone. As much as we coach the defensive zone as "the work zone," the same has to be said about the offensive zone. The difference is the motivation to stay on offense. If we can illustrate that playing "at the pace I want you play at" will give us the chance to play on offence much more, we have a chance to create consistency in the motivation to have great effort habits. [21]

Exit kill is directly connected and dependent upon offensive zone shape. If you lose your shape, you will lose your exit kill capacity. All the roles in exit kill are interchangeable and in a given shift every player on the ice may be in every role at different times. Recognizing, and, more importantly, anticipating the role change as the conditions of the play fluidly change with the movement of the puck, and as the clock ticks down and the score changes, factoring in the game conditions into your decision making is what we want players to truly understand.

---

[21] *https://www.instagram.com/reel/CrRLvIdgH_O/?igshid=YmMyMTA2M2Y=*

OFFENSIVE ZONE EXIT KILL

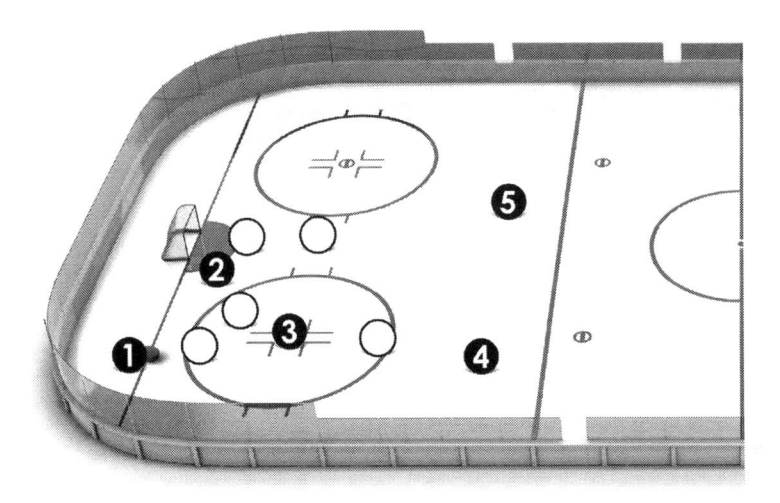

Figure 86:

In the original play, we have a regular offensive zone shape and roles,

The play changes sides and now the weak-side defender becomes part of the primary attack triangle.

Now when the puck turns over, the original weak-side D, the original strong-side D and the F3 are responsible for immediate transition. With 1 and 2 working to get above their check and pressure the puck from behind. From a role perspective, the weak-side D is furthest away from the puck to start the play, but in a second, he is part of the primary offensive triangle as the puck changes sides. Then in a split second, he is in the primary exit kill transition triangle with F3 and his partner. So in three seconds, he has three different roles in the play. Recognizing these role changes is a big part of hockey IQ. Now watch F3, their effort on the side change offensively puts him in position to be above their check when the puck turns over and get above their speed to kill the exit. The duality of the movement and the understanding that it's a dual purpose improves with effort willingness, because the player understands how vital the role is and the offensive opportunities the hustle represents.

BELFRY OFFENSE

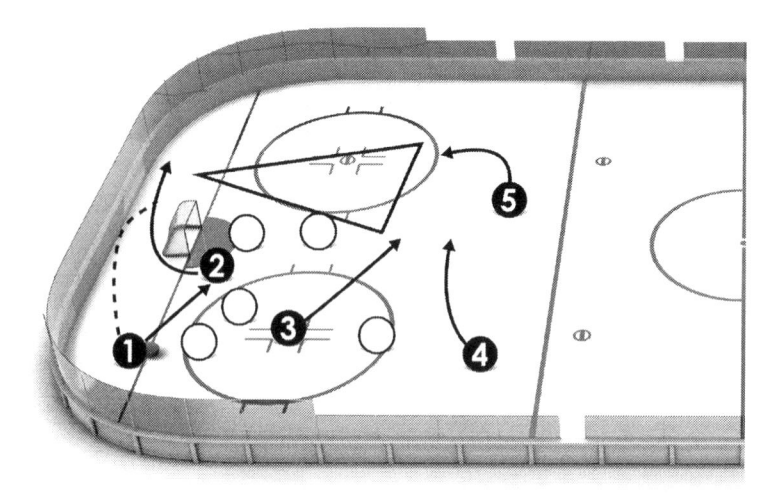

Figure 87:

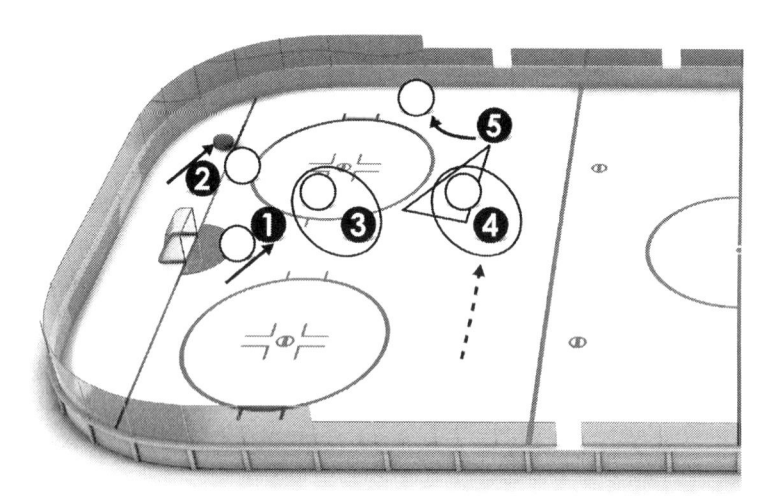

Figure 88:

All of us have been in situations where an ill-timed pinch at the wrong time in the game with no support leads to an odd-man rush against. For the longest time, when this happened I was lamenting the pinching D for not recognizing the game situation (the score, the clock, the time in the shift, the opponent on the ice, etc.) and not double-checking if we had an F3 to support and instead the D recklessly pinches and costs us a goal. Then I evolved to thinking, why is this always on the pinching D? It felt like the D was left with the hot potato. Why doesn't the F3 share responsibility of also recognizing the game situation and not making sure that they are reliable? Surely, F3 shares this responsibility. That's when my mindset shifted to include F3 with equal parts responsibility. Now, I'm all in with this being a five-man responsibility. Everyone is responsible. If all our players understand the duality of offensive zone play with the puck and transition exit kill or rush defense, depending on the conditions of the puck and the game situation.

The most advantageous time to kill an exit is when the new puck carrier has a tough puck and is on an island (they don't have immediate puck support). An example would be a rimmed puck to the weak side, the weak-side winger has to sprint to the puck and field it off the boards. The conditions of the puck and the difficulty of the opponent being able to get immediate puck support (their best chance is the strong-side winger slashing for support. In both situations, the weak-side winger fielding a rim in the DZ and the slash forward, they are on an island and perfect for exit kill. So long as our transition shape allows us to get to their speed before it gets organized (full possession, support arriving and speed building). If we can get to the exit before the opponent has full control of the puck, and we can attach to the speed threat of the slash support, we can move aggressively to kill the exit without exposure.

BELFRY OFFENSE

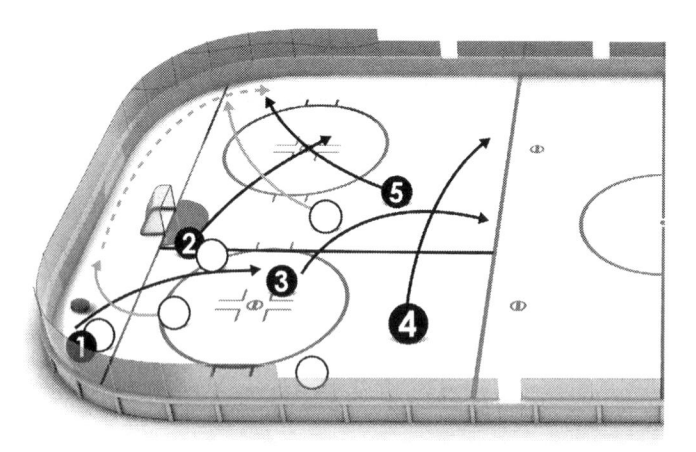

Figure 89:

Now if the transition shape isn't set up right (we have too many of our players on the outside), and we can't get the speed attached and the pursuit angle, well, if we are aggressive, we are at exposure. This is the "team" and group play that is required in exit kill.

We have the three high players above the play working together to attach to speed and support the interchange of roles between players. We also need a one in and one out approach to the dot line to aggressively pressure the puck while protecting the middle of the ice at the same time.

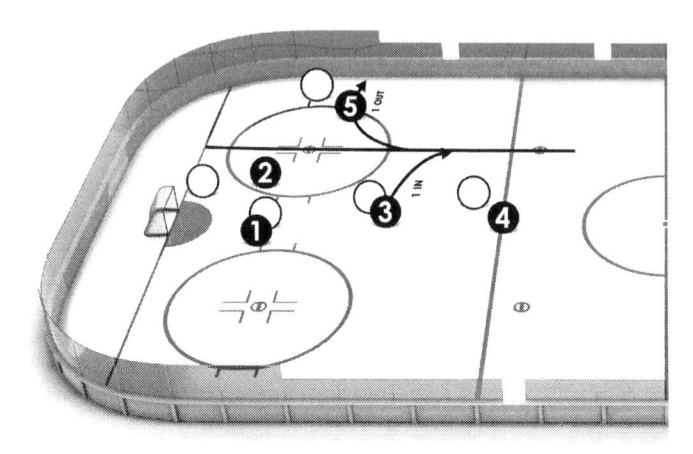

Figure 90:

192

OFFENSIVE ZONE EXIT KILL

If F2 and F1 are aggressive in their reloading, then we should have a great deal of pressure coming from below the puck and we maintain the integrity of our shape. In other words, we stay "connected." If we aren't connected and we lose our shape because we aren't sprinting from behind the puck, then we allow too much space between our D and our Fs which reduces the support to be aggressive and now we have to concede the lines.

The shape has two dimensions, the interior connectivity and the total distance between points (players). When we are in a good offensive position and have the right players on the inside and the puck turns over and we are on defense, we can now react quickly defensively to get the puck back. In the pursuit of getting the puck back, we want to stay on the inside of our check, so when that puck turns back again quickly to where we are on offense, we automatically have players on the inside to threaten the net.

Conceding the lines refers to the offensive blue line, the red line and the defensive blue line. These three lines are critical markers for us to make decisions on how aggressive we can be in getting the puck back. Sometimes you have to concede the lines and shift from exit kill to rush defense. The first priority, though, is exit kill. We don't want to concede anything if we don't have to. However, the conditions surrounding the possession of the puck decide. We have to weigh the percentages and make the highest percentage play for the conditions of the puck. When we are playing well, we have great movement and a strong shape to support, now we can react to change of possession or undetermined possession and initiate exit kill before the exit gets organized and that becomes the key to territorial advantage.

One of the key breakthroughs I had in my understanding of exit kill was when I started to see the duality of the transition shape. At the beginning, I thought of it more from the offense (being in the offensive zone with the puck, to losing the puck and now trying to defend swiftly to get the puck back). As I looked at it closer, I realized that the better the transition shape is the stronger leverage we have in both successive

BELFRY OFFENSE

transitions. The offensive to defensive transition to get the puck back AND the offensive shape to generate a dangerous chance in the window of time afforded by the transition. There is a window of time when the opponent, who was on defense, then gets the puck briefly. They think they are going on offense, and then, they lose the puck just as fast as they got it and are now back on defense. There is a window of time available to us to attack while they are recovering their defensive position. In looking at it from this perspective, the transition shape isn't just about getting the puck back. It's about getting the puck back AND being ready to attack in the transition window, which is usually 2-3 seconds after turnover.

BELFRY OFFENSIVE ZONE

(ZONE CONTROL) = (ELEVATED SPEED OF SHAPE) X (HABITS + PERCENTAGES)

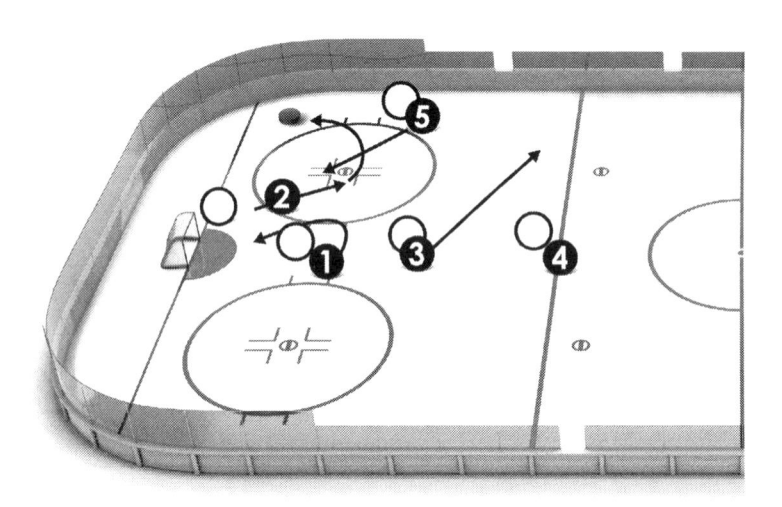

Figure 91:

This is where speed kills. The speed at which we can get the puck back and get it into a threatening position, the higher the quality of chances we can create. Now if you couple exit kill with cumulative shift effect, possession line changes and our goal of creating deficit shifts, you can see how exit kill fits lock and step into the entire philosophy. In all of it, the core structure remains.

In exit kill, we start with our offensive zone structure zone control = elevated speed of shape + (habits + percentages). This doesn't change. All the components here lend itself through cumulative shift and possession changes and in extending offensive zone time with exit kill. If we want to continue to have offensive zone control, we have to elevate the speed of our shape and then leverage our habits to improve our percentages.

The habits of exit kill are rooted in positional awareness and discipline to shape, the rest of the habits are all about effort detail. Positional awareness is reflected in rotations, and discipline to shape is reflected in the effort off the puck.

Defensive Forward Skating

For defensemen, exit kill is about forward defensive skating. It's interesting because it isn't just about skating forward. There are a lot of nuances to it. Situationally, it often starts with an offensive zone surf. Surfing is when the defender controls their skating but skates forward coming down in the offensive zone from the offensive blue line to the short porch. Surfing is an anticipation skating skill whereby the defenseman controls their skating and moves into position to make the next play (either catch a low-to-high pass inside the surf and use the middle distance position to shoot or to surf to preserve the space behind them (between the short porch and the blueline) that they can backpedal into with the puck and open up the space in the offensive zone, pass to their partner, attack down.

BELFRY OFFENSE

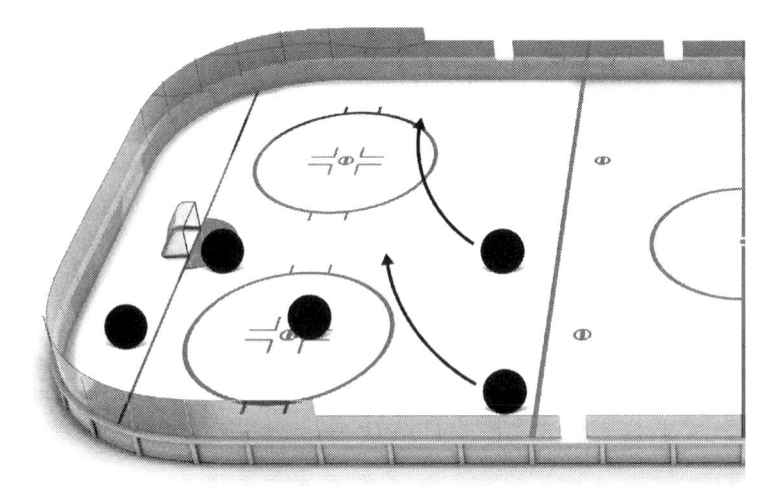

Figure 92: Forward Surf

Another situation is the weak-side fold. The weak-side D surfs down and recognizes an opportunity to attack the puck carrier in front of the strong-side D. The fold language reflects the tactical action of folding over to the other side.

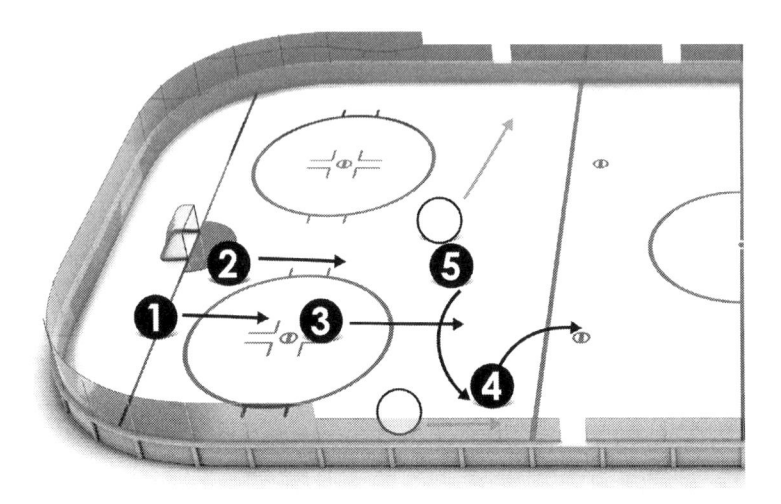

Figure 93:

196

OFFENSIVE ZONE EXIT KILL

The weak-side rim exit kill is a perfect situation for defensive forward skating. This is the weak-side D skating forward on an angle to win the puck back against the breakout forward trying to field the rim.

There are a lot of nuances in the execution of defensive forward skating. Those nuances include:

1. It all starts with a surf. The defender controls their skating using side push, weight shift or glide or all combinations therein. The defender uses the surf to get into position to then forward defend. This is such a critical part of defensive forward skating defending that is often misunderstood. Surf with anticipation of the next play.

2. Crossover skating on an arc with a counter lean to the outside of the arc with stick position on the outside of the arc with the stick on the ice the entire duration. The player must be able to skate with the upper and lower body separated. Combining a leading stick that is slightly ahead of the skates, but to the side of the body, the stick can't fall behind the skates as that'll affect the player's balance. In this posture, the player crossover skates in acceleration. At different points in that acceleration, depending on the handedness of the puck carrier, the interior options and the closing speed the defender can get, the defender must then bring the stick over to the opposite side of the body protecting the inside. If the defender was right-handed and moving to the left, they would start with two hands on their stick on the forehand on the outside, and then when they bring the stick inside, they switch to one hand on the stick, again keeping the stick blade out in front of the skates but to the side.

3. Sometimes the approach requires the defender to control their speed and to control their approach by using a side push skating technique. The side push is when the outside skate inside edge and the inside skate outside edge work as a push and pull piston action that allows the defender to use their skates to protect passing lanes and control speed until it's appropriate to close into the contact.

4. The defender must skate on a closing angle that lines their outside shoulder up with the inside shoulder of the puck carrier. If they are slightly behind, they will invite the puck carrier to cut in front of them, and if they are slightly ahead, they'll invite the puck carrier to attack their heels.

5. As the defender closes the space, they'll have to establish a stick in the passing lane. They want to keep the puck on the stick of the puck carrier. While keeping their head active to take in as much surrounding information as they can about the play environment, what hand is the puck carrier, how much space does the puck carrier have between them and the boards, do they have immediate inside pass support and what immediate support do you have? A lot of information to take in, process and execute. Need a lot of situational reps with variance.

6. In the moment of truth, which is the moment just before contact, the defender needs to speed up slightly to get their outside shoulder slightly inside the outside shoulder of the puck carrier. This allows you to cut their hands. One cue I like to use to help the defender understand this is "skate through the defender's hands." This encourages the defender to take one more aggressive crossover to get a nudge body position on the check.

7. Inside the contact the defender has to become exceptional with the outside foot inside edge balance and strength on that edge as it's critical to drive through the puck carrier.

8. Inside the contact, the defender can also use "hand fighting" to help secure the body position. Hand fighting is using your outside arm to both jar the arm of the puck carrier and help you set the space.

9. As the player cuts through the hands of the check, they target their hips to drive through the hands of the puck carrier, close enough to influence the posture of the puck carrier - kind of stand them up.

10. As the defensive player is gaining inside position, they also target the stick and puck of the puck carrier, attacking the inside of the puck to win it.
11. Now we need a weight-shift crossover to create separation off the wall.

A lot of detail in setting the closing angle, defending the right spaces with your stick, using good crossover acceleration with upper- and lower-body separation, then all the contact details. A lot goes into these habits, so it's a lot of reps for the defender to understand the basic approach, contact and separation. Once the basic approach is functional, now there is a need to work with variance, bigger players, smaller players, faster players, slower players, change of speed, trick players who want to come inside, players attacking your triangle. There is a ton to learn and adjust to.

This is where just playing games may not get it all done. You may have to put together a skill development progression to pull these details up the surface and get them plugged into the defensive players' habits. Then create situations in the drill progression where there is opportunity for significant variance, where the defender is forced to feel the situation, make adjustments, make decisions.

Tracking

There isn't much difference really in tracking the puck and in defensive forward skating in terms of the actual track approach details. The process of closing has the exact same objectives and skating strategies. The difference between defensive forward skating and tracking is defensive forward skating has more risk if you miss the angle and the check gets north above you. Tracking, you are still originating from above the puck, and it's usually done on a slight angle, but it's a beeline. The tracker is aggressive, the tracker is coming hard and looking to get on top of the puck as quick as possible. The biggest challenge of the tracker is to make sure that inside the track that the puck doesn't beat them inside.

The tracker, while in a beeline to pressure the puck carrier, must have a great pursuit angle and a discouraging stick. The stick has to be disruptive to the pass. The objective of the tracker is to win the puck back, but the responsibility of the tracker is to contain the puck on that side of the ice. The role of the tracker is very similar to the role of F1 on a forecheck. F1 is in hard pursuit, in a good angle and pushes the puck toward the wall and contains the puck on one side of the ice and finishes the check to not allow the puck carrier back in the play. The same is true for the tracker. Don't let the puck beat you inside and don't let your check beat you back in the play.

The best trackers are in anticipation of the responsibility. They read the possession change and are already in pursuit. When the puck carrier gets a handle on the puck, the tracker is already a problem. Great tracking comes from a reliable F3 presence with a clear understanding of the duality of the position, and that clarity is leveraged into anticipation and able to get the jump on the play. Poor tracking is late reacting, a step behind and unable to create stress for the puck carrier and concedes the exit.

Backpressure

The last component of exit kill is back pressure. We want to have as much defending happening from above the puck and above the opponent's speed, however when you are defending, it most often comes from when you were just on offense. Therefore, you will have players who are still in offensive positions and not above the puck or an opponent, rather on the offensive side. Players in these positions have to sprint to work from behind the puck to create back pressure. The back pressure hurries the offende into rushed plays, into punts or they can steal the puck.

OFFENSIVE ZONE EXIT KILL

Tactically, to back pressure with the most opportunity to stack the percentages in our favor, you want to force the puck carrier to his backhand or at least off a playmaking position. When chasing the puck carrier from behind when they are trying to exit the zone, we should first approach on the puck carrier's forehand side and threaten to swipe the puck on that side, make the puck carrier tentative to have the puck on his forehand and playmaking position for any length of time. The more we can have the puck carrier carry the puck in the middle of their body or have to move the puck across the midline of their body towards the backhand, they aren't in near as strong a playmaking position.

The objective of the back pressure is to pressure the puck into either a rushed play, or force the puck carrier to over-handle the puck and carry it for too long. We want to impact the speed at which the opponent can organize a counter rush against us. To impact the speed means to force the puck carrier to rush a play before the play gets moving and the speed gets started, or force the puck carrier to hold onto the puck longer, thus extending the routes of the players building speed. As the routes get longer, the player begins to slow down waiting for the puck, thus we have effectively controlled the speed through our pressure.

Back pressure is about affecting the speed the offensive team has to make plays, to make them play at our speed and not theirs. Without back pressure, there is more opportunity for the rush players to get "on time." In other words, the puck carrier and the speed supports are able to get organized and the puck can be delivered at the right time. Back pressure compresses the time available and is disruptive, creating bad passes or making plays to decelerating or stopped players. Offense is about movement and defense is stopping movement, so by disrupting the timing and forcing the support to slow down or stop, we are pushing the offense into a deficit to continue the play, improving our chances of getting the puck back.

Technically, when a player is pressuring the puck from behind, there are a few elements that come together to position the back pressure to get a steal.

BELFRY OFFENSE

1. The back pressure continues to skate; one of the biggest fallacies of back pressure is the pursuer stops skating when they get inside a stick length. There is a real discipline of skating into the takeaway attempt.

2. The intellect in the art of the steal is to get the puck out of the forehand while in pursuit of the puck, to keep the puck carrier from easily making a play. Then force the player to their forehand side by threatening the backhand side with your stick. Whether it is tapping the puck carrier with your stick on the backhand side hip, or having an actual presence on that side or combination of both, there has to be a threat that pulls the puck carrier into vulnerability on the forehand side.

3. Then, of course, as the puck carrier looks to protect the puck on the forehand side, as they move the puck there, the thief is already there awaiting for the stick to be exposed and attacks the stick for the takeaway.

4. Back pressure strips are an art form that require learning the tells and the timing. Using the tells to set up the timing, providing false information to the puck carrier to bait them into exposing the puck and then the second it's exposed, the pursuer steals it.

Another great steal that has picked up a lot of traction lately has been the "hook steal." In this steal technique, the pursuer does everything as we've discussed to get the puck exposed. Once it's exposed, the thief will bring the top hand of their stick down to the ice, so not bending at the waist, rather going down on one knee while in motion and the top hand on the stick goes to the ice, creating a flat stick with the blade angled out or flat on the ice. Then using a hook motion, the puck carrier uses the shaft close to the blade and the blade to "hook" the puck backward off the stick of the puck carrier. While the "hook" part is being executed at the puck, the pursuant will actually come up off their knee in preparation for a turn or change of direction in reaction to the steal.

OFFENSIVE ZONE EXIT KILL

The third back pressure steal approach is actually the one you should start with, and that's a contact disruption on the puck carrier. In this play, the objective is to finish your back pressure skating alongside the puck carrier so you can make a contact bump and dislodge the puck off the puck carrier.

What this does is it solidifies the habit of skating through the steal attempt. By demanding that the steal be a contact steal, the pursuant has to continue to skate hard through the stick length. If the puck carrier feels the pressure on the one side of their body and turns away from the contact, they are also turning away from the speed counter play. This is part of the desired effect of the back pressure in the first place. We want the pressure to delay delivering the puck and allow as many of our players to recover their position above the puck. This does all that in spades.

I like to start with the contact steal attempt first for all these reasons, but most importantly, the success rate of an actual steal is lower than the surgical strips we discussed before. What I love to see in my players is a physical contact disruption to force the puck carrier to escape and then get the strip or hook steal immediately following the contact. So the tactics are combined. This is my favorite expression of the technique.

The main objective of back pressure is to disrupt the next play. The best benefit of disrupting the next play is either you get a steal attempt or the puck carrier makes a play that gives us the puck back and you are in a perfect position to attack right away. Back pressure is about improving our chances of creating the opportunity for quick transition leading to uncontested or poorly defended chances.

NEUTRAL ZONE TRANSITION RE-ENTRY

Once we get into the offensive zone, we want to stay there as long as we can, win the puck back and sustain offense. We want to get into cumulative shift effect and invest in shifts that we can stack on top of each other to create momentum. At worst, we want our exit kill activation to force the opponent into a chip out. Once the puck is chipped out, we are presented with an opportunity for a neutral zone transition re-entry.

Controlling the neutral zone is a big part of controlling the game, and there are four situations that give you a chance to take control of the neutral zone. In the interconnected game model, the chances to control the neutral zone are revealed in this order.

1. Neutral zone transition re-entry
2. Rush defense or entry denial
3. Rush entry
4. Neutral zone defense

This is where looking at things from a different perspective can make all the difference. Most of the time, when we think of controlling the neutral zone, we think first to neutral zone defense and some forecheck system, 1-1-3 or 2-3 or any other way you want to configure your personnel to defend the neutral zone. When you view it from the interconnected game model, neutral zone defense is last and neutral zone transition re-entry is first. The reason it's first is because we start our team development by understanding the offensive zone and work back to the defensive zone. That change of perspective makes all the difference.

How meticulous you are in articulating the opportunities for offense in neutral zone transition re-entry is a big part of what teaching offensive hockey IQ in all your players. As soon as the puck comes out of the

NEUTRAL ZONE TRANSITION RE-ENTRY

offensive zone, it's a race against the clock to see if your group can capitalize on the inherent advantages of re-entry. If your group is galvanized and sprinting, you can find a ton of opportunity. If you can't get organized quickly enough, then you have to go to a more slow regroup. You might possession change, you might bait them in to a change. What matters is that you prioritize speed of re-entry. We want to come right back in just as fast as the puck came out as the first priority. If that re-entry play is not there because we can't get our people out quick enough or we don't get a good first touch in the neutral zone, then we can fall back into a more deliberate re-entry.

The re-entry is directly connected to the exit kill pressure and routes. If we are committed to our exit kill as a five-man unit, then if the puck is chipped out, we have everyone sprinting forward and organizing quickly to take advantage of the natural disadvantage the opponent has in contesting the blue line on re-entry. It's very difficult to get the defensemen up to contest the line. The defense will be back of the line, and if it's contested at all, it'll be with forwards. The opportunity to gain depth in the zone without being heavily contested is almost too good to be true. Moreover, the opportunity to use the middle of the ice, either through an "on-time" F2 driver or with a middle-entry possession. We can pressure the opponent on re-entry right away, with either depth or middle threat. The advantage of starting with a speed advantage in the offensive zone by using the depth available to get speed. This sets up the offensive zone to begin with an elevated speed shape.

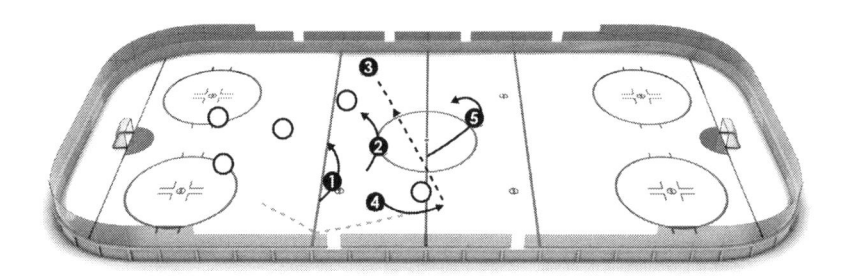

Figure 94

BELFRY OFFENSE

The more competitive the level you are playing at and the more competitive the two teams that are playing, the less true rush scoring chances are going to be available. True rush chances meaning a rush involving a numerical advantage and opportunity to attack east-west. In the NHL, most rush plays are at numerical disadvantages, or at best, you have even numbers. The rush is a major part of offense, whether you can create scoring chances off of it or not. The rush is really speed in the neutral zone that you can carry into the offensive zone, either in direct rush scoring chances, in setting up the forecheck recovery or in just setting up the offensive zone where it can get in motion. On re-entry, the possibilities for numerical advantage are high, because the defensive group will have a hard time consistently getting their D up to the blue line to contest the line. We want a 2v1 on the anchor or entry play and another 2v1 possibility when the anchor gets the puck and someone on the back side with speed.

In a game this season between the Dallas Stars and New York Islanders on January 19, 2023, on a first period breakout, the Islander winger misses the slashing winger with a pass. The Dallas D gets to the puck for a quick up to the strong-side anchor. The anchor holds the puck on entry and allows the middle-presence driver to set the space by driving the dot line. The anchor then passes in the space behind the middle driver to the weak-side dot. The weak-side dot player then has a 2v1 vs. the Islanders weak-side D and the driver who continues to the back post. This is an easy goal for Dallas to open the scoring.

In the 2023 playoffs in the first round, Carolina scores an overtime winner vs. the Islanders on a re-entry play where they leverage the two 2v1s to create two side changes. On the play, the Islanders commit an errant breakout pass to the winger that gets out in the neutral zone. When Brent Burns touches the puck on the Islanders' side of center ice, there are two Carolina Hurricanes defensemen in the NZ and three of their forwards already above the top of the circle in the offensive zone sprinting out of the zone. Burns makes an uncontested cross-ice pass to the Hurricanes anchor. Jordan Martinook is middle support and re-enters on the dot line against the two Islanders defensemen who are just now getting up to the top of the circle. That leaves a massive cross ice pass in behind the driving Martinook to Jesper Fast who is on the weak-side dot line. The pass goes from anchor to cross-ice dot line in a blink of an eye and it's an easy catch and shoot for Fast, and Carolina wins Game 2 in overtime.

So the elements that we need to improve rush entry are available if we are quick about it.

On re-entry, there are a couple shape elements that offer opportunity.

If we can re-enter quickly enough, before they get their D up, there will be space between their D and their F nearly immediately upon reentry that allows us to change sides to speed on the back side. This is dangerous in its own right, if our original strong-side speed or middle-entry player keeps skating, we can find him on a second-side change for a tap in.

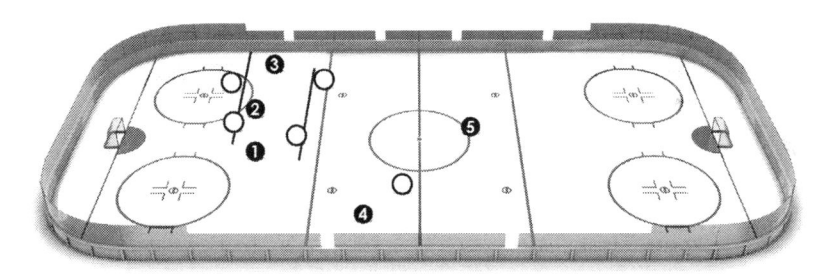

Figure 95:

1. A forward hinge by the partner

This is where the game has changed over the last few years. In counter situations previously, the role of the weak-side D was to try to get "underneath" their partner. When the puck came out of the zone, the weak-side D used to sprint forward to the middle of the ice, many of us wanted that D to go through the middle faceoff dot and pivot backward to open up for their partner. Now, the underneath hinge is less automatic and more situational. Now, we prioritize the weak-side D to look to hinge forward

BELFRY OFFENSE

and get ahead of the puck looking to time a possession re-entry with a speed advantage. If the play isn't there, then we can look to be more deliberate. The reason the forward hinge by the D partner is important is that we now have a speed option on both dot lines on re-entry on a quick up to the strong side. If the entry goes on the strong-side quick up, then the forward hinge by partner will work with the weak side forward to determine who is in position to have the depth and get into the cross-ice passing lane and who will provide second layer pass support.

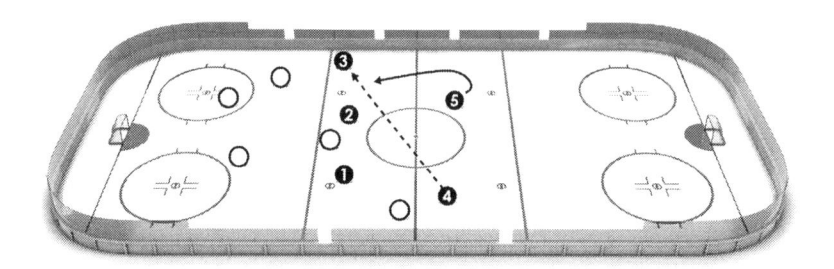

Figure 96:

2. A quick up anchor

The first option on that chip recovery is to try to come right back in as quickly as possible with a lot of speed. The anchor post up at the offensive blue line on either the strong side of the chip or the weak side of the chip with a quick uncontested soft gap contested re-entry is the clear first option. The key to the quick-up anchor is quickly getting everyone onside and come right back in by hitting the anchor and bringing speed through the middle or on the dot line.

The first player to the puck has to get vision of the options prior to puck touch. Many players will either fully pivot and gather the puck going backward. We also see players use a quick pivot to expand their vision momentarily prior to picking up the puck. Then you have shoulder checks and relying on your teammates communication to understand the re-entry game conditions upon first touch.

The anchor player wants to get quickly stopped just outside the line and square to the passer. The key on the play for the anchor is to catch the pass and get everyone onside. The anchor needs to be close enough to the blue line that they can catch and cross at the same time if everyone is already onside, but has to be aware of where everyone is as they may have to catch it and hold it outside the line to buy time to get everyone onside and then get over the line to get everyone onside on the re-entry. The anchor job is not easy. There is a lot of awareness of where everyone is and responsibility to ensure we can enter at the first possible second there is an opportunity.

3. A middle presence

On a possession re-entry, we need someone in the middle of the ice or on the dot line with speed upon entry. A forward in the middle of the ice coming toward the anchor, or the forward hinge D on the dot line on the side of the anchor is another strong option. The middle presence is flying and working towards the anchor, so that we can quickly 2v1 the likely forward who will contest the line. We need the middle presence to be carrying a lot of speed because we need the depth. Not only to capitalize on the speed differential versus the poorly gapped defensemen but to open up a cross-ice pass in behind that speed.

One of the best examples of this is from a New York Rangers game this year vs. the Columbus Blue Jackets on March 28, 2023. This is an awesome example because of the relationship between offensive zone possession and neutral zone re-entry. In the shift, the Rangers have a heavy forecheck that results in a turnover chance as F3. Patrick Kane jumps on the turnover and attacks on a slant and hits the post on a backhand shot. Kane recovers the rebound and his pass to the point comes out of the zone. The Rangers defenseman pulls the puck back waiting for the Rangers to get onside and then stretches a puck to Kane in the middle of the ice. Kane and Chris Kreider execute a cross exchange that gives Kreider a middle re-entry before passing to the right side. Kane continues his route on the dot line on the left. Kreider pushes the D back by driving and creates a passing lane for a cross-ice, dot-to-dot, pass to Kane. Kane upon touch has Kreider on a 2v1, Kreider's play has created two 2v1s for both dot-line attackers. Kane uses the threat to Kreider as a disguise for his shot and he scores the third Rangers' goal of the first period.

Don't forget, in the second period we may be able to bait them into a change. We need to be aware of the shift clock as they may be looking for a change and double down on the chance available.

On a line change, this is where our D prioritizing getting on a forward hinge can put them in position to threaten offensively. There was a goal this season on March 13, 2023 by the Colorado Avalanche in Montreal on a first period re-entry, where the Canadiens tried to change when Colorado had the puck in the neutral zone. The puck came out on the side of the ice away from the benches, the Colorado D, Samuel Girard executes a first-touch quick up. What's interesting, though, is his quick up was a board pass to his slashing D partner Bowen Byram. Byram read the line change and jumped through on slash support and before Montreal knew it, he was already driving the net. The Montreal D were caught with a bad gap and Byram had a significant speed differential allowing him to easily take the corner and walk across the crease to score. Just a brilliant understanding of the situation by both D, and Byram became Colorado's center in the play and attacked fearlessly because of the vulnerability of the change.

This is the effect you want to have on teams, like Colorado has. Don't dare change when they have the puck or they will make you pay. This isn't just a read or a system. This goal is created because Byram is in the right position in the shape. This allows him to see the opportune re-entry due to the brazen Montreal change attempt and he doesn't hesitate. Colorado is a great re-entry team, because they prioritize it and have the shape and the habits to stack the percentages.

Now, if we are unable to quick up quickly, and it's better to pull back into a more deliberate re-entry, we now have a couple ideas we can work off of.

NEUTRAL ZONE TRANSITION RE-ENTRY

1. Neutral Zone Regroup

    Traditionally, a chip recovery would fall into a neutral zone regroup, where the play would first change sides with the D in an underneath hinge. Once the puck goes D to D, then any number of options open up:

    a. The original D who passed it to their partner, then works to get underneath the puck and in the middle and is an option coming up the ice. A good play to manipulate the opponents F1 and create attack space in the middle.

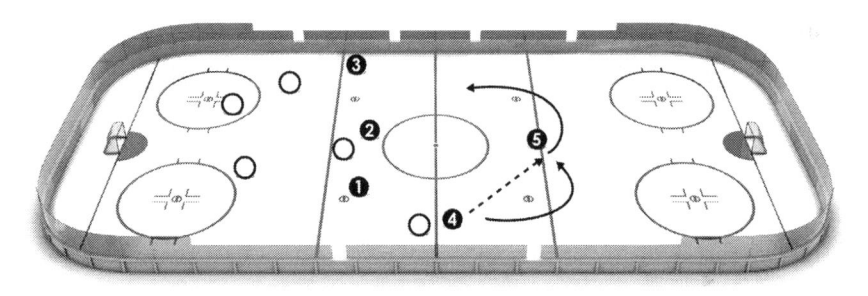

Figure 97:

   b. Over and up. The D to would go D to D and the up to the anchor.

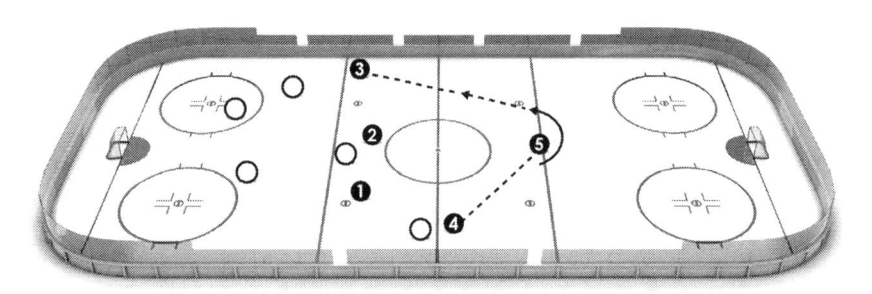

Figure 98:

211

BELFRY OFFENSE

c. Over and in. The D would go D to D and then find the middle of the ice.

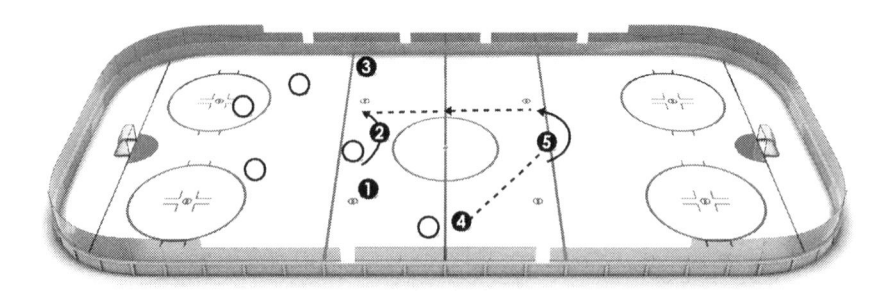

Figure 99:

In the opening minutes of Game 4 of the 2023 Stanley Cup Final, Vegas scores on a re-entry middle play that leads to a breakaway goal to open the scoring. On the play, Vegas has an extended possession in the offensive zone including shots and shot recoveries, taxing the Florida defenders. The puck comes out of the zone to Zach Whitecloud, who immediately looks for re-entry. Florida is looking to change and Vegas has both Mark Stone and Chandler Stephenson curl in the middle of the ice for re-entry. Whitecloud finds Stephenson in the middle, Florida's weak-side D changed leaving the middle of the ice open. This is a critical opening goal in Game 4 and comes from a middle-ice re-entry. [22]

d. Over and dump it in. The D would go D to D and then that D would skate it to the red line to dump it in.

e. Over and into the flats. The D would go D to D and then the weak-side forward would take back ice to get as even with the puck as they can and present themselves in the flats.

---

[22] https://twitter.com/belfryhockey/status/1670249820857016320?s=20

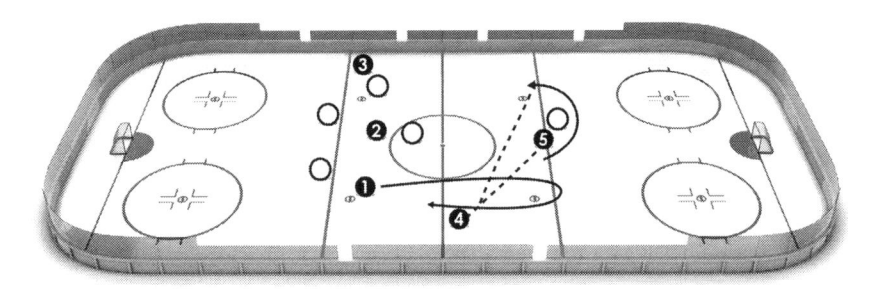

Figure 100:

2. Swing

On the swing, the D pulls the puck back into the middle of the ice and waits for the rest of the group to organize. Often teams will take the opportunity to change during this time. The idea behind the swing is to beat F1. F1 is important to beat regardless of where you are on the rink. On the swing re-entry, as the puck carrier establishes the puck in the middle of the ice, two forwards will swing to one side of the puck and the D's partner will swing on the other. The third forward has stretched the ice and could be positioned in a variety of tactical positions. They could be anchored on the boards on either side at the offensive blue line, they could also be stationed in the middle of the offensive blue line. It's really at the coach's discretion. The two forwards swinging on the one side are staggered, with the first one getting ahead of the second. By staggering the two forwards, the lead forward insulates space for the second one. The lead forward is attacking the neutral zone with speed trying to drive back the defenders and create a runway for the second forward. The puck carrier should pass to the second forward who has now a runway of speed. This works the same as speed coming from behind the puck, the lead forward is a speed decoy that pushes the defenders back in an effort to have them gapped to the wrong guy, the actual threat is the speed coming in from underneath that speed. This is the differential we hope to leverage to gain depth into the offensive zone.

BELFRY OFFENSE

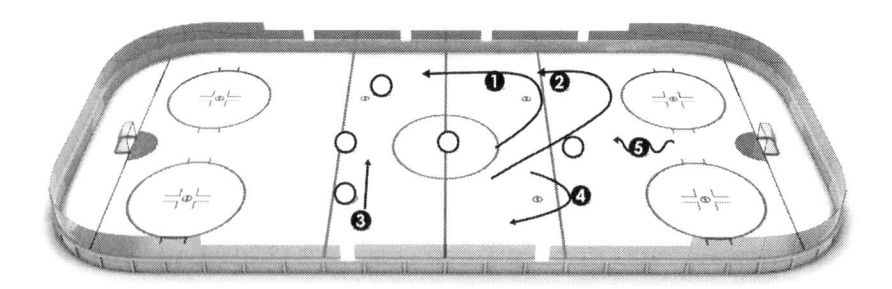

Figure 101:

The D could also use his partner on the other side while the swing is going on the other side. The partner swings to get above the puck and then looks to try to use the space created by the first swing forward on the other side to pass cross ice to the second forward swing in the flats. This creates an opportunity to attack on the weak side. If we bring the stretch forward to the puck with speed, when the lead forward stops prior to entry to stay onside, we can potentially 2v1 the defender with overwhelming speed.

In situations where the opposing team is able to get their defensemen up to contest the line, we can use our re-entry speed off the puck to attack the space in behind them in an overlap entry or initiate the forecheck.

3. Overlap Entry

When ether opposition is able to get their D up to contest the line and a direct pass to our speed isn't available or the time available to our anchor is limited, they can soft chip the puck in behind the strong-side D to lead our dot-line speed into the puck to resume our offensive zone possession.

NEUTRAL ZONE TRANSITION RE-ENTRY

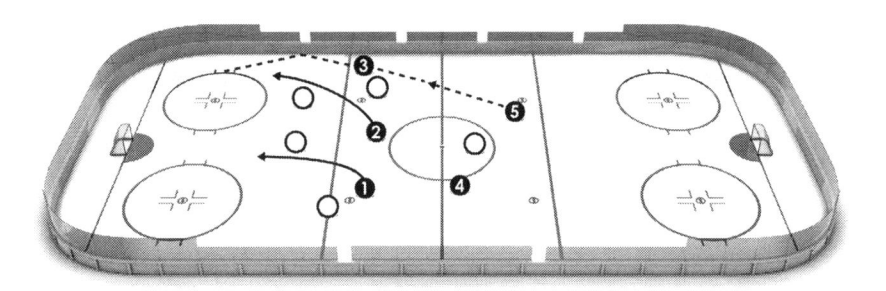

Figure 102:

4. Forecheck Entry

   On the re-entry, we may use the anchor to knife the puck back into the zone, or use the middle speed to get it in deep and we can use our dot line speed on either side to get first touch.

   In either situation, whether we can get a possession entry, or we put the puck in behind the D, we have to recognize where the opponent's D are on our re-entry and execute based on the advantages that that positioning offers us. The entry decision is based on habits which puts us in position to stack the percentages in our favor. The importance of the investment and diligence in the offensive zone will play a big factor in the positioning of the opposition's defensemen and their eagerness to contest the re-entry. Understanding how the game stitches together is what makes these decisions so much easier for us to make collectively.

   One of the best indicators of offensive hockey sense that after I came to realize how interesting it was, I couldn't unsee it, is the timing players have when they cross the offensive zone blue line. Players with high-end offensive hockey sense time the line, so their entry timing creates opportunity for competitive advantage. They adjust their routes well before the line and they time the line. A good example is watching top offensive players when they are the stretch or above the puck, watch how they stay alive on the play to make the adjustments they need on their routes. This was my first exposure to what I call a "dip accel." A dip accel is when the stretch player or player above the puck in the neutral zone arrives at the offensive blue line before the puck, and rather than slow down or stop at the line, they will make a subtle weight shift toward the redline by 3-6 feet while watching the puck carrier intently and are still able to properly time the line on the entry. They maintain their speed, they use the dip to create angles on the entry and they are on time on the play. They arrive on time with the right speed and dangerous plays can be made because of their diligence. When they are the puck carrier, they are conscious of the entry in the way they handle the puck. They'll reach the puck across the line early to free the route speed of the players off the puck. There are conscious decisions that you can clearly see being made to facilitate the entry for the group. Players who struggle to make plays or turn pucks over on entry will do so because they approach the entry with greater concern over their own play on the puck. Players who make elite entry plays know that as the puck carrier they are serving their linemates and that paradigm shift is why they make plays. The last consideration they have is what they are going to do. They are seeing the play develop (the movement of their linemates and doing what they need to do (speed the play up, slow it down, move the D) to create the entry conditions. They are in service of the play.

Where this really jumps off the screen and slaps me across the face is in re-entry situations. The play of the anchor when they get the puck offers fascinating insight into that players offensive hockey sense. You can see as soon as they get the puck and their approach to the entry as to whether they are in service of the play or they are immersed in their play on top of the puck. It becomes so clear, not only in their play and then as you watch the players around them as they time the entry. When you watch enough of these events, you'll see players off the puck sprinting the neutral zone exclusively watching the D and not paying attention to the puck carrier until the last second, and if the puck isn't going to cross the line on time

NEUTRAL ZONE TRANSITION RE-ENTRY

with their skating, you'll see them make a dramatic play to stay on side. They'll slam on the breaks or they'll make a 90-degree turn on the line or they'll just end up offside.

I am convinced this is a massive opportunity in the rush game. Not only in re-entry, but in all rush-entry situations. I think re-entry offers a lot of fascinating challenges and nuances for the players and that's an area I'd start to introduce a lot of these concepts. What does the puck carrier do when they are ready to re-enter but one of their linemates is still fighting to get out of the zone? What does the other forward or the D do who is trying to time the line in relationship to the puck carrier AND the player fighting to get onside when you re-enter? If you want to really take a stab and try to teach hockey sense, table your 3v3 games for a minute and come up with a teaching progression that challenges re-entry timing, then turn that into a game and see what happens. You may be surprised at who actually excels at this in your group. Then, of course, attach it to exit kill. Then build up the rush re-entry defending and then let them go.

The next step to this is when you find a puck carrier (you won't have to look long) in your group who struggles as the anchor or re-entry in both plays and facilitating the entry (getting the puck to cross the line to free the routes of the players coming in. This is an opportunity to get into area passes, the weight of a puck placed in behind their D, leading passes to the direct support. Flipping their mindset to service of the entry play is the conduit to playmaking, which in turn, is a pathway to continued possession and ultimately scoring chances.

RUSH ENTRY DENIAL

If the opponent is able to exit their zone with possession and we are unable to exit kill or force the puck into a neutral zone re-entry, we shift to rush entry denial. The best teams don't take much time to get through the neutral zone, they skate the neutral zone fast and they move the puck forward. If they change sides, they do it to skate onto the puck with speed. The key to rush-entry denial is to do the work on in offensive zone defending. Where we get above the puck and get attached to the speed on exit, we can limit the play moving forward with possession and we can carry the numerical advantage in the NZ. When we carry the numerical advantage, we can control the middle of the ice and push the puck to the outside. The numbers also allow the defensemen to hold a tight gap to contest the red line and or the defensive blue line. If we don't do our work upon loss of possession in the offensive zone, we will concede the speed and the better rush chances.

    The interesting battle in the neutral zone is the control of the middle of the ice and stretching our defensive spacing. If we get stretched out, where our D are separated from our forwards, the D will have to concede the entry and not be able to contest either of the two lines (red line or blue line). If we lose our defensive presence in the middle, we will not only concede speed through the neutral zone, but we will also concede side change. Side change at speed where the defensive spacing is stretched eliminates back pressure on the rush, now the rush can play at their speed and not our speed. When the defensive team has middle defending presence and good defensive spacing, as they go hand in hand, it's hard to have one without the other, then they can force the rush to play at the defensive speed. In rush defense, the defensive speed is to force the puck carrier to make a play prior to the red line, which puts icing the puck as an option, or our defensive blue line, which puts an offside play, or ideally, a forced turnover for transition or dump in

RUSH ENTRY DENIAL

transition in play. Either way, we are stalling the rush threat against and put ourselves in position to get the puck back.

The way I view this is from the perspective of what are the play conditions that give us the best chance to get the puck back quickly or force a stoppage. If we have to concede the entry, how can we do it with the least amount of exposure.

The priority tree for us on entry denial is as follows:

1. To force a turnover in the neutral zone that we can counter on.

   Situations where our D are supported with back pressure numbers and can hold their defensive spacing to contest the lines (red line and blue line) and force a turnover that we can counter on.

2. To force an icing.

   The D are supported with immediate back pressure numbers and the puck carrier is vulnerable to heavy pressure prior to gaining the red line and we force an icing.

3. To force an offside.

   The D are supported with immediate back pressure numbers and can control their gap timing their pressure on the puck carrier near the defensive blue line where the puck carrier has to make a rushed lateral play and puts his support offside.

4. To force a dump in that our goalie can handle.

   The D are supported with immediate back pressure numbers and can control their gap timing their pressure on the puck carrier near the defensive blue line and the puck carrier is rushed into a dump in that they can't control and our goalie can get out and get first touch.

5. To force a dump in we can retrieve (first touch).

   The D are supported with immediate back pressure numbers and can control their gap timing and pressure on the puck carrier near the defensive blue line and the puck carrier dumps it in and we get first touch.

6. To defend an unrecovered dump in (lose first touch).

    Our D have good support to hold their gap and apply pressure to the puck carrier on entry forcing a dump in, but the speed differential favors the offensive team and they are able to win the first touch on the puck.

7. To defend a possession entry.

    Our D are not supposed with good back pressure numbers and have to absorb the rush and not able to put pressure on the puck up the ice and have to try to delay the rush for help later in the rush play. The defenders protect the middle and deflect the play outside and as the play gets deeper in the zone and back pressure catches up, they can apply pressure.

8. To defend a shot against.

    Our D and the back pressure numbers are not able to pressure the puck carrier enough to disrupt the play and the entry leads to shot against.

9. To defend an odd-man rush against.

    There was a failure somewhere up the ice in the offensive zone defending and rush defense that led to a mistake that conceded an odd-man rush against.

Our ability to effectively deny the rush entry is a group activity that starts with our reaction speed to defending in the offensive zone and in the moments on the exit. The more back pressure speed and numbers we have in support of the defenders, the more aggressive we can be to get the puck back quickly and get back on offence.

One of the key coordinations in rush-entry denial is between the D,

RUSH ENTRY DENIAL

the first back pressure forward and the dot line. This is a one-in and one-out coordination of pressure in relationship to the dot line.

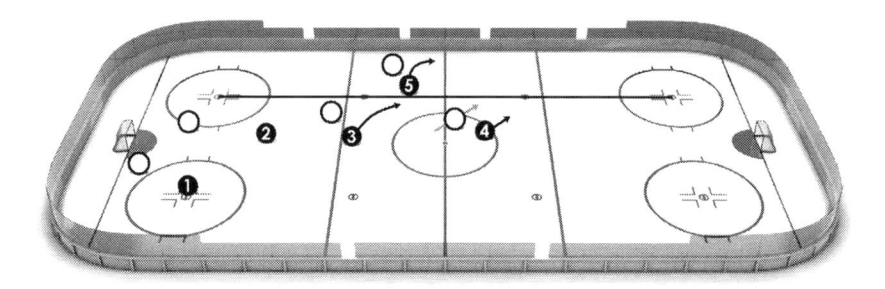

Figure 103:

We want the puck back quickly, but we don't want to degrade our rush defense leverage. We want pressure on the puck carrier to force a play before the offensive play organizes, but we can only have one of our D or our back pressure forward in pressure pursuit outside the dots. The strong-side D, in most situations, is making this decision. Coaches will often get frustrated with indecision or poor execution and implement a hard rule that the back pressure forward is going all the time and the D holds the dot line. I'd like to work with the defensemen to improve their ability to assess the pressure, the speed and the spacing in relationship to the clock and the score to make clean and advantageous situations for us to get the puck back as quickly as we can with limited risk. The hard rule becomes frustrating when the D is in a perfect position to pressure and the puck carrier is not a high-level offensive threat. Now we allow the play to advance further than it needs to and with time and space, the puck carrier's options and decisions will improve. The reality is any time a defender pursues the puck outside the dots, there is a risk to degrade the rush defense leverage (inside position, spacing and pressure). However by trying to minimize the risk and pressure outside the dots, we are giving ourselves a chance to disrupt the rush before it gets organized and get the puck back quickly. I don't want to concede lines unless the offense has earned the advantage and we have to absorb.

The best part about one in and one out is this is a shape consideration we can apply everywhere on the ice. Once our players get enough variance of reps to recognize the signs of elevated risk in the rush situation (which forwards are reliable in back pressure and which are not), they can leverage the defending shape and habits to make decisions based on those percentages.

As much as the strong-side defensemen and the back pressure is the primary focus of rush-entry denial, the weak-side defender is the heartbeat of transition. The weak-side D is responsible for:

- Counting the numbers (what is the rush against situation 3v3, 3v2, etc.).
- Determines weak-side fold situations - numerical advantage and a puck carrier on an island.
- Directs the setting of gap spacing by organizing the defending shape. Coordinating with the strong-side defender and the back pressure support.
- Works to ensure we have control of the middle and discourage side change.
- Absorbs the middle speed.
- Intercepts cross-ice plays.
- Gathers loose pucks behind the strong-side D.
- Retrieves dump-ins.

The weak-side D puts us in position for transition by directing and supporting the defending shape. The skating and stick defending has to have purpose and a strong sense of spacing. We can't have the weak-side D stretching the gap space because they don't have updated footwork. Most of the exposure in entry denial comes from skating habits and skill limitations of the weak-side defender. When the D is on the offensive blue line when the rush against initiates, the weak-side D will often sag in their gap because they crossover accel violently off the offensive blue line and open up too much gap and also move curvilinear as many will use multiple crossovers in a row on an arc to get off the line. Once they start the backward curvilinear accel off the offensive blue line, the defenseman is continually recovering their position. The more efficient control skating backpedal accel is to use a step back (a step back is when the player moves like they are walking backward up the stairs, the inside skate outside edge pushes forward to propel the momentum backward while the outside skate steps back), followed by backward striding (consecutive C-cuts in a straight line) and ladder steps (moving laterally by replacing the foot rather than crossover), as the play develops. This will allow them to control their skating in direct association to the speed of the oncoming rush and control their line. The more controlled the skating is, the more mobility they have to anticipate and react to transition opportunities.

If the weak-side D is active in the offensive zone, then I would generally like them to be skating forward in a surf when the rush against initiates. In this case, as the oncoming rush begins the weak-side D should be most concerned with setting the defending shape and controlling their skating. To this, they would turn both skates facing their own net and use a step back inside their pivot to control their skating line and speed. Then settle into backward striding and make any adjustments to their line using ladder steps This is good rush defense footwork.

The defender also can hide their reach to present the appearance of a false passing lane to bait the pass across. Defensemen will use two hands on their stick and hold the stick slightly to the side of their body and are mindful to keep it out of the passing lane, can create false passing lanes to encourage passes to intercept. D who declare their reach will have one hand on the stick outstretched. This shows the passer exactly where the reach is of the defender. The weak-side defender has to be clever and sly in the way they present the lane, so to encourage the pass across and provide an opportunity for a pass interception transition.

BELFRY OFFENSE

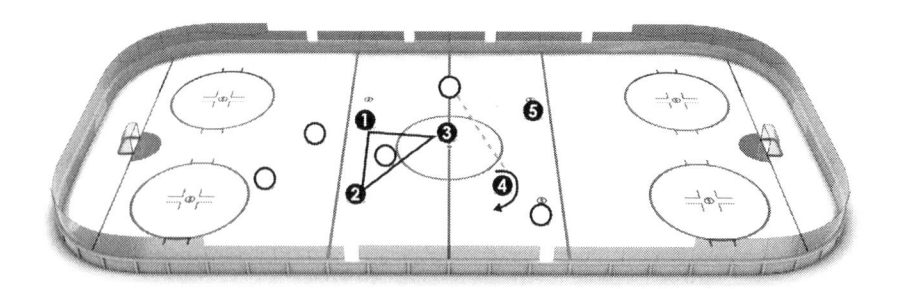

Figure 104:

The transition opportunity comes in a few different play situations:

1. The strong-side D invites the puck carrier into their defensive triangle (the space between the blade of their stick and their skates) and makes a stick play on the puck, creating a loose puck or direct turnover.
2. The strong-side D invites the puck carrier into the contact range the defender forces the turnover through their checking skill, which separates the puck from the puck carrier. This could be a personal takeaway from the strong-side D with an acceleration off the wall.
    a. Or the strong-side D could invite the puck carrier into contact range and create a loose puck for the weak-side D or for the back pressure forward to pick up upon separating the puck carrier from the puck in contact.
3. Weak-side D pass intercept.
4. Weak-side D loose puck recovery.
5. Weak-side D pass deflection.
6. Weak-side D disruption takeaway when attaching to the speed on entry
7. Weak-side D spacing forces the puck carrier to keep the puck as there is no passing lane. Thus pushing the puck carrier into either contact or a chip takeaway.

8. The weak-side D absorbs the speed but also defends the cross ice passing lane for pass intercept or deflection.

The rush-entry denial detail starts with the shape we get into upon exit. This sets up our strong-side D, weak-side D and back pressure forward to get into a transition triangle right away. The other two forwards are sprinting back through the inside of the dot lines to hold our defensive shape and be ready in the transition triangle if we can turn on offence. They also sprint all the way back as we need them to pick up second-layer pass defending.

The potential for offense on a turnover on entry denial is tremendous. The numbers of chances generated and goals scored on turnovers on the blue line is staggering. While we desperately want to keep the puck in the offensive zone once we get there, or track the puck and capitalize quickly on a re-entry situation, if we miss both of those opportunities but can get organized in a transition triangle to force the rush into a turnover at our blue line, there still is a tremendous offensive opportunity.

I use the term "transition triangles" because I want to connect the player's mind to associate a shape to an action.

In rush-entry denial, just like the offensive zone, it is two triangles connected by a single player. The roles of these triangles change depending on the location of the puck. All the roles and positions in the triangles are interchangeable.

Some examples of common role changes in recurring situations: A defenseman activates and the puck turns over when they are in the corner, the covering forward is now the weak-side D, the reloading forward is the new F3, the net-front forward is the F2 track and the D who is in the corner is the F1 strip and steal back pressure. Now if we aren't able to control their breakout and they organize a rush against, we have to organize our transition triangles and work our shape and spacing to get the puck back.

Now in working to get the puck, we execute a one-in-and-one-out shape consideration with the strong-side D pressuring for the turnover.

BELFRY OFFENSE

Our F3 back pressure holds the dot line and the strong-side D forces a chip by the puck carrier that F3 recovers. The pressure D could become the F3 middle support, or the weak-side D position being played by the original F3 forward would forward hinge on the pass and skate the puck and become the middle.

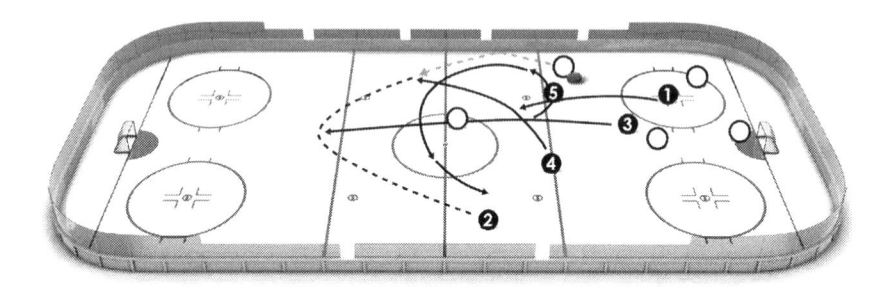

Figure 105:

There is a great clip of this on October 20, 2022 when the Washington Capitals were visiting the Ottawa Senators. In the play, Ottawa is in the offensive zone and Washington gains control of the puck and initiates an exit. Thomas Chabot is the strong-side D and pinches down forcing the chip out. The weak-side D, Artyom Zub, swings over and makes contact on the slash support forward, Lars Eller. This creates a loose puck situation for the back pressure forward who picks up the puck. Now in transition, Drake Batherson, the back pressure forward passes to Josh Norris on the weak side. In transition, the third player back is Chabot, so he becomes the center in transition and swings through the middle of the ice to provide middle support to Norris. Norris finds him in the middle of the ice and Chabot has a speed differential he leverages into the 1v1 and beats the defensemen to generate a shot. Just a brilliant example of the interchange of these roles. [23]

---

[23] Becoming the Center Chabot https://twitter.com/belfryhockey/status/1660411296536297475?s=20

These positions are interchangeable and players move to maintain the integrity of the shape. They react in transition to quickly organize a rush entry. We need to capitalize on the rush denial spacing from the transition. If we attack quickly, we can push the spacing even further apart between their D and their forwards and that represents opportunity to change sides of the ice with the puck easily. We can also isolate the defenders into two 2v1s. The chance quality potential is exponentially better without back pressure dictating the time, the offense can play on their time, not on the defense's time.

RETRIEVALS

In the interconnected game model, like every other major game situation we've covered so far, the consistent success of our retrievals will be reliant upon the consistency and commitment to the work we do in rush-entry denial. To consistently force a dump-in, our D need to feel comfortable to leverage a tight gap that encourages the opponent to send the puck in. In order for our D to feel comfortable in a tight gap, we have to have hard back pressure they can rely on. Now once the puck is sent in, we want to be as "quick to 3" as possible. A retrieval by definition is transition, and in any transition, time is of the essence. We need to be quick to be organized and decisive in execution before the forecheck can get organized.

Teams organize their forecheck any number of ways, but by and large, forechecking is about cutting the ice in half, having a good F1 to steer and/or pressure the puck, inviting the puck into small area, don't allow more than one player to get trapped or beat at any one time, forcing the puck and the player to come to a stop (effectively stalling the puck and forcing the retrieval team to stop) and creating a turnover that can lead to transition offense. Any offensive zone forecheck is about advancing the puck into their offensive zone with a coordinated plan to get the puck back and use the transition advantage to create scoring chances. If this is forechecking, then retrievals must be: creating access to both sides of the rink, beating F1, alleviating pressure on the puck, beating/trapping more than one forechecker, keeping the puck and our players in motion and moving the puck into big areas to advance the puck out of the zone just as fast as it came in.

One of the more misleading depictions of retrievals is that the bulk of the responsibility to escape the pressure and make the exit play is on the retrieving D or the player getting first touch. I think this is not at all representative of what is most frequent. Compounding this assertion is every night in the NHL we will see a clip of Cale Makar, Miro Heiskanen or a number of unbelievable skating defensemen with a ridiculous self-skating breakout on a retrieval. That end-to-end clip starts trending on social media and the idea that defensemen need to carry the bulk of the retrieval responsibility perpetuates. When you dig into all the retrievals of these D in a five- or 10-game stretch, you see that the ridiculous self-breakout on a retrieval is actually a low-frequency event, maybe once or twice a game they may find themselves into a play that they can create daylight and execute a self-skating breakout. The highest-frequency event on a retrieval is actually a play where they pull F1 in one direction and execute a bump off their heels to their support, trapping F1. I just don't view retrievals as one player's primary responsibility and don't train it like that anymore, I view it as a five-man responsibility with two triangle shapes, a quick to 3 and a transition triangle.

On the retrieval, the number one thing I'm concerned about is getting "quick to 3," I want the puck carrier supported. Now there are a number of ways you can set up the three, you can stack them, you can wing them, you can do whatever you want with them, but you need to have three at the puck as quick as possible. The most likely play under pressure is a bump off the checkers heels, so offering that option will open up other escape options.

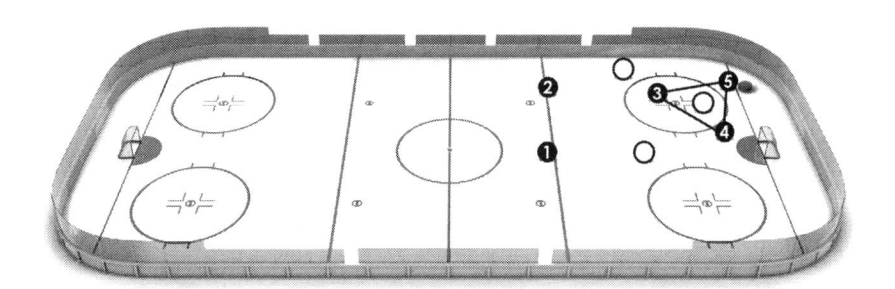

Figure 106: Quick to 3

If our rush-entry denial habits are good, then we will have an opportunity to cut off their F1 and perhaps their F2 on their way to their forecheck

BELFRY OFFENSE

responsibilities to buy enough time for our first touch to get a favorable first play on the puck. Like any loose-puck play, first touch is critical. A favorable play at the puck is a first touch before contact, a chance to change speeds, an ability to manipulate their skates to provide false information on F1 and effectively trap F1, a play made before their F1 is in the contact space or a chance to get the back of the net uncontested. The result of our "quick to 3" has to be two immediate pass options. The forecheck is unlikely to bring three players to that first touch, so we should initially outnumber F1 and maybe F2 on the first touch. If the first touch is quickly and properly supported and we can beat F1.

The exit play, in most situations, is on the second touch. The first touch beats/traps their F1, the second touch makes the play that is most frequently the one that leads to the exit. This is why I think we miss an opportunity when we place so much responsibility on our first touch. Yes, of course, the first touch is really important, but the first touch doesn't shoulder all the responsibility. If the second touch is most frequency the one that sets the exit, then that's just as important. Retrievals for me are a group exercise, when the puck is dumped in, we have two triangles. A primary triangle at the puck (quick to 3) and then the transition triangle which are our exit options.

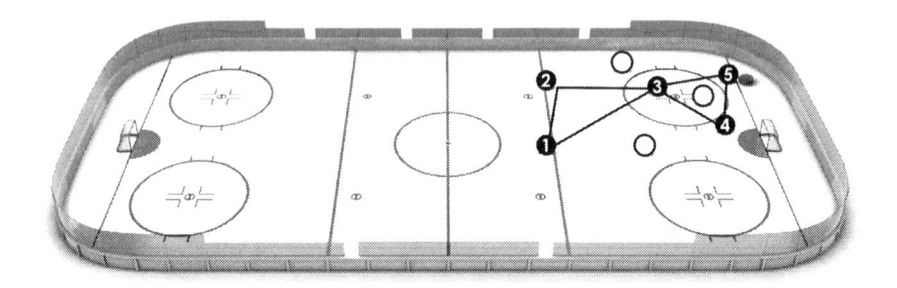

Figure 107: Primary Quick to 3 to Transition Triangle

There is a great example in a game this season when the Kings Los Angeles were playing in Colorado. Los Angeles rims an entry and sends

Devon Toews back for a corner puck retrieval with the puck tight to the wall. Los Angeles F1 is Anze Kopitar who cuts off the back of the net play to Makar. Their F2 is Adrian Kempe, who is one of my favorite players in the NHL, he takes away a forehand wall rim for Toews, but because Nathan MacKinnon is back to create a quick to 3, Toews has a quick bump to the middle to MacKinnon who is in perfect position and they easily beat the two Los Angeles forechecking forwards The Los Angeles F3 is low on the weak-side dot line, with the speed MacKinnon has and no immediate F3, Los Angeles concedes the neutral zone and an easy entry.[24]

There are some interesting things you can do when you view the triangles in this way. The primary triangle beats F1, the second touch gets it to the transition triangle and sets up our exit. The cleaner you can exit, the better chance you have of getting through the neutral zone quickly and your exit leads to entry. When you view it this way, you would track it and build your metrics in a sequence and not in isolated events. The ideal objective of a retrieval is possession exits leading to possession entries that lead to a shot. Now there are any number of results that can occur in that sequence and tracking those in the sequence order gives us a clear event (sequence model) frequency metric. How often do these different event sequences occur and at what success rate? I also want to know who (the players), frequency and success rate of first and second touch. These are elements inside the tracking sequence. Over time, we will get to know the context of contribution and role frequency. We also know where in the sequence it is breaking down and that'll give us more specific clips to review to determine exactly why and what we need to do to improve.

Handling the retrieval to exit cleanly and consistently opens up some more interesting exit to entry options. For example, if we are comfortable that we can beat and trap F1 consistently and we can get our second

---

[24] Retrieval Quick to 3 Colorado: https://twitter.com/belfryhockey/status/1660412595650670592?s=20

touch to be in a good position to make the next play, we can stretch the high forwards out of the zone and begin the process of stretching their forecheck shape at the seams. If we can stretch our high forwards under control of the puck with our second touch, then we can get really long on our opponent and dramatically elevate the risk they have in keeping their D aggressive in the offensive zone for pinch situations. Now instead of holding the blue line or pinching down on our board plays, they are flying out of the zone to defend our stretch threat, then we can control their forecheck support. We also stretch their transition support, so even if they are able to force a turnover, their transition space is too big. We could also stretch our high forwards for the purpose of setting the attack space in the neutral zone and bumping to speed coming behind.

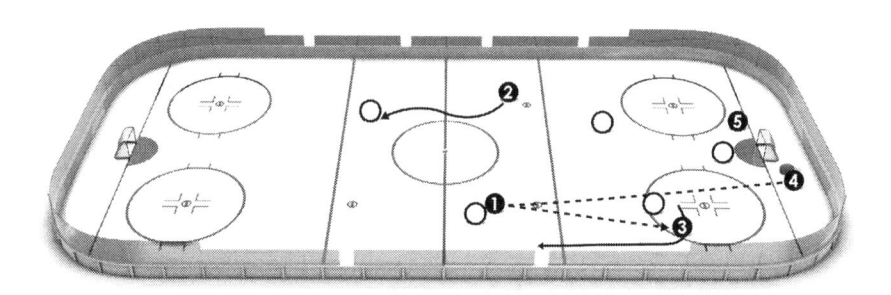

Figure 108:

There is a great example of this in the February 15, 2023 game where the Detroit Red Wings are in Edmonton. In the third period, the score is 4-4 with under eight minutes to go in regulation time. Detroit gets a retrieval where the first touch takes the back of the net and invites Edmonton to settle into a 1-2-2. To start the play, the Detroit superstar centerman Dylan Larkin opens up on the half-wall as an option. Then the Detroit defensemen steps out from behind the net on the same side as Larkin's support and sends a long pass up the middle to the stretch forward who has "fronted" the Edmonton defenseman. "Fronting the defender" means the offensive player threatens to get behind the defender to push him back on the stretch, but then gets directly in front of the defender, so the defender is on his back. Now when the puck is set the stretch, he is fronting the D and has the body position to bump it back to the next layer of speed. Now the fronted stretch man just bumps it back to Larkin who continued his speed and picks the puck up with a massive speed differential in the neutral zone. The defenseman who was fronted by the stretch is pre-occupied with the stretch and is in no position to then defend Larkin, so Larkin sprints right by. While all this is going on, Tyler Bertuzzi is on the weak side of the play and reads the stretch to bump play on the opposite side and sprints to join the play. Upon entry, Larkin and Bertuzzi are on a long 2v1 that they turn into a grade-A scoring chance with a one-knee, one-timer shot on a great pass from Larkin to Bertuzzi. From first touch on the retrieval to shot on goal, a clean 10 seconds. [25]

There is another great example, November 6, 2022 in a game between Detroit visiting the New York Rangers. In this game, halfway in the first period, the Rangers are on a retrieval under moderate pressure from Detroit. On first touch, the Rangers D rims the puck to the weak side to the quick to 3 low forward. The low forward invites the pressure to him and bumps it back to the original retrieving defenseman. The defenseman passes it in front his net to an open partner who then stretches the puck to a posted winger who fronts the defenseman. The posted winger then bumps the puck to the underneath speed. The speed differential leads to a scoring chance. [26]

These types of plays are more and more available when you have confidence in your quick to 3 to beat one or two forecheckers. Then the two high forwards can pull the opposition's D out of the zone and create a speed runway underneath.

Regardless of the plays we'd like to explore, it starts with execution inside that primary triangle with the first touch and second play. Without

---

[25] Detroit Stretch Speed: *https://twitter.com/belfryhockey/status/1660413498579382272?s=20*

[26] NYR Stretch Speed: *https://twitter.com/belfryhockey/status/1660413967385108482?s=20*

that, we aren't going to have the exit confidence to beat the forecheck consistency. Without exit confidence to beat the forecheck, we will be more likely to want to "just get it out" which will lead to re-entries against. We want to limit our time in our defensive zone, so we need to be able to beat the forecheck consistently.

When I look at retrievals, I prefer to have my "quick to 3" tight and on the same side of the ice. I like my weak-side D or net player to be on the inside or "front post." I think the options presented by "front post" support offer the most solutions for the retrieval.

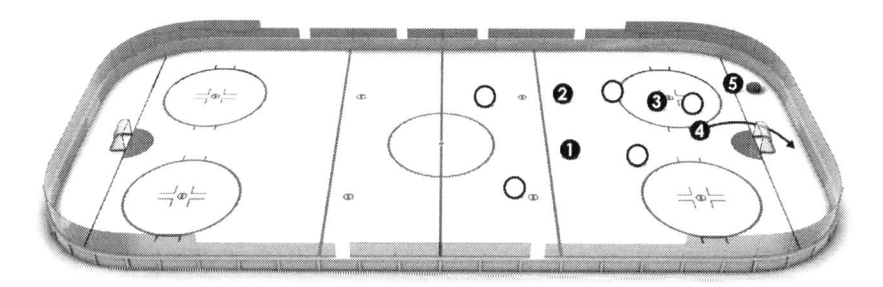

Figure 109: Front Post

I did a study of the 2019 Stanley Cup champion St. Louis Blues, specifically watching Alex Pietrangelo and Colton Parayko's shifts in the final vs Boston. The original reason for the study was I wanted to know more about the utility of the weak-side D on both teams. The Pietrangelo and Parayko pairing was especially proficient in both their ability to influence the game at the weak-side D. Not unlike every other study I've done, I started tracking and studying one thing, and in the course of that study, something else pops up that causes a pause and start again for further exploration. What jumped out was how frequently they "bumped the puck" to the weak-side D on the front post in retrievals, breakouts and defensive zone faceoff plays. It was so pronounced, I went back and tracked both teams' instances and pulled the video to take a deeper look.

There are many clips, one of which was in Game 1 with 9:26 left in the second with St. Louis up 2-1. St. Louis dumped the puck in and sent Boston into a retrieval. What I like about this clip is the commitment of the Boston D to get to the front post. The play was a cross dump from St. Louis, so the original strong-side D, who was on the dot line when the puck dumped in, he sprinted to the near post of the puck. The puck was a difficult puck to pick up for the D, who was picking it up on his backhand. He sent the puck to the front post and the front-post D escaped the pressure and found the middle for the exit inside their quick to 3. If you follow the exit, you see the retrieval D joins the rush and leads the rush on entry. This is fantastic clip example of the utility of the front post on retrieval but also how committed Boston is to its retrieval to exit to entry habits. [27]

While I prefer front-post support, and I feel like the weak-side D supporting the play on the "back post" and falls off the net, the next play can be harder, this is not to say I don't want to see any back-post support. I just want to see the front post much more frequently. Then when the D decide to use more of a spread exit, it becomes more impactful.

In the rush-entry denial section, I mentioned the value of a "goalie first touch." In retrievals, we love a goalie first touch. There are two main values to a goalie first touch that impact our ability to breakout vs the forecheck:

1. The goalie can stop the puck behind the net and the first touch of our defenseman is protected behind the net. This is important because now we can breakout more on our time and not on the forecheck's time. Depending on the game situation (time and score), the opposition may need to be more aggressive in their forecheck, and a goalie first touch where they stop the puck behind our net for our defensemen, we may see the opponent look to flush the puck out

---

[27] 2019 Boston vs St Louis D Front Post: *https://twitter.com/belfryhockey/status/1689676985449029644?s=20*

BELFRY OFFENSE

and pressure behind the net, this inherently beats F1 and that pushes our first defense touch to effectively be the second touch which can lead directly to exit. The entire first touch play of the retrieval is protected by the net.

a. We can take control of the time, the opponent will have a harder time putting pressure on the first touch.

b. The opponents F1 may chase behind the net.

c. On close goalie-to-player hand-offs, the goalie can set a pick or screen for our player on their F1.

d. The goalie settles the puck and pulls it off the wall for our D to pick it up, so the collection is much cleaner.

e. The goalie and our "quick to 3" makes our first touch a 4v1 or a 4v2, we will potentially have at least two and sometimes three direct and unchecked options or the first pass or second touch.

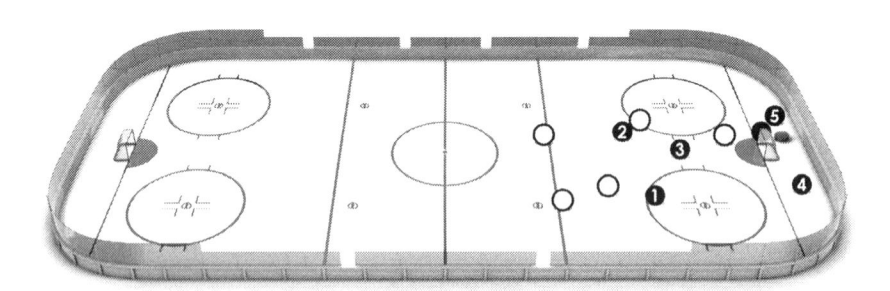

Figure 110:

2. The location of the forecheck is now undetermined until the goalie makes a play. On a forecheck that the goalie doesn't get a touch on it, the forecheck can anticipate where the puck will end up and organize its forecheck immediately on that anticipated location. When the goalie gets the first touch, the goalie could hold the puck behind the net for a hand-off to their defensemen or first player

back, the goalie could invite F1 deep into the zone and pass the puck on F1's heels effectively beating F1. The goalie could invite F1 deep in the zone and when F1 gets close, then push the puck over to the D, trapping F1 deep in the zone and on the opposite side of the net. The value of when the goalie can make a direct play to one of our "quick to 3" players. They can get a clean touch and their shoulders up the ice. They have a much better situation to make the next play.

The goalie-to-player plays and manipulations of F1 are reliant upon good communication and understanding of the play situation (score, time, ability to get the back of the net, F1 pressure) and being able to execute cleanly. This takes a lot of reps. While there are advantages to a goalie first touch, we have all seen what happens when the goalie to "quick to 3" play fails. It usually ends up as an easy goal for the opposition.

In retrievals we have to keep the main objective in mind, connecting exit to entry as quickly as possible. We want to be transitioning the puck out of our zone just as fast as it came in and get right back on offense.

COVERAGE EXIT TO RUSH ENTRY

The first part of this section, the defending in the defensive zone, admittedly is going to be a "fly by" of defensive details. Out of the entire book, this section is far and away the most difficult. The problem is there is an entire book that can be written on the defensive zone tactics and skill details alone. I've struggled with how much to dig into here. In writing and rewriting this section many times, I found myself diving head-first down the rabbit hole and the actual "exit-to-rush entry" part was very nearly never to be heard from again. What I've landed on is to acknowledge that there is a lot of detail missing here, but feel I can try to give the important details that relate to the actual puck acquisition and keep the focus on the transition aspect of exit-to-rush Entry. With the disclaimer now in place, let's get into it.

The coverage exit means we are starting without the puck in our defensive zone and we have to defend to get the puck back before we can exit. I view defensive zone coverage to exit the same way as the offensive zone, only instead of offense to defense, it applies defense to offense. Positionally, this is two triangles for me. A primary defensive triangle at the puck and a transition triangle. These roles change for the player depending on where the puck moves to. The understanding of what your role is and what triangle you are really part of as the puck moves and the conditions change is the most critical aspect of the positional discipline we will need to defend well enough to win the puck back and transition.

COVERAGE EXIT TO RUSH ENTRY

Return to the Defensive Zone

BELFRY DEFENSIVE ZONE

ZONE CONTROL = COMPRESS SHAPE X HABITS + PERCENTAGES

Figure 111: Defensive Zone Equation

The return to the defensive zone sounds straightforward, and it largely is ... but it has some nuances that are important. The straightforward part of it is we want to come back to our "house" with urgency of purpose and getting tight. We want to get tight and protect the middle of the ice as the first priority. Which again sounds straightforward. The practical application of that of course is nuanced. You aren't going to leave pressure on the puck to sprint back to the crease, or are you? We have a defensive shape we want to get to quickly, but when? What about the puck carrier? How do we move together to compress the space? Have we seen enough examples of the dangers of over-backchecking and leaving players wide open move and make plays to. So the answer is straightforward, we want zone control and to accomplish that we use the equation:

Compress Shape = Habits + Percentages

However, we have to work through some of the nuances to get it just right. What is the answer to the nuanced pressure on the puck, while getting to our shape, while protecting the middle ice? A big part of the answer for me is in the failed rush defense.

How did we get in the defensive zone in the first place? The premise of the interconnected game model is to do our work up the ice to get the puck back before a possession rush against becomes a problem. A possession entry against means mistakes were made in the offensive zone and in the neutral zone, so a possession rush against is technically a defensive recovery. We are coming back to the defensive zone, not defending the rush, but recovering our defensive position. This perspective change really helped me understand what I really want in terms of a return to the defensive zone.

DEFENSIVE ZONE LOGIC

SHAPE INTEGRITY = HABITS X PERCENTAGES

ROLE CHANGES

ANTICIPATION   AUTOMATION

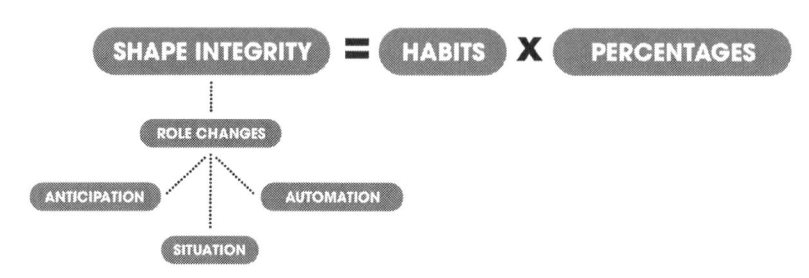

SITUATION

Figure 112:

When we return to the defensive zone, we need to accomplish the following objective tree:

- Deflect the puck out of the middle of the ice as soon as possible, do everything possible not to give up interior shots.
- Recover our shape.
- Outnumber in the middle of the ice as quickly as we can.
- Leverage our shape to compress the space.
- Use the compressed space to create an engagement trigger.
- Jump on the engagement trigger to get into transition quickly or force the puck to come to a stop.

The mindset is active patience. We aren't running around, we recognize our place in the shape and we start there. We support the initial pressure on the puck and we try to leverage our shape to contain the puck, so we can compress the space. Once the space is compressed, we anticipate an engagement trigger (puck carrier turns their back on the play, there is a bobble or a loose puck) then we jump on the engagement trigger to either get to the transition triangle or get the puck stopped and give us a chance to compete for transition.

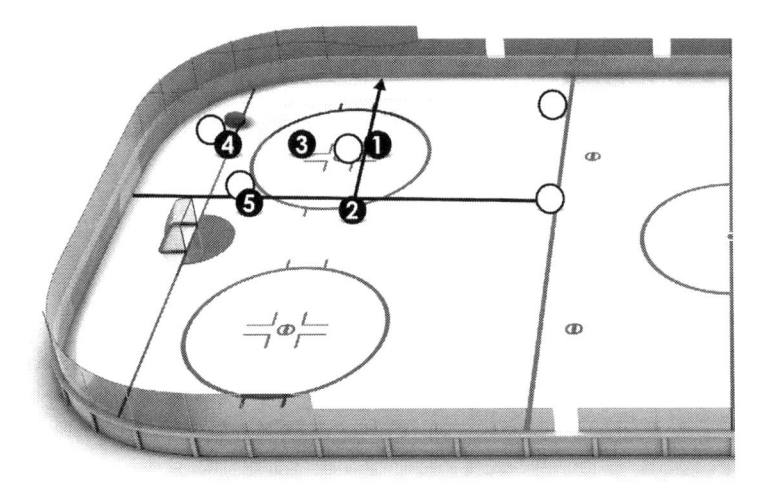

Figure 113:

The bottom line is I don't want to give up interior shots, and I want to connect an exit to an entry as much as possible. The defensive zone offence if executed well should lead us into the neutral zone with a chance to create a strong entry. We have to get the puck back, but be ready to activate as a group once we do.

There is an entire book to write on the details of defending in the defensive zone, so I'm not going to get too detailed in the defensive zone defending skills. I'll highlight a few of the most important aspects of defending while I keep the focus on initiating an attack. However, just like when we were in the offensive zone, you can't discuss initiating an attack from the defensive zone without first talking about how you are going to get the puck back. The way the book is designed is to focus on shape, habits and percentages, so that's where I'll center the discussion. However, know that there is a lot of detail still left to mine, just not in this book.

Defensive Shape

The defensive shape is essentially, two triangles connected in the middle. Commonly referred to as "5 on a dice." This is how it starts:

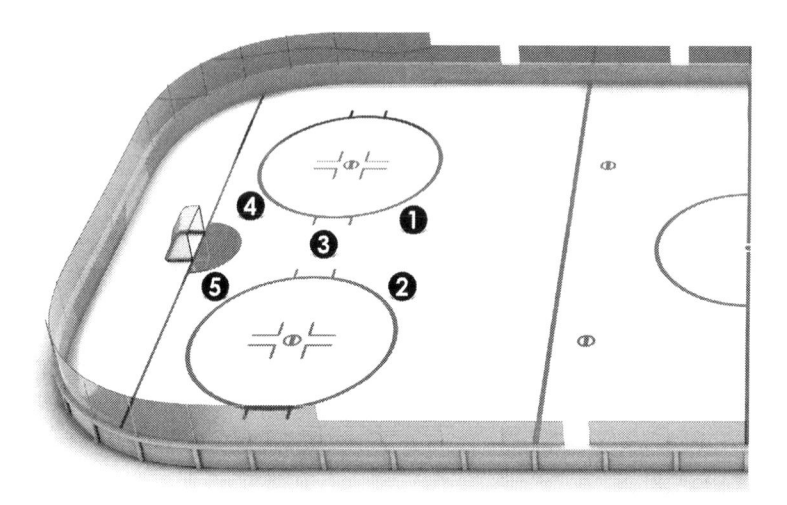

Figure 114: 5 on a Dice

When the puck is in the corner, this is an opportunity to compress the space, but we have to be clear on where the triggers are, what we are willing to concede and what we are not. The biggest difference in the game now versus a few years ago is a few years ago there was a big effort for the winger to "cut off the top," and now you just can't have your strong-side winger trapped on the wall. The bottom line is once we have the puck in either of the corners, we are organizing to get the play stalled and to get the back and look to organize and exit.

One of my favorite defensive plays is to get inside position on the puck in all points of our primary defensive triangle.

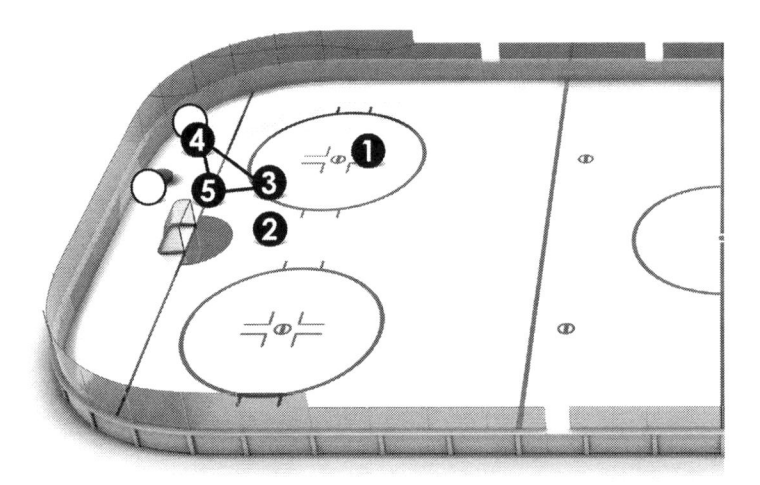

Figure 115: Playing inside the puck

This is a good example of a defensive concept of playing inside the puck. Working in the corner to win wedge body position and insulate the puck to get off the wall.

To get there with this, the first order of business on this section is to reconcile that all three low positions are truly interchangeable. When I say truly interchangeable, I mean that both defensively and in transition. Defensively, we are all there, we all want the low forward to be defensively competitive, have a great stick, force stops, work in tandem with the corner defensemen, when two D go to the corner the low forward holds the net front, all that stuff. We are all there on that. What I don't see as much of is the D becoming the center in exit transition and joining the rush. That seems like the best place to start rolling up our sleeves on this section.

As the defending shell game is going in in the corner and the center the corner defender and the weak-side defender are all engaged in defending to get the puck, when the puck turns, whomever is furthest up ice is the center. We have to reconcile this to be automatic. Otherwise, we will most often struggle to get numbers in the rush. We will attack in 1s and 2s and in 3s when the puck turns over in an advantageous position for the low forward to be able to join.

This is why playing center in the NHL is so difficult, because it takes a tremendous amount of speed, determination and transition reads to be a consistent factor on rushes that originate deep in the defensive zone. If we can agree on the assertion that if you want to win in the NHL playoffs, you will have to have a great low offense game. Usually starts with a great forecheck and then the forecheck becomes a heavy offensive zone back wall dominant game. Now our low forward, often the center, is competing down low against an elite forecheck to offensive zone back wall juggernaut team. When we win the puck and the play turns over, upon exit, the low forward is 30-50 feet behind the exit play. Now you add no real delay game to speak of because the back pressure is so committed and intense, getting into the rush and being a factor as the low forward is incredibly challenging.

Now, if it challenging for the low forward to consistently get into the rush because they are often 30-50 feet behind the exit play due to the back wall and corner nature of the defending, then how do we get meaningful numbers on the rush consistently? We activate the weak-side D, right? Well, kind of. For me, it's not about activating the weak-side D as much as its activating whomever is highest of our low defensive triangle. The term I use is the D becomes the center. The role of the net-front defender, whomever that is, depending on the rotations and situation automatically is the center. So any puck that goes from the corner to the high forwards, that net-front player "becomes the C." I phase the role as anytime there are two of our players below the goal line, you are the center and you play as the center throughout the exit to entry sequence. This player is sprinting the neutral zone, filling lanes and understands entries. Or do they?

COVERAGE EXIT TO RUSH ENTRY

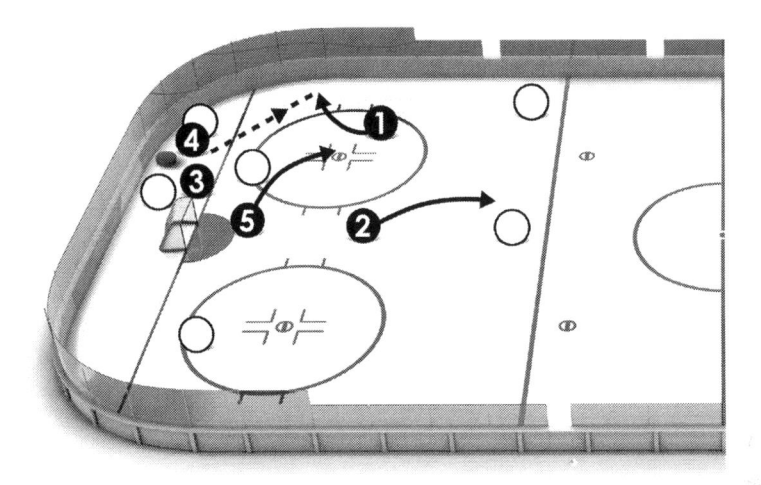

Figure 116:

This is a player development and a coaching challenge. How many reps in practice or training does your D take where they are leading the rush? Now when they don't do it well, they miss assignments or turn pucks over for poor decision-making, we can accuse them of not having good enough "hockey IQ," or we can recognize that we may not have given them a fair chance to develop this in their game. We need the D to be comfortable on the rush because we need more numbers on the rush. Developing defensemen with offensive rush skills has to become a priority because it's too much to ask the center to consistently make up 30-50 feet of space to even become factor on the rush entry.

The transition triangle in the defensive zone initially consists of the player who has the puck (could be either of the two D or the low forward) and the two high forwards. Now once the puck gets to the high forwards, the exit triangle shifts, it's no longer the puck carrier and the two high forwards, it's the puck carrier and two players on the weak side.

BELFRY OFFENSE

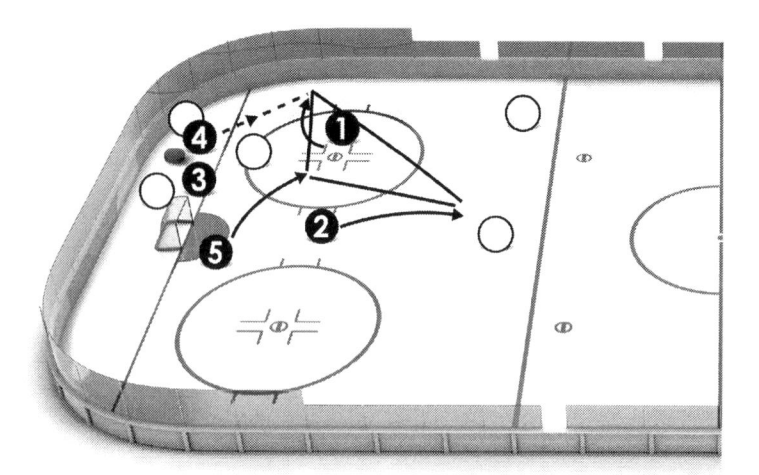

Figure 117:

I go back to what we said in the offensive zone play. When you have an isolation versus a low forward, we need to take him on and challenge him defensively. Not just challenge them defensively because we know no matter how good they are as a defensive forward, they aren't a defenseman and often that can mean getting better offensive chances by recognizing, isolating and taking them on, but also because the more we engage the low forward defensively the more unlikely it will be that he can become a consistent factor in transition rushes against that originate deep in the zone. If the opponent doesn't have a consistent activation strategy of the highest low defender in the rush, they will attack with a high percentage of rushes with just two attackers in the neutral zone. This becomes significant if we trace back the interconnected game model in the offensive zone.

In our interconnected game model in the offensive zone, our priority is to get the puck back before the rush against gets organized (speed, numbers, routes). If the opposition has to use their board side high forward on the breakout and that leaves them with the weak-side winger. If they don't jump the highest low defender in the play in a timely fashion, we have a 1v2 vs a forward on an island. With this situation, we are going to get the puck back a lot and sustain offensive zone game control.

COVERAGE EXIT TO RUSH ENTRY

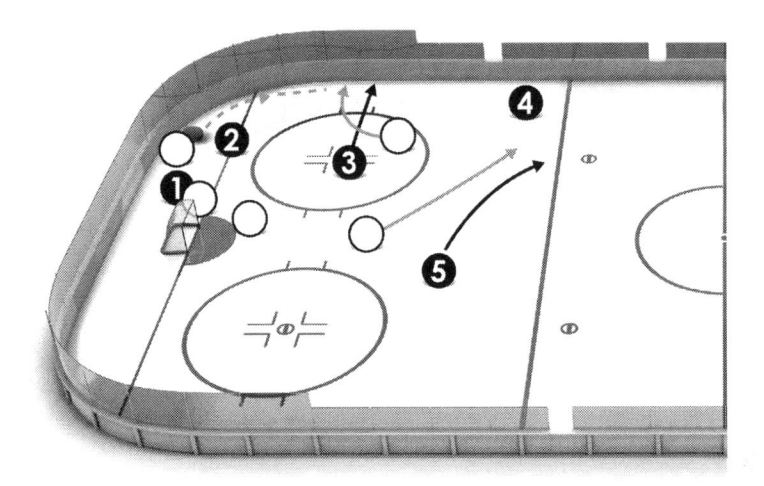

Figure 118:

The reason the triangle changes once the puck gets to the high forward and includes the players on the weak side is due to the premium I place on a control exit that beats the tracker and gets the puck in the middle of the ice or in side change. I can only assume that every coach is thinking the same as I am in terms of how hard he wants his team to track the puck and back pressure to get the puck back quickly, and I know how much I want the puck to stay on one side, so I can alienate the puck carrier and get the puck back. I have to assume every coach is thinking similarly, and if that's the case, then we have to solve the tracker.

One of my longest and best clients is Kyle Okposo, captain of the Buffalo Sabres. I started working with Kyle when we was playing for the New York Islanders. When Kyle was with the Islanders, he was playing top-line minutes with John Tavares and developed a very nice offensive game that took advantage of his strengths. In his time in Buffalo, the challenge was to just get into the offensive zone in the first place. The Sabres went through a rebuild and Kyle's game was tangled up in that. Now the offensive zone time was chopped almost in a third almost immediately. The defensive zone play was long and with few

247

BELFRY OFFENSE

rush situations where he was getting a pass in flight. The reality of the situation was the touches he was getting were mostly DZ touches that were either rims or contested loose pucks. Not ideal to get out of the defensive zone with possession much less get organize consistent rush chances. In order to find his way through, he had to commit to becoming elite on the defensive zone wall. The process to becoming elite was a wonderful journey for both of us.

To start, he had to resign himself to the fact that the majority of the pucks he was going to have a play on were going to be extremely difficult to make a play with. He was getting a steady dose of rims to the weak side, shoveled pucks up the strong-side wall with a pinching D or an F3 all over him, contested loose pucks and blocked shots to recover. Many of which would be later in the shift and his linemates would be looking to get off rather than orchestrate a counter attack on the rush. With all this stacked against him, the game doesn't care about what's fair. It's up to Kyle to figure it out.

After coming to terms that these were going to be the majority of the pucks, next he needs to figure out which pucks were ones he could make a play on and which ones he had to just get it out. Determining the difference was a big step. The only thing worse than chipping out a playable puck is trying to do something with a puck that you just need to chip out and turning it over in the defensive zone. This was a first step towards playing the percentages. What I didn't understand until I engaged deeply into this process with Kyle was the percentages for one player are different than the percentages for another. As a player, there are things you can do to improve your percentages on pucks that would be unplayable for most other players. This is the leveraging of good habits. Which begs the question, what are the good habits for a high forward in the defensive zone?

The success habits of a high forward in the defensive zone are as follows:

Before you even start...

COVERAGE EXIT TO RUSH ENTRY

1. Start in the right position.

The game is too fast to start out of position and expect to be able to make consistent plays. There just isn't a consistent substitute for being out of position. Positional discipline is of outmost importance.

2. Anticipate role changes as the puck moves to maintain good positioning.

Once you are in good position, anticipate how that positioning will change with the movement of the puck and the opposition. Anticipating role change as the puck moves allows you to make better positional decisions and movements to stay in the right spot.

3. A smart stick, in the right place for the situation.

In the defensive zone, the puck is going to come through seams either intentionally or getting knocked, having the stick on the ice and in the right lane is important. Many good possessions will come from pass intercepts or deflected passes that come to you. This is especially true for when you are on the weak side. Many of Kyle's best exits come from when he's on the weak side. Knowing this is a high possibility and being engaged and ready for them when they come can save a lot of unnecessary time in the defensive zone.

4. Body position allows quick response movement.

Skate positional discipline is another key aspect. Skate position allows you to react quickly. So many loose pucks and contested pucks are going to be won by a half a step, a half a step you can find by being in the right position with your skates facing the right way. For example, when you are on the strong side and the puck is in the corner, your feet should be facing the wall, perpendicular to the wall, which will allow you to move and react quicker. Your head is on a swivel, but your hips and skates are

BELFRY OFFENSE

facing the wall. The strong-side defensive forward runs into trouble the most when his skates are facing the puck in the corner. This reduces vision and awareness of where the strong-side, potentially-pinching D is, and also players whose feet are facing the corner will likely drift to the corner, unwittingly moving out of position.

Habits on the play at a contested puck...

5. Body position first.

Win the puck line first, then make the puck play.

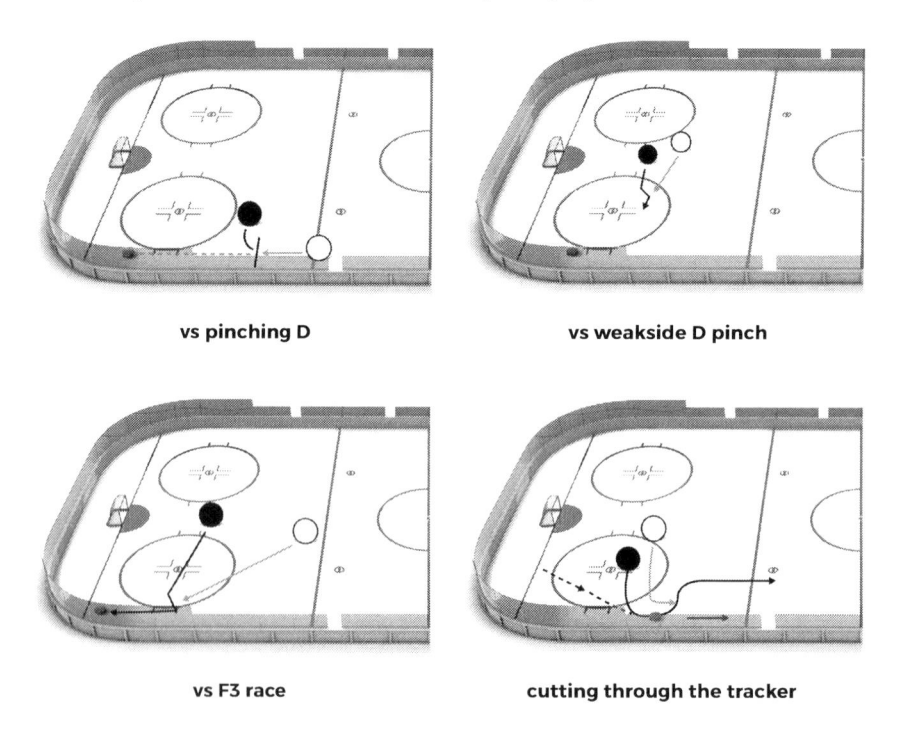

vs pinching D   vs weakside D pinch

vs F3 race   cutting through the tracker

In all these scenarios, the commonality is winning the puck line translates to the ability to cut the hands and get the check on your back to protection the puck.

Winning the puck line is critical to protecting the puck, it allows you to take momentary control of time.

6. Protection paves the way to patience.

The immediate threat determines the direction the protection time is going to be. If it's a pinching D, then the protection time is going to be going back toward the goal line. If it's the tracking forward, then the protection time is going to be in a cut off or cut under. If the pressure is coming from underneath, then the protection time is up toward the blue line. Once you leverage protection and have momentary control of time, this allows the options to reveal themselves.

7. Patience paves the way to plays.

The poised plays that come from the opportunity to be patient. Patience is being able to make the play on your time When you are making a play on the defender's time is a big part of how the forecheck forces turnovers.

Where are the plays?

In the defensive zone on the strong-side wall, there are generally three plays to make.

1. The most common play is to find the other high forward, often in slash support or holding wide width in the NZ to change sides. This can coincide with the strong-side forward cutting the hands of the tracker. This strong-side forward is moving forwards out of the zone. Many times, the strong-side forward is making a play through the tracker or the forward skating defender to find their other high forward.
2. The weak-side D position. This is where the net-front defender can jump up the ice and provide a weak-side option. Often a play where the strong-side forward has body position on a check coming down on him and he gets the check on his back and passes to an activating weak-side D. The other way is he starts moving forward toward the

blue line and to beat the tracker, either stops or makes a quick cut under to make a play underneath the tracker.
3. Side change out the back. This is where the winger is moving toward his own goal line and moves the puck behind the net to the weak side of the ice.

The right play reveals itself once you take control of time. Kyle Okposo, when he became world class on the DZ wall, what followed was a clear relationship to problem solving a defensive puck and making a play that improved the conditions of the puck and a subsequent second possession in the offensive zone in the same possession sequence. There is a clear link between the forward making the exit play and the puck following him around. With this understanding and clear relationship, Kyle was able to convert his strong defensive zone play into offensive zone touches. His influence over the game and ability to transport the puck from the defensive zone and into the offensive zone through multiple puck touches became a leverage-able game performance asset.

I first discovered this relationship in my work with Patrick Kane. The relationship though was his use of the weak-side D. Patrick is a left shot winger who plays primarily on the right side. His defensive zone touches are his forehand when going back toward his own net and backhand when going toward the blue line. Patrick would get body position on the pinching D and snap a pass to the weak-side D and initiate the rush. He would often turn up and sprint the neutral zone and join the rush and get it back on a cross-ice play and would now control the entry. Then of course, he would likely find the weak side of the ice after entry in a pull up or inside cut play, then get it back in the offensive zone. By making a play in the DZ to the weak-side D, he would convert that into three possessions in the same sequence. We know the more frequently a player gets the puck in the same sequence, the quality of the possession conditions improve with each possession. With three puck touches in succession in all three zones with three side changes, the puck he would get in the offensive zone was right in his offensive zone wheelhouse, climbing the wall.

Once I noticed this with Kane, I started to track it with other players and study random players in the league and see if the correlation existed for them, or was this just a special player doing special things. The more I looked at it, the more I saw that this is something all high defensive zone forwards should know and understand. By the time the need to work with Kyle Okposo had presented itself, my understanding of how he could connect plays was already solid. Now it was a matter of Kyle figuring out how to use his body and turn it into gaining body position and then leveraging the body position to take momentary control of time.

The other role we need to discuss at length in defensive zone exits is the primary defender. The primary defender has a very difficult task, and depending on the skill set of the puck carrier, it can be a real tall order to be effective. The primary defender's responsibility is to take control of the puck carrier's space. If the primary defender can take control of the puck carrier's space, they can lead them into smaller area and...

1. Force the puck to stop.
2. Pressure the puck carrier to degrade the quality of the puck conditions for the next player.
3. Outright force the puck carrier to turn the puck over.

To do this, the primary defender has to use their body position and stick to lead the puck carrier into small space. Once they have them there, now force them to turn into that small space and move in to contact for puck separation. This requires a lot of good skating skills and the understanding of how pressure influences. A big part of the details of the primary defender is how they use their hands. When to have one hand on the stick, when to have two hands on the stick, how to use cross checks effectively, when to use hand fighting. The list is extensive. When the defender is outside of contact space, but is clearly the primary defender (usually inside a stick length), I want the defender to have one hand on their stick when they have to try to influence the puck carrier on the backhand side, as they are using their stick to "herd," lead, pressure and force the puck carrier into small space. When the puck carrier is moving on their forehand side, then of course I want them to have two hands on their stick. When they get into contact range, I'm not a big "wrap" guy. A wrap is to have one hand on the stick and have it wrapped around the defender on that side and then use your free hand to push the puck carrier in. The wrap can be really effective in controlling the movement of the puck carrier and forcing them to come to a stop. The limiting part is you are susceptible to taking a holding penalty if the puck carrier is insistent on that top-hand side where you have the puck carrier wrapped up. There are also limitations to having your stick trapped around the outside of the puck carrier and your ability to get a self-takeaway. I personally prefer to use pushes and hand fighting with the puck carrier to push them into small space, have two hands on the stick and use cross checks and then move in for wedges and seals once you have the puck carrier stopped. Kobe Bryant has an excellent video on hand fighting in basketball that I loved. [28] In the video, Kobe is talking about defending the ball handler and wanting to press the ball handler's free arm against their own body, which limits their ability to come back to that hand and makes them much easier to defend. In hockey, the control hand of the puck carrier is the top hand, so anytime the defender can knock or press or disrupt that top hand and top-hand elbow, they can force a bobble from the puck carrier. There are many different ways to use hand fighting when defending as the primary defender, the challenge is to be able to do it without reaching or overextending. When you overextend or reach, the puck carrier will spin on you and you'll lose the coverage. The primary defender also needs to know how to close the "doors."

    The doors are the back wall/ We don't want the puck carrier to be able to skate the puck behind the net. Cutting off the back is important to containing the puck in the corner. Working in concert with the other

---

[28] *https://www.instagram.com/reel/CrQsK-KPdme/?igshid=YmMyMTA2M2Y=*

low defenders, sometimes the primary defender can lead the puck carrier into the next defender who is in a better position to exert greater pressure or initiate the contact.

The other door is the half-wall. Trying to force the puck carrier to cut back to the wall, this improves our ability to bring the puck carrier to a stop. Now if he can move it to the top or move it to the bottom, we can at least bring the puck carrier to a stop. In low defending situations, I want the primary low defenders to force the puck carrier into a stop, whether they still have the puck on their stick or not. Finishing that check and forcing the stop breaks the rhythm of the offense. That puck carrier when they try to get back into the play is now a little later than they would have been if we let them just continue on. This delay in reloading into the play applies pressure to the next puck carrier even by just taking one more passing option off the table. These are the little battles we want to cumulate and ultimately lead to quicker possession changes for us in the defensive zone.

The last role in the defensive zone is the weak-side forward. The weak-side forward while defending the interior high slot, the middle point and any activating defensemen on the backside, they are critical to our transition. As I spoke about in the Kyle Okposo example, the most successful area in creating transition for the defensive team was that weak-side position. The weak-side defensive forward has the following considerations:

1. Good positioning in the defensive zone and awareness of priorities. For example, normally the weak-side defensive forward would position themselves on the outside or inside hash marks (depending on the specifics of the defensive zone coverage implemented by the coach) and responsible to have a good stick to deny pucks into the high F3 when in the middle, any cross-seam passes through the slot, to the weak-side offensive defensemen or rotations and activations to the weak side. However, if the primary low defensive triangle can get a stop in the corner, they will look to push the attacker in to the

BELFRY OFFENSE

wall, and the weak-side defender may shade to the corner as the offensive puck support moves more to the wall. This means the weak-side defensive forward has to slide down to the net and protect the net. In the event that a defender gets beat off the wall or the puck moves quickly out of the pile and gets inside our weak side defender, our weak-side defensive forward would cover this area in his absence.

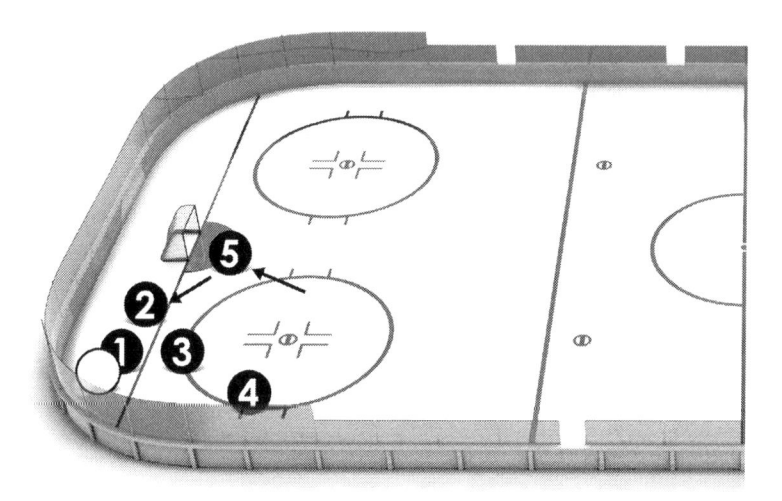

Figure 123:

2. Deciding between slash support and weak-side availability while getting vertical on exit. What I personally prefer is that the weak-side winger would sprint up the ice first (getting vertical) and then slash after the red line, if they are going to slash. I like the weak-side winger to have more of a committed decoy route, where they are primarily looking to push the defensemen back. Once he pushes the defensemen back, then he can slash, to just slash is inviting island play (where the puck carrier doesn't have puck support) on the rush and allows the defensive transition triangle to compress the space in the neutral zone.

COVERAGE EXIT TO RUSH ENTRY

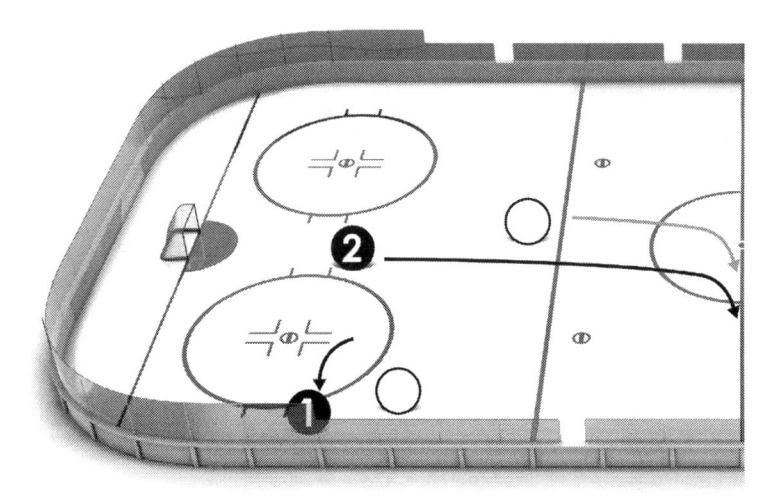

Figure 124:

The better offensive wingers I've worked with say when they are making a play as the strong-side high forward, they prefer the weak-side support to stay wide. They don't like the immediate slash support, because now the play options limit as does the space. They'd like the weak-side forward to clear space for plays underneath the space they create by getting vertical. Once they've got vertical and then they want to come to the puck between the checks, the play has had a fair chance to materialize, and if the puck carrier is still with the puck, then chip it forward. However, the vertical-to-slash skating route has expanded the plays available and that's the job. If they just slash immediately, it compresses the time the weak-side D has to get in the play and draws more people into the puck carrier's space thus reducing the time on the play.

The other advantage of getting vertical first is if the play does go to the weak side, they are pass options that can be used for bump back plays, or they can become a strong-side anchor, they can dip accel to time the entry. There are just too many good reasons for the weak-side forward not to go vertical first in most situations.

3. The anticipation to win weak-side rims. It is critical that the weak-side high forward is ready and anticipating weak-side rim situations. The purpose of a weak-side rim is to open up the ice that's been compressed by the offensive zone forecheck and use the weak side of the ice to alleviate that pressure. If the weak-side defensive forward can anticipate and win those races to the puck, we can draw their weak-side D low in the offensive zone when they don't have the puck and beat that pinch leading to rushes versus forwards defending going backward.

Line Rush For

Once we get a controlled exit, now we need to organize an entry that prioritizes chance generation. Exit to entry to chance generation is the sequence. The earlier you can threaten the middle and/or move the puck through the middle of the ice the higher the probability of chance generation. If we sprint the puck through the neutral zone, create an entry and generate a shot, but stay on the outside the entire time, it's going to be difficult to score. If we can get through the neutral zone and create a side change prior to entry, then get another side change or get into the middle with the puck then we are going to have a chance to generate. All sounds good, how do we do it?

It starts with understanding the strategic areas of the ice.

1. Hot Zone

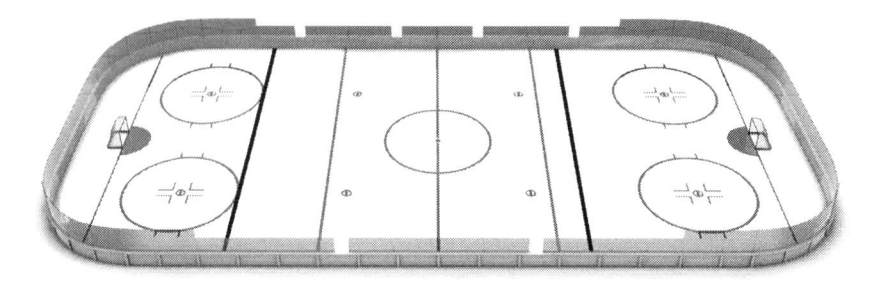

Figure 125: Hot Zone

The hot zone is a term for the extended neutral zone as an area to highlight that the D should be active here. That's why I call it HOT. When I say active, I mean I want the D to get into this area and sprint the middle as F2, or the weak-side dot line as a pull up option for the puck carrier, get on a forward hinge and beat F1, dump the puck and get in on the forecheck or recover a self-chip, fill a lane, be a dot wide catch-and-shoot option, run a ladder play with the anchor, fill a role. What I don't like to see is the defenseman carrying the puck through the neutral zone through to the entry.

Even when a defenseman is world class offensively, there still aren't many situations that when a D is underneath forwards (they have the puck but are the third player on the rush to cross the red line) on the rush where they carry the puck between the blue lines and it is going to lead to a dynamic rush entry chance. We all know D who lead the rush between the blue lines and force the players who are with them to slow down or stop at the offensive blue line. This isn't an elite offensive rushing defenseman for me. This is a defensemen who has an unsophisticated understanding of chance generation and reduces the rush down to whatever they can do on their own. What's worse is when they do this 5-10 times a game only to paint themselves into the corner and in the moment they realize they don't have a personal chance to shoot, they now start to look for someone to pass to and are rattled that their teammates have stopped moving with any sense of purpose. The smart ones just land on the net, waiting for a bad angle throw in once they have no other options. In most team situations, this is a disgusting abuse of leverage and should not be tolerated for a second. If you are an offensive rushing defensemen, learning the hot zone is a critical part of developing true sophistication in your offensive game. This goes back to my assertion that rush-entry development should include the defensemen in all roles to develop fluency. They just don't get enough reps.

BELFRY OFFENSE

2. "2 and 2"

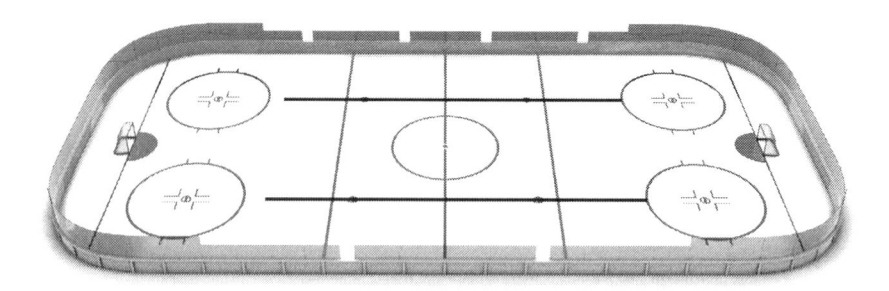

Figure 126: 3 Lanes

When I first started, the rush had three lanes. The two lanes outside the dots and the middle was defined as the the between the dots. This led to a 1-2-3 principle of attack where the No. 1 is the puck carrier and he drives the puck wide, the No. 2 is the middle driver who drives to the net, and the No. 3 is the high forward who over the years we have moved this responsibility around. It went from being "high" wherever that means, then dot wide. The challenge with this is there isn't much in the way of manipulating the D as we sprint straight down the wall and we are fighting against the good back checking rules that most teams would have in place. The two D would play the F1 and the F2 driver and the backchecker would pick up F3. We would have the backchecker sprint back through the center ice dot and then "pick up the trailer."

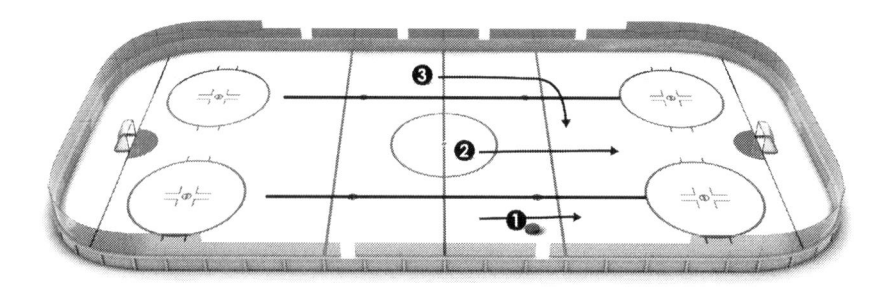

Figure 127:

COVERAGE EXIT TO RUSH ENTRY

Then went to more of a diamond which indicated an expectation that one of the D would be joining the rush. So this is still largely the 1-2-3 principle, but we now want the No. 3 to be dot wide on the weak side and the No. 4 is in the high middle. The diamond was particularly effective for the high production rush delay players. They could pull up and find a threat on the back side of the ice, or they could find the late guy in the middle. The diamond was a good way to test the backchecking rules of the opponent. The backchecker was sprinting through the middle of the ice and our F3 was on the dot line, so that left a window of opportunity to go dot to dot. If the backchecker did a great job of taking this away, then we could find the fourtyh guy late. The need to have a four attacker in the rush was huge, because we can count on the opposition to have one hard backchecking forward, but would they have two? Well, jumping the D in the rush would certainly test this.

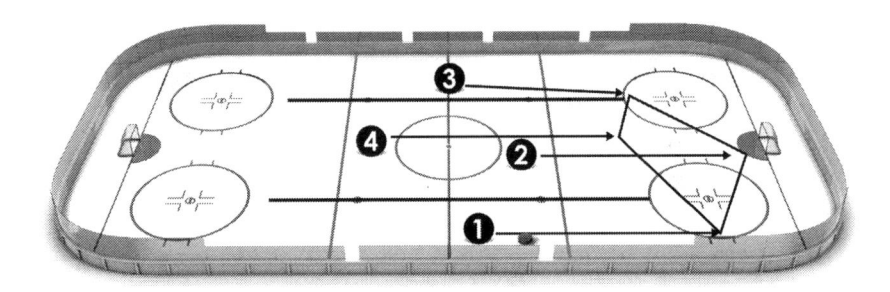

Figure 128: Diamond Entry

Now that brings us to "2 and 2." Is it as simple as we now have four players in the rush, but we only have three lanes? I don't think it's that simple, no. What I like about the "2 and 2," is that it divides the space between the dots in half. Now this is not to have four players in the rush with one in each of now four lanes. This is to describe the interaction between the F1 and F2 forwards in entry philosophy.

261

BELFRY OFFENSE

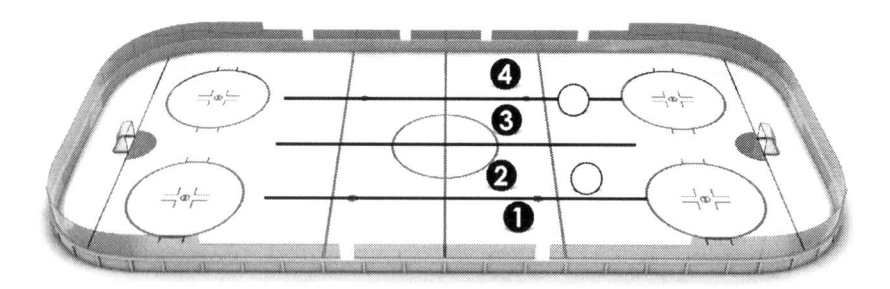

Figure 129: 2 and 2

The entry philosophy is not just to enter wide. We can't be doing that exclusively anymore, we have found great success in being able to enter in the middle or on the dot line. So the four chambers is a way of how we are going to manipulate the defensemen on entry. At some point, we want the entry to be deducted to a 2v1 vs one of the D. This could happen on either side of the ice.

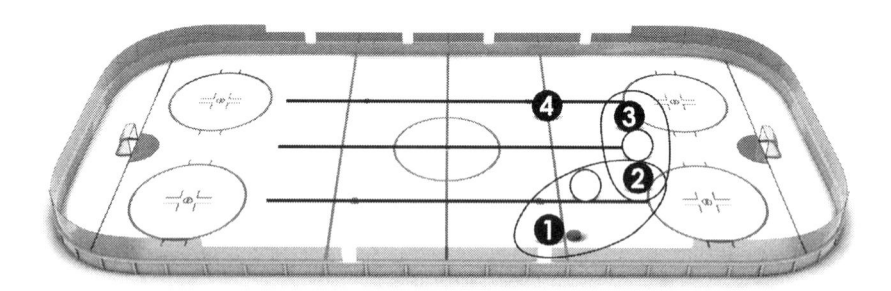

Figure 130: Two 2v1's

This is why it was so important to ensure we are thinking about our entry as we exit. If we don't incorporate how we want to enter into our exit, then our exit will never lead to the entries we want. The entry is dependent upon the exit. If we go slash support right away in the neutral zone and encourage both D to slide over, we are looking at an outside entry most frequently in this situation. Well, that doesn't match the objectives and opportunities of a "4 chamber," where we want to isolate

262

COVERAGE EXIT TO RUSH ENTRY

and manipulate the primary defensive defender. That's why we have to have routes from our exit that set up the entry routes.

3. Dot line

The dot line is a critical ice marking in rush entry. The distance from the dot to the boards is 35 feet. Now defensemen are taught to play their outside shoulder with the inside shoulder of the attacker. This side-gap positioning puts the defender in a great position to encourage the attacker to take the outside space. With the puck carrier having to go all the way across the defender's body, it's much harder for them to take the inside. If the puck carrier carries the puck outside the dots, then the defender can play on the dot line with opportunity to close if needed. When the defensemen can hold the dot line and use the dots it's familiar with and the spacing is good for them to be able to settle into rush-entry defense. However, if the puck carrier is on the dot line, and the defenseman plays the outside shoulder to inside shoulder, they would have to play 8-10 feet inside the dot line. Now instead of the space being 35 feet to the wall, it's now 40-45 feet. That is much more difficult for the defensemen to compress that kind of space. The extra 5-10 feet of space is a lot.

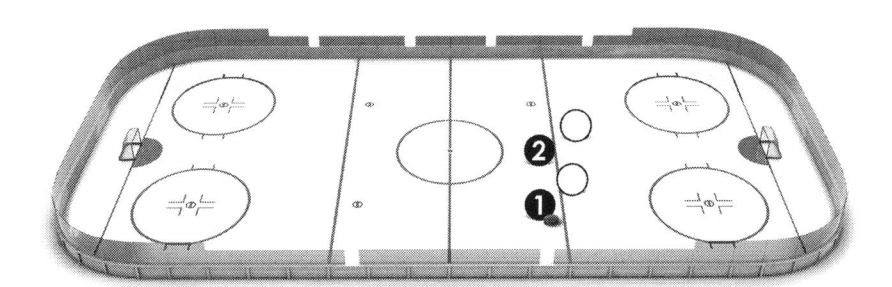

Figure 131: Dot Line Space

Outside entry with proper support, the D can play more aggressively and compress the outside space.

BELFRY OFFENSE

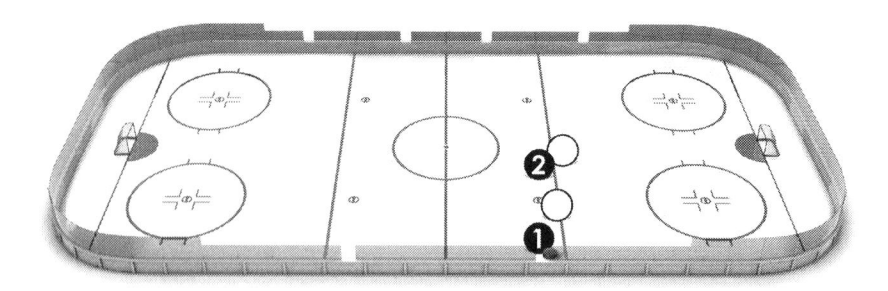

Figure 132:

Dot-line entry, now the D is pushed inside the dot, offering a lot more side gap space for the defender to have to try to close after entry.

Now if we combine the dot line with "2 and 2," there is opportunity to manipulate the defender and make plays either inside out or outside in.

The big part of the manipulation is angle entry. Angle entry refers to prioritizing skating crossing the line on an actual angle to create space to make a play through on off the D's heels and to see if we can pull the D on an angle. Defensemen are more vulnerable when we can move them on angles.

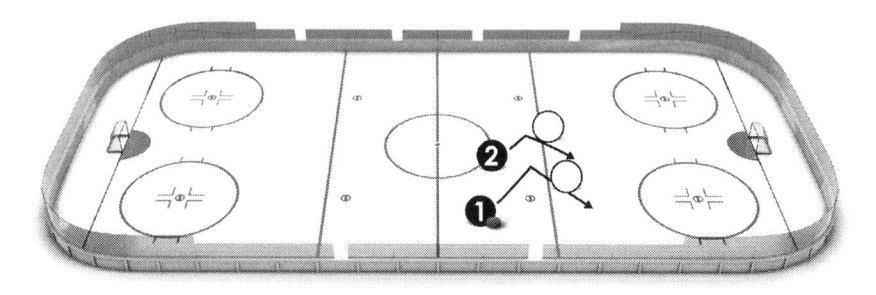

Figure 133: Inside Out Angle Entry

264

COVERAGE EXIT TO RUSH ENTRY

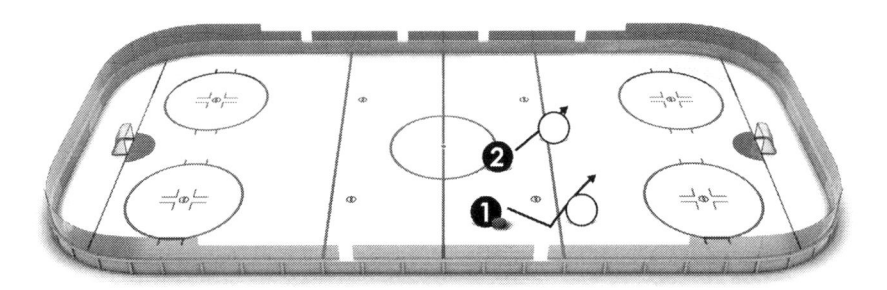

Figure 134: Outside In Angle Entry

Exit play to the dot line and then angle entry offers those who understand the difference between a crosscut and a linear crossover an advantage. Crosscuts and linear crossovers have been confused with each other ever since I coined linear crossover years ago. A linear crossover is just that, it's a crossover executed in a completely straight line of directional skating travel. A crosscut is a crossover that pulls you slightly or more off the straight line of directional travel. Crosscuts usually are done one way and one the other because the first crossover pulls you off the line. These are not the same skating skills. They are very different and used for different tactical advantages. A linear crossover is executed to change speed at a speed when a change of speed when the player is at or near full speed without losing the straight line direction of travel. The analogy I like to use is it's like when you are riding your bike and you are either going to go up a hill or you want to go a little faster. To do this, you raise your butt off the seat and stand up on the pedals as you drive the pedal down and at the same time drive the down pedal up. By raising your butt off the seat, you are maximizing the down force and power production available and can now get up the hill easier or go faster, quicker. This is what a linear crossover is for. It maximizes the down force and power production when you are at a skating striding speed where this is difficult to do. The linear crossover is not better than the crosscut. They are different, and when they are utilized in proper sequence, it's stepping on the gas for speed.

BELFRY OFFENSE

When we look at the exit to dot line to entry neutral zone skating opportunity in rush entry, we see how good patterning can leverage the best of the manipulation of the defensemen on entry. If, as an example, we take the strong-side winger and the weak-side winger on exit and follow them through the neutral zone in one of the patterns that lead us to the entry we want and looked at it from a skating pattern, we would see something like this:

The strong-side winger receives a pass inside a pivot on the boards. Inside the catch, the player is in a pivot, and when they land the outside foot, the skate is loaded with weight on the catch. The player uses that skate to initiate a crossover to get off the wall and into the dot line. They use a second crossover to get vertical up the dot line. The weak-side forward uses a linear crossover acceleration pattern to get vertical and drive the D back. The strong-side forward once they get up the ice on the dot line uses a linear crossover to get vertical up the dot line. The strong-side forward now uses a dot line to inside and inside to outside crosscut for an angle entry and try to pull the D with them and draw the D on an angle.

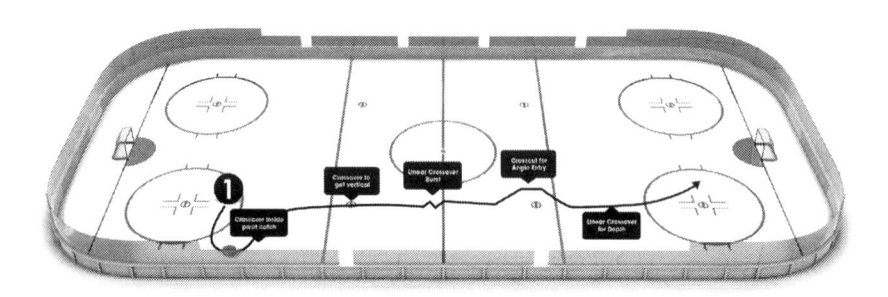

Figure 135: Strong Side Winger Skating Route

The weak-side forward after getting vertical with their linear crossover also execute crosscut for an angle entry to get on the heels of the primary defender as a pass threat and building depth into the offensive zone. This is a good example of how tactical skating patterns work inside a game situation route. You can train this footwork and its situational variations to be automatic. This pattern I detailed would be a baseline for footwork and pattern that the players can then work off of.

The other detail I really like in rush-entry skating patterning is for the puck carrier to shoulder check with the puck while in acceleration. This detail is not as embedded in the habits of all players as much as it should. The shoulder check in the neutral zone suggests you have an understanding that there is dangerous offensive opportunity in the people coming in from behind you. Not just for delay situations, but back-diagonal plays can be tremendous in terms of ramping up the shot quality on the rush. Too many times at every level, the puck carrier falls victim to the shrinking ice effect. The further you skate up the ice, the less ice is in front of you and the more ice is behind you. Not enough players have the awareness skills or the reps to truly understand how to use ALL the threats on the rush. The shrinking ice effect is a major limitation for most rushing defensemen. This is why they find themselves getting painted into the corner so easily and miss chances to create dangerous rush plays.

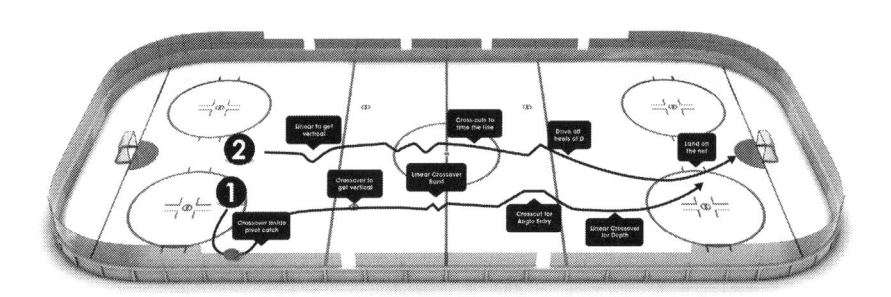

Figure 136: Strong Side and Weakside Winger Routes

I do a lot of this this kind of skating patterning work with all my players. In the NHL, it is critical you can find your way through the neutral zone and contribute to the rush in any role in the play you find yourself in. If the play leaves you behind, that will be limiting. It's critical that every player have a foundation of these skating skills and understand how they

BELFRY OFFENSE

can be worked together. Once these skills and patterns are solidified, they can be transferred into many other situations in the game.

The crossover-per-stride-ratio study I did many years ago pulled me right into this world, and that study, which was originally intended to see how players utilize crossovers, changed into acceleration patterning. The original intended results of the study was seeing a clear difference between first line and fourth line players in their utility of crossovers. The evidence of the study slapped me in the face. It was clear. When you are skating forward, cross your feet! Then when I saw the patterning of the actual skating and the routes the study became invaluable in understudying how top players work skating combinations and routes to create advantages.

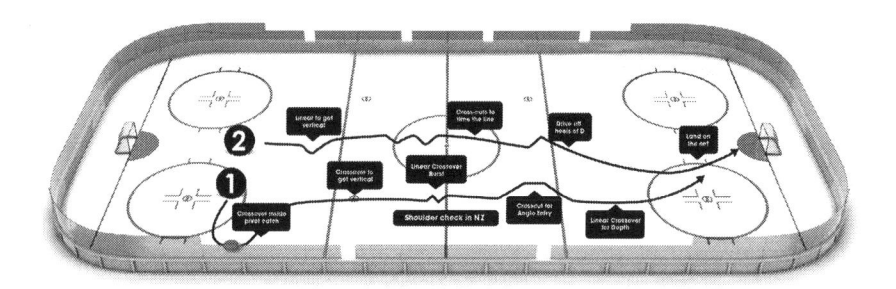

Figure 137:

I remember distinctly back in the day when I was coaching in minor hockey, one of the coaches I coached against for years and I met in the lobby, and he said to me that he saw one of my players playing in a tournament, a spring tournament that we weren't at as a team. "I knew it was one your guys by the way he skates," he said. He was referring to the amount the player crossed over when he skated. In the late 1990s, I had read the book *Overspeed* by Jack Blatherwick, and by the early 2000s, you couldn't attend an ice time of mine without doing a ton of outside edge and crossover work. Every practice we were accelerating through corners in crossover acceleration and doing everything I could do to challenge the outside edge. The result was all of our players were crossing their feet everywhere. During that time, so much of the skating development was centered around stride development and I completely left stride development in favor of an almost exclusive investment in crossover and outside development.

4. The critical role of F2

The importance of F2 on a rush can't be understated. F2 is responsible for the depth of the play in the moments immediately following entry. F2 has to time the line and work in a sprint to gain as much depth as possible. There are coaches who want him to go right to the heels of the puck-side defender so we can threaten to get into behind him. There are other coaches who just want the threat and an available stick but not get too far on the puck side. There are many variations of routes to make the strong-side defender uncomfortable, what's important is that you are threatening the space in behind him with speed and open the possibility of two 2v1s.

When we were talking about rushing defensemen and my distain and frustration for rushing defensemen who slow forwards up or make them come to a complete stop at the offensive blue line, I believe what limits them is not understanding how to be a great F2. This is where the rush ladder plays for defensemen could be a real game changer in their rush entry effectiveness.

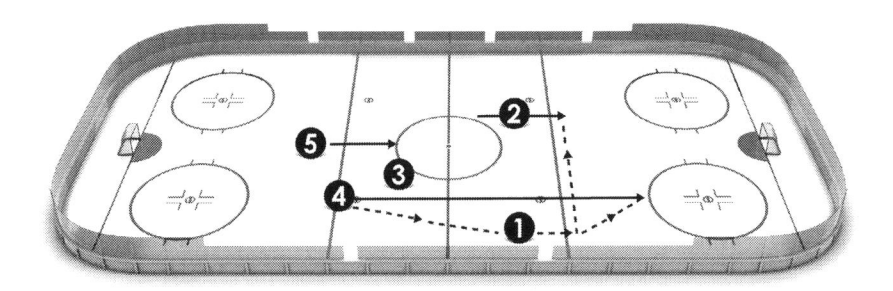

Figure 138:

This is a D (4) using a ladder play and keeps the forwards speed on the entry. Also commonly referred to as a kick and drive, I prefer the "ladder" term because it depicts the idea of jumping ahead.

5. Forecheck routes

In the media buildup for the 2023 NHL Stanley Cup Conference Final between the Carolina Hurricanes and the Florida Panthers, the Panthers head coach Paul Maurice had an extended interview with Sportsnet's Christine Simpson. In the interview, Simpson asks, "I heard that in game 82 of the regular season this year, Carolina is in Florida playing the Panthers, and you said, Rod Brind'Amour is the best coach in the NHL." The always immaculately articulate Maurice responds, "Correct, I don't think there's a more consistent team in terms of style of game. What are we responsible for? We're not really responsible for the talent, we're certainly responsible for getting the most out of the talent. But we will design a game and teach our team that game and hold them accountable to that game, and I think he's the best at it." [29]

The Carolina "game" is a game that leverages its shape to dismantle yours. The Hurricanes have become elite at managing the puck in a way that makes it difficult for you to make plays. They will often give you the puck, only to take it right back. But they don't just give you the puck anywhere. They give it to you in difficult places with difficult pucks to manage and force you to have to problem solve that puck under tremendous pressure. That's forechecking - not just in the offensive zone though, that's everywhere on the ice. The Carolina Hurricanes forecheck is a relentless 200-feet-by-85-feet forecheck. It's every inch of the rink. They don't come with one guy, they come with everyone. However, their real game is what I refer to as "tandem forecheck." They excel with their F1 and F2, they have great speed, they move automatically as the puck is sent into space and F1 and F2 work together to get the puck back.

---

[29] https://twitter.com/sportsnet/status/1659342790554271745?s=46

But it doesn't stop there. Once they get the puck, they quickly threaten. They can threaten from anywhere on the ice and they do it with speed and numbers.

When they are in the defensive zone, the defense will flip the puck high into the neutral zone, so your D have to come off the offensive blue line and field a "pop fly" or settle a bouncing puck, while their F1 and F2 are charging at you. This results in odd-man rush for them. They don't need you to have an unsupported pinch or defensive rotation miscue to get an odd-man rush. They can get it off awkward puck placement and immediate pressure. They have five players in the screen (meaning when you watch the broadcast, they have five players in the viewing screen an awful lot), and they counter you with numbers and shape. Their automation comes from the clarity of the purpose of how they manage the puck. Carolina manages the puck by minimizing their risk by not trying to make plays or hold the puck in situations that aren't favorable. In those situations, which there are many of them, they advance the puck in areas that they know are difficult for the opposition to make a play. So they turn an unfavorable offensive puck for them, into an unfavorable puck for you and try to pressure that puck to get it back, leaving you in a compromised position on the turnover.

What I have described to you throughout the book is much more of a game control style of play by actually possessing the puck. Carolina's game control style of puck is through puck management and fast and organized pressure. They excel in transition. They built their roster to support this game control approach. They have a ton of speed in their forward group, they have offensive weapons who excel in quick odd-man rushes, they have D who can both make stops (their D with Jaccob Slavin, Brent Burns, Brett Pesce, Brad Skjei and Jalen Chatfield are all big, rangy D who defend really well, can make a play and get up the ice quickly. They added Shayne Gostisbehere and he adds a nice puck-handling element to that group. They have a roster whose individual skill assets match their game control objectives.

What I've described to you is a game control approach that is centered around excelling in the spaces between. The transitions between situations from offensive zone possession offense to offensive zone defense to stay on offense, excelling in the transitions or the space between. For decades our game has been taught in isolated game situations. We work on the breakout, then we work on the forecheck, then we work on offensive zone. We teach it all separately. We track the game in isolated events. That was a zone exit play, that was a shot, that was a defensive stop, that was a zone entry, but the game isn't played that way. The game is fluid and is more in transition BETWEEN events than actually in each event. In my mind, the advantage is in developing a fluidity and a speed in that space between and have that be the core of your game. Rod Brind'Amour and Carolina are the same ... but different. Then you look at Colorado and when the MacKinnon line is out, they do one thing and play a certain way, and then when the other lines come out, they don't play like that they play differently. With Colorado, they've taken the top of their talent and put them all together in a unit of five and they invented a way to play that highlights every strength. Every new player that gets moved into that unit due to injury has to figure out how to play that way, because the other lines don't play that way. They won a Stanley Cup, convincingly, with a structure like this. Then you have Carolina, they have four lines who come at you and everyone is doing the same thing. The point being, a little creativity goes a long way in our sport. Why handcuff MacKinnon, Landeskog, Rantanen, Makar and Toews in a style of play that doesn't bring out their unique strengths? If you have unique personnel, it's in everyone's best interest to build room to maximize it. Whatever assets you have in your group ... that's the potential for where you can go in your style of play. Style of play is EVERYTHING. Style of play is your direct pathway to player development. If your style of play is in alignment with the assets of your players, then your style of play can be positionally gasoline on their individual and collective development. It is a multiplier. However, if your style of play is restricting on the development of individual assets, your team cannot and will not grow. The key to player development is a congruent game control approach that is lock and step with individual assets. Coaching a team where every player fits perfectly to the style of play is extremely rare. Most of the time, you have a Colorado situation, where you may have to have a few things going on. Perhaps your top six plays differently than your bottom sox. On most teams, this is probably the starting point of building an identity that can compete with a singular style of play. In every NHL situation I have studied, if there is a problem, this is the root of it. From your game control style of play, you can then create the space for them to be competitive. We talk all the time about having competitive people, people who love to compete and win, but then their game control style of play doesn't create the space for them to be competitive. In the game control style of play that I've walked you through, where is the inherent space for them to be competitive? Well, it's everywhere, it's at every turn, it's written on every page, it's the foundation for the entire thing. The space is there for players to grow. In Rod Brind'Amour's puck management approach to game control style of play, where is the space to be competitive? Pretty clear, right? The very phase of "putting players in position to be successful." This is what that means.

What about Paul Maurice's Florida Panthers, what's their game control style of play in the 2023 Stanley Cup Playoffs? Forecheck physicality. Now take a look at the roster, now take a closer look at their best players. Why did they trade Jonathan Huberdeau for Matthew Tkachuk? Watching them play in the playoffs this year, that's now obvious. Take a look at their defense, and then pay attention to their shape on the forecheck and more importantly what happens when they get the puck back. You could argue they also excel in puck management, they don't handle the puck or make plays when it isn't favorable. When it isn't favorable, they give the puck back to you, but in a tough spot and make you have to problem solve it under pressure. That's game control style of play, in direct congruence with personnel assets. What I'm describing is a game control approach where I don't want to willingly give you the puck, I want to work to improve the conditions of the puck. I'm in player development, I love the puck and I love when players make plays. I don't want to give you the puck, but when you get it, which you will, I'm not coming to get the puck back, I'm already there, because of the duality of my shapes. That's the essence of Belfry Offense. However, that's not the only way to do it. You may have unique players on your team you have to make some space for in order for them to grow. Nothing you can't figure out with a whole lot of study, a little creativity, a fascination with real competitiveness and determination.

In the NHL, there are clear situations, not many clearer than the Carolina example, where the approach to game control and style of play is in congruence with player assets. When this happens, you don't have many players, if any, who are adapting their game to fill a role. Their role is to "Do You." Just be the best version of yourself in the most competitive way you can express yourself. You ARE your role. In the NHL, situation is most important, because if you are in a situation where your asset base is not in congruence with the team's approach to game control, you are not going to excel. There are very few players in the NHL who can outperform their situation. If you are a D who likes to handle and carry the puck, escape checking pressure, play 1v1 and rush the puck every chance you get ... where is the space for that in Carolina?

As a player development coach, I think it's critical that I understand all of this and study the team's game control style of play for every one of my clients. What happens if I don't know how they want to play? Well, I run the risk of suggesting my client do something that runs counter to their style of play. This is not going to lead them to more success. In my role with my players, my job is to find ways they can be more successful in what they already do at a high frequency. The frequency is influenced by the team's style of play. If I don't study how the team plays and match that against what my client's high frequency events are and their asset base ... I don't have a chance to make an impact. I would say, if anything gave me my greatest competitive advantage over anyone else in my industry, this is it. This is a major separator that gives me access to the top players in the game. I know the space they can grow.

As soon as we say forecheck, the first thing I think about is exit to entry routes. If you want to set up your forecheck, we have to look back at one zone earlier, how did we exit? Are we in position and organized to set up a forecheck for puck recovery?

What is the order of priority of the forecheck?

1. Indirect pass – a forecheck recovery in which the opponent never touches the puck. A hard rim, cross-corner dump in or a self-chip are good examples.

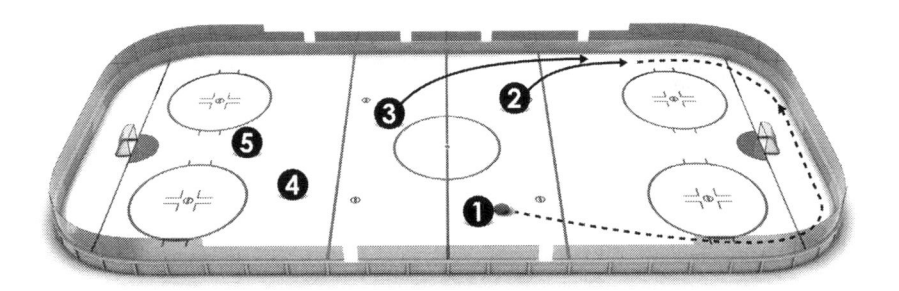

Figure 139: Hard Rim

On a hard rim, we like to have two retrievers on the rim to offer a number of more options both in the retrieval and in the next play.

On a self-chip, it's important to crossover inside first, to pull the D inside, then chip it in behind the D. The reason is because it encourages a loopy pivot by the D and you can get inside position for recovery.

I would also include shooting dump-ins on the goalie as an indirect pass. This is a great tactic to keep a mobile goalie in the net and not disrupt your forecheck by stopping it behind the net. Shoot it on the goalie, so they redirect it into the corner and start your forecheck.

The same is for shooting it off the end wall to have it rebound into the slot. These are excellent and creative ways to get first touch.

First touch is everything. The more we can get first touch or

BELFRY OFFENSE

contest first touch, the percentages for consistent success on our forecheck will skyrocket.

2. Contesting on touch – a forecheck recovery in which our F1 arrives to compete for the puck at the same time as the defender. A flip in that dies in the corner or a soft lay in is a good example.

3. Contesting after touch – a forecheck recovery in which the defender gets first touch and we are trying to rush his first play, so the first touch stays on the wall.

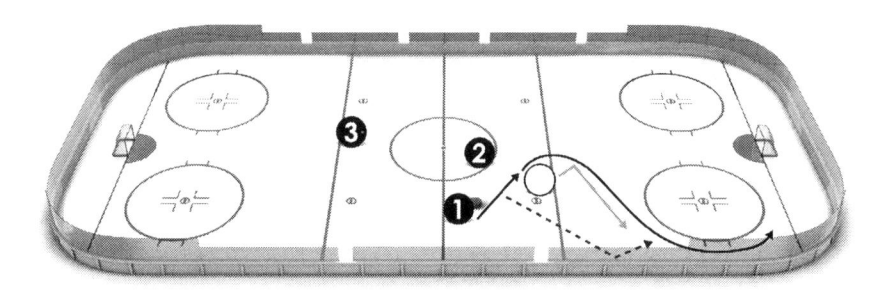

Figure 140: Self Chip

4. Conceding the first touch and influencing the second touch – a forecheck which concedes the first touch and falls into a more conservative pressure on the first puck carrier and tries to limit the passing options of the puck carrier before gradually closing off the space.

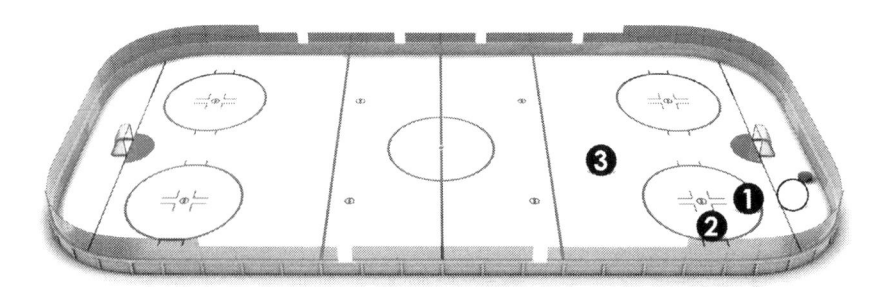

Figure 141:

So much of the forecheck is our F1, what kind of pressure can we get on the first touch will impact how we can forecheck. The pressure we can get on the first touch is directly related to how quickly we can get through the neutral zone and how quickly we can get organized with our support. This is all reliant upon how you exit. The forecheck is just as reliant upon exiting well as possession entries.

The Role of the 2nd

If you study contested forecheck, the two biggest determine factors of success in puck placement on the shoot in and how quickly the second can get in position. In any forecheck, the second player makes the whole thing work in contested situations or not. How quickly can you get your second player in position. When you watch great forechecking teams like Carolina, Florida or Vegas, their second is in position and ready to work in tandem with F1. That's the important distinction. The second is not just coming to get a loose puck that was forced by F1, the second is there to work in tandem with F1. F1 initially pressures the puck and cuts the ice in half and leads the puck into small space, often into the second who helps stop the puck and the player, then F1 picks up the loose puck. The actual contact often comes from the second who the puck was steered to them by F1. In tandem forechecks, F1 doesn't have to do all of it, he just has to lead and steer.

Now imagine if tandem forecheck was now something you viewed as any loose puck, anywhere on the rink. Now you are approaching the forecheck in accordance to the Belfry Offense Shape + Habits and Percentages. Everyone on the shape could be F1 and the next closest player is our second and anywhere and everywhere on the ice that there is a loose puck, we work with tandem forecheck. That's a concept that offers great space for players to learn to have competitive effectiveness.

PLAY OF THE CENTER

The play of the center is no longer a single player responsibility. It's way too big a job for any one person. In today's game, save the goaltender, at some point, you'll be the center. My thinking about the center position has evolved from a person to a stewardship of a responsibility. It's about controlling the middle corridor of the ice in all three zones, both offensively and defensively, and the glue holding the shape.

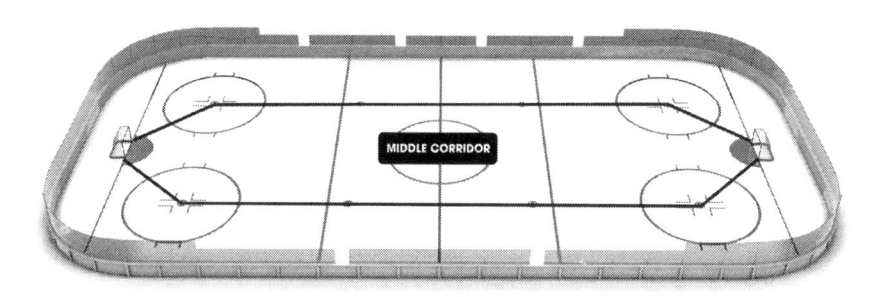

Figure 142:

After the 2014 Winter Olympics, I asked John Tavares what made Patrice Bergeron so special to play with as a center and he said, "He's always available." He is always in the right spot. Every time you need an out, he's there. Every time you turn and you need to make a play, he's there. He makes the game so much easier. John was talking about his offensive play, but he's also won the Selke Trophy five times. Ok, so let me get this straight. Bergeron is always in the right position offensively, but also is in the right position defensively? How is that possible?

When you study Bergeron closely, there are a few habits he has that stand out. The first is his positional discipline is just that, a discipline. He is most often positioned in the middle of the "5 on a dice" visual of the connectivity and duality of being between the two triangles. He is inside the dots both offensively and defensively. His availability as a dot release or middle release is constant. His pursuit angles are impeccable, largely because of the consistency he has in his original positioning. He is a master of making decisions based on the percentages.

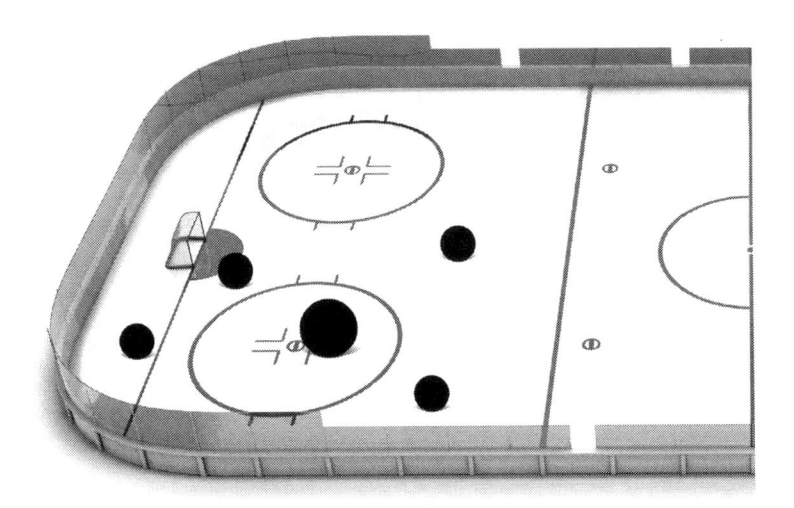

Figure 143:

What's the biggest difference between the way he plays and the way other centermen play? He doesn't rotate himself out of the middle nearly as often. He only rotates out of that middle connective position when there is a high percentage tactical reason. Otherwise, he is a steward to the shape. There is an entire book to be written on his play as a center and the genius behind the discipline of how he plays. This, admittedly, is an elevator snapshot of what he does. The purpose in mentioning him is he is the best of this era to do it. He has scored 20 goals or more in each of the last 10 seasons. However, 2018-2019 is his only season over a point a game, and that was the only season he flirted with registering an 80-plus point season. If he is in the middle connective position most often and many plays have to go through him, because he's so easy to play with and is always in the right position to give you an out, why then is he not more offensively prolific? This is not to say he needs to be or a slight on his play in any way. I raise the question only in the context of how difficult it is to truly consistently play the center position properly, which he would be the gold standard AND prolifically produce offensively. Somewhere along the way, he's making choices that affect his ability to consistently generate offense to hold the duality of the position or shift more to a defensive position. We also know, it is challenging to generate consistent offense without having an elite rush offense. Bergeron's foot speed may hold him back from getting in the rush as F1 and F2 as often as you need to generate. His low defensive zone position to facilitate coverage breakouts, which is a masterclass, can prevent him from leading the rush. Perhaps, this is a factor, as his best rush threats would be transition opportunities, as the late guy, or in re-entry.

Nathan MacKinnon's performance in the 2022 Stanley Cup Playoffs was the signature performance of playing center in the NHL at the highest level it can be played. The performance was everything you could want in a center. He was offensively prolific, leading the Avalanche in goals. He was literally everywhere the puck was on the ice. His positioning, his tracking routes, his positional discipline ... but then it was his speed. In a blink of an eye, he would go from corner defending in the defensive zone to leading an odd-man rush, to then reloading above their exit and tracking the puck to get it back, then leading the re-entry, then working the puck high and low and then tracking the puck to keep offensive sequences alive. He was everywhere. It's not just speed either, it's the refining of his positioning and habits that made his speed a determining factor. I put together an entire presentation of what his play was as a center in those playoffs and how it's put an unrealistic expectation on others to realistically play the position like that. It just isn't possible for nearly every other player in the league to duplicate the way he played. So he set the bar, the only problem is he pushed it to a level that is out of reach.

For my Belfry Hockey Podcast, in Episode 3, I studied Martin Necas of the Carolina Hurricanes in the 2021-2022 season. Necas is one of my favorite players in the NHL because of how interesting the way he plays is. Necas' play patterns offered me the insight I needed to reinvent the way I think about playing center. Necas is a right-shot right winger who loves to play in the middle of the ice. When I studied him, he was playing with Vincent Trocheck, who was the center on the line and phenom left-shot sniper Andrei Svechnikov. When I watched that line play, and in particular watched Necas, I was immediately struck by the amount of time Necas played in the middle of the ice. He and Trocheck were constantly switching in and out of the center position, in essence, sharing the position.

The more I studied Necas, the more I began to see that the comfort he had in playing center and the frequency he was rotating into the middle, that the center position was always filled. When you watch other lines, when the center rotates out of the position, the center position is either not refilled until he returns, or the player who assumes the position is not as comfortable and there is vulnerability by the center not being in the center position. Now we have a winger who is very effective in the middle of the ice, who now is sharing the position with the center. Aside from the obvious comfort of having the center position "covered," my mind goes to where the advantages might be. Let's go back to Bergeron. In order for Bergeron to play the position as responsibly as he does, he doesn't rotate out of the position very often. When he does, the percentages have to be stacked in his favor and for it to make tactical sense, otherwise he holds his position. Now if Necas wants to play the middle of the ice, and is constantly rotating in and out, and when he does play the middle of the ice, he is effective, what can that do for Trocheck offensively? If the position is truly shared by two capable centermen, now they can rotate out of the middle more comfortably, but also more strategically. Can both guys drive the effectiveness of the center position through their strategic rotations in and out? I see nothing but opportunity with something like this.

If Bergeron is in the right place all the time, but has to often make conservative decisions offensively to hold the integrity of the position on the "next play," and MacKinnon's superhuman characteristics make the way he plays the position unreasonable for others, then maybe Necas and Carolina have cracked the code and offered insight into another way to play center.

Playing center is incredibly difficult to do really well. It's really difficult to be in perfect defensive position all the time, while also threatening the net offensively. Centers are constantly weighing the percentages and most with an offensive acumen have to have the defensive responsibility win out more. Or you have centermen who sit on the defensive side exclusively and make no meaningful contribution to the offense. It's much easier to play center when you sit on the defensive side of the puck and don't have the burden of generating offense. When you have the burden of generating offense, alongside the responsibility of defending, it's more than a challenge. Playing center, and hitting all the objectives of being an effective center, is too much for one player with the speed of the game today. Encouraging center play from wingers and developing winger skills (defensive zone board play in particular) to centers, coupled with teaching D how to lead the rush effectively as F1 and F2 and the weak-side D becoming the center. From a development perspective, we have a lot of work to do to prepare our players to control the middle of the ice.

In Belfry Offense, with shape + habits and percentages equation as its core, it's more than rotating the winger or jumping the D in as the center. Center is not a position, it's a role. The key to Belfry Offense is players recognizing role change in advance of the play and execution the skills and tactics needed to perform that role from a position of strength.

WHAT MAKES THEM GREAT

Friends of ours in Florida have a son-in-law who has a degree from Harvard and was in the process of finishing a second degree from Columbia University. Definitely someone you have to find a way to ask a good question to. Over dinner, I was searching for a question to ask that would open him up. I asked him if there were any classes that he had taken in either school that were especially interesting or changed his thinking. After taking a second, he said that he loved one of the art classes as "now he can enjoy going through art museums so much more." What he learned in that class about art history and the different techniques used to produce the greatest art pieces our world has ever seen gives him the opportunity to now truly enjoy art because he can understand "the genius behind the pieces." It completely changed his ability to appreciate the differences in art.

During the re-writing stage of this book, our family went on vacation to Italy, where the entire country seemingly everywhere you go is an art history lesson. Brilliant art, painting, sculptures, music, even the street art is everywhere, you are surrounded by many of the greatest art pieces in the history of the world. I, unfortunately, have no idea how to differentiate between the genius. I don't know enough about art to recognize the genius. While on our trip, we did a number of tours of the major art museums and churches in both Florence and in Rome. On our last day in Rome, we visited the Borghese Gallery and Museum. Our tour guide was an art history major and did it ever come through in her tour. Her passion and knowledge was remarkable in explaining the brilliance in the art and its perspective for the period. In the Borghese Gallery, there are a number of Gian Lorenzo Bernini sculptures. Bernini has been credited with creating the Baroque style of sculpture. Our guide's ability to articulate the intricate brilliance in the sculpture and its impact on a generation of artists gave all of us on the tour an ability to see the sculpture through a different lens. This lens of understanding gave me an opportunity to truly appreciate the art.

My career-long study of offense in hockey has taken on this for me. A beautiful goal on a SportsCenter highlight reel gives me just enough understanding that something great happened, but I really didn't know enough about it to recognize where the genius was is in the movement or the genius of someone else moments before that was responsible for creating the conditions. The more I started to make connections in how players, lines, units and teams create offense, the more I can start the process of learning how to truly appreciate the genius in the game of hockey. Many of the greatest expressions of genius in our game don't result in a goal or end up on the highlight reel. The genius in the NHL is everywhere. The game is played so fast that it's impossible to notice it all. Now when I watch a game, I notice the genius in repetitive pattern recognition and making a simple play nine out of 10 times. But that one time, the conditions of the play surrounding the pattern create an opportunity to attack, and the player recognizes the opening and BANG! Or that same pattern happens the same way each time, but one time, one of the players sees an opportunity inside the repetitiveness to do something slightly different, which alters the spacing and the timing to create an opportunity. This is the kind of thing that is happening. It's not just a one-on-one dangle or a seeing-eye shot or a pass intercept, it's not the isolated play. It's what led up to that play that offers insight into why it became possible in the first place. One of my friends watched a live game with me and asked me to narrate what I was looking at when I watched the game. After a few minutes, he told me to stop as I was "ruining the game for him." Ruining it because I am focused on what's happening away from the puck as much as I'm watching what's happening on the puck or watching a shape develop or a subtlety of decision-making. Sometimes, you just want to just enjoy the game for entertainment.

One of the best parts of my career is the study of "What Makes Them Great." Studying players to discern what really makes them great. What do they do that unlocks the genius on a consistent basis? Where is their individual genius and how do they express it in a team game? How can others, at breakneck speed, see what is happening and also contribute to creating the conditions of genius? This is what is truly fascinating and is a lifelong study. Every time I have a breakthrough of understanding, it opens up an entire new world to explore and I'm right back to feeling like I'm at a the beginning.

In 2016 at the World Cup of Hockey, I had a couple of my clients playing for "Team North America." I was all about the entire idea of "Team North America." I thought it was a fascinating concept to spice up international best on best. Like everyone else, I couldn't wait to see what was going to happen. As soon as they played their first game, they captured the hearts of everyone. They were absolutely electric. I was able to go to a couple games in Toronto and watch them live, and it was so intriguing as everyone was trying to process what was unfolding.

To start the tournament, Auston Matthews was the 13th forward, working his way into different lines. Auston hadn't played a single game in the NHL and was just coming out of playing in Zurich, Switzerland. He had played in the World Championships that spring as a preparation for the NHL, and the 2016 World Cup was timed perfectly just before the NHL season. It didn't take long for Auston to work his way onto a line alongside Connor McDavid and Mark Schiefele. It was an instant explosion. In hockey terms, the "chemistry" that followed was incredible. The speed they played at the plays they were making at that speed gave insight into another level. While it was a short tournament, the impact was felt long after. Matthews went on to score four goals in his NHL debut and along with McDavid and MacKinnon have skyrocketed to top of the best players in the world lists. What stood out for me was the speed that team wanted to play at, the speed of the puck movement and the speed off the puck was phenomenal to watch. They blew the doors off of Finland and then the overtime win over Sweden put everyone on notice. Something special happened at that tournament that felt like a springboard for many of the players on that team to new levels in their NHL careers.

Two summers later in the summer of 2018, I hosted a Belfry Hockey NHL Skills and Tactics Camp in Florida. This was the second summer we had hosted a preseason camp for NHL players, and this time we wanted to take it to the next level. I had read an article about Richard Sherman inviting the top cornerbacks in the NFL to workout with him and go over film. I sent this article to Patrick Kane and asked him if he thought we could do something similar. We had many of the top players attending, we should try it and see what would happen. I dubbed it "The 88 Summit," and it ended up taking on a life of its own. The players really got into the collaboration and the experience became an immediate paradigm shift for me. [30] During the on-ice part of that camp, Patrick and I talked about having him and Auston paired on the same team, so they would have a chance to play a lot together over the week, with an eye ahead to possibly playing internationally with each other at the upcoming Olympics. The Olympics never happened, but they did play together during that camp and we all watched in excitement to see what would happen.

I watched it live, rewatched the video, I pulled the clips and sliced, diced and dissected every second of their time together that week. I didn't know what I was looking for, but I was convinced there was something to find, not just between those two, but from everyone in the group. At that time, when I finished my analysis and talked to the players, my conclusion was similar to what we all saw when Matthews played with McDavid in 2016, the speed they could play at, and the speed they could make plays at. When they were really going at the camp, the obvious discernible characteristic was speed. They just played faster when they were together than they did when they were apart. he depth of Matthews' playmaking skills revealed itself more clearly. He could see plays and think on the same plane as Kane. They could anticipate off of each other which was reflected in the way they moved off the puck. My takeaways at that time were:

---

[30] *https://www.si.com/nhl/2018/09/20/88-summit-darryl-belfry-hockey-film-breakdown*

- Elevated speed of play.
- Anticipation reflected in speed off the puck.
- Playing with expectation, if they sprinted to a space, the puck would be there.
- The craftiness of plays through people was something to watch, how they attacked defensive triangles (space between the defenders stick and skates), or passing off the heels, or pulling a defender closer to them to buy a little extra time to let the play develop enough to send the other into attack space.
- The passes to each other were most often leading passes, putting pucks into an area that the other was skating into.
- A lot of plays when both players were skating on the arc.

In 2021, I was asked by my longtime friend Andy O'Brien to run the on-ice part of the BioSteel Camp. The BioSteel Camp was again a preseason camp that players were looking forward to get themselves ready for the start of the season. Andy said, "Sidney (Crosby) and Connor (McDavid) want to play a lot together at this camp with an eye on potentially playing together at the Olympics." Perfect, here we go again. What can I learn from this? How different would Crosby/McDavid be than Kane/Matthews? More importantly, how has my lens changed and will I be able to see more or see it differently because I know more now than I did back in 2018?

The BioSteel Camp, Crosby/McDavid played out very similar to the Kane/Matthews. I saw the same kind of effect. The speed elevated, the plays were made at high speed, they made a lot of plays through the defender and they made a lot of passes to space. What was different was my lens. What I was able to do was ask better questions. Do they take consistent routes to attack? How do they get the speed to elevate? Is there something they do to make the advantage they create greater? With this being my second go around, I was able to watch it differently and therefore see different things. This time, I was able to see:

- Most often, they make a play to make a play. The one pattern was give and go, but the give was to space and the pass back was to the next space. The "give" is to possession space and the "go" is to attack space. McDavid would put a puck to the outside space to Crosby, then sprint behind the defender for the puck back. Possession plays are made to improve the chances of attacking on the next play.

- When they pass the puck softly to space, the receiver has time to shoulder check to see where the "go" is going while the puck is on its way, allowing him to make the next play faster. Players who are receiving a harder pass have to concentrate more on the pass reception and while the puck gets there faster, the receiver has to find the next play after reception rather than prior.

- When they attack heels of the defender, they tend to go inside. They don't just attack heels, they create heels of a defender angling inside out and make a play to the inside. The pass receiver is splitting off the heels expecting to be able to attack.

- They use speed of the play with the puck to win the puck back quickly, a lot of strips, steals and shot recoveries. Often uncontested, they are moving so quickly offensively that they can use that speed to get the next puck. A lot of goals scored after a strip or steal to extend the possession.

I'm certain that I'll learn more if I'm fortunate to have the opportunity to do this again, as now I'm at another level of understanding, so now I can have my eyes open for other things. The next challenge is to take all that I learned from these "generational" athletes and see what aspects would be useful for all players in the league. In everything we learn from the best of the best, there is always something inside those skills or tactics that every player can benefit from. The difference is awareness. I just need to find a better way to communicate it and provide a platform for them to explore ... space to grow.

The habits of using leading passes and not passing so hard all the time. Use leading passes with more emphasis on:

- Using the right weight of the puck.
- Building the habit of the receiver to look for the next play, while the puck is on its way to space.
- Move purposely to the next spot as you send the puck to space.

These are all skills I can teach to the masses. If I do, our group can play faster offensively. If I can elevate their offensive speed above the defensive speed, we can now have a better chance to win the puck back. All things that are fundamental to Belfry Offense.

Another big advantage I've enjoyed in my career is capitalizing on the common viewpoint that what special players do is not applicable to everyone else. There are so many people who are dismissive of what the best players in the world do because they can't see the relatability. This has always been a mission of mine and has led me to some amazing breakthroughs for players who aren't at that same level of skill.

Belfry Offense is about providing "the space to grow." It's about aligning players to a decision-making equation that they can make all their decision from, without imposing a laundry list of principles and rules that the bog players down. It's about the opportunity and freedom that we can find when we move past the fear of causing overthinking in our athletes and teaching players to be able to think (anticipate, recognize patterns, play in forethought) when they are playing, but it doesn't negatively affect their movement rather enhances it. This is the objective.

These are the skills that separate.

Made in the USA
Monee, IL
15 August 2023

735bb4c9-34e3-4e60-86f2-0ff8c9a0b912R01